Foraging
for
Survival

Foraging
for
Survival

Edible Wild Plants of North America

MYKEL HAWKE

AND

DOUGLAS BOUDREAU

Skyhorse Publishing

Foraging has real and potential hazards and risks. Consult your local foraging experts to ensure that plants have been properly and safely identified prior to consumption. Many "false" plants may be confused for safe-to-eat plants. This book is not a field guide; it is a book about using edible plants in survival planning. Be smart and be safe.

Skyhorse Publishing books may be purchased in bulk at special discounts for sales promotion, corporate gifts, fund-raising, or educational purposes. Special editions can also be created to specifications. For details, contact the Special Sales Department, Skyhorse Publishing, 307 West 36th Street, 11th Floor, New York, NY 10018 or info@skyhorsepublishing.com.

Skyhorse® and Skyhorse Publishing® are registered trademarks of Skyhorse Publishing, Inc.®, a Delaware corporation.

Visit our website at www.skyhorsepublishing.com.

10 9 8 7 6 5 4 3

Library of Congress Cataloging-in-Publication Data is available on file.

Cover design by Tom Lau
Cover photo credits: Mykel Hawke, Douglas Boudreau, and Getty Images

Print ISBN: 978-1-5107-3833-1
Ebook ISBN: 978-1-5107-3835-5

Printed in China

Table of Contents

Disclaimer

In any situation that could be deemed a survival scenario, the laws are relaxed on foraging even on protected land. However, the act of foraging aside from that is mildly prohibited in most jurisdictions and more so in others. Doug teaches what we can forage on, if we have to someday, but only encourages experimentation on edibles for the purpose of becoming familiar with them, how to prepare them, and what they taste like. Doug completely discourages using wild edibles for regular use. It should be a knowledge useful to our survival and be experimented with once identification and preparation requirements are 100 percent certain. *Minors should never attempt to forage for wild edibles without adult supervision.* No one can be held responsible for any mistakes made in any way by anyone using this guide as a reference, as no one will put wild plants in your mouth but you. The reader assumes full and all responsibility for his or her own health. Neither the authors nor the publishers are liable for any illness or discomfort the reader may experience while using this book. Use caution and common sense!

Please understand that there are so many variables and variations when it comes to wild edibles. Some plants may have pesticides on them. Some may have some sort of disease or fungus. Some plants may simply have dirt or animal excrement on them. Any one of those substances alone could cause illness in humans. Some plants may have very close looking kin that are not edible. Some plants may be evolving as new subspecies. It is for these extremely varied and highly possible reasons that foraging for wild edibles must be approached with a great deal of precaution and common sense.

Even with an expert right beside you, to make a 100 percent positive identification of the plant, it would not be humanly possible for the expert to know if some mosquito control insecticide might have been sprayed in that region, as but one example of some of the realistic possible dangers and risks. It is also for this reason that Doug and I encourage you to study, learn, and practice enough to know what you need, but not to make it a regular habit of wild foraging, unless you know the area and can wash your edibles. Otherwise, it's better to learn what is around your area where you live, work, or travel and then try to grow some of those native plants in your own yard, where you do know the environment under which the plants grow and you can control the history of any herbicides or pesticides, in order to make the enjoyment of wild edibles the safest experience possible.

It's also important to realize that plants have life cycles, too. That means you should learn the plants in their varied forms from winter, spring, summer, and fall. Some plants are not fully ripe and ready to eat until the second or third year, and some don't produce edible substances after so many life cycles. You must learn, study, research, and memorize anything you may put in your mouth. No one book or source can teach you everything. Maximize all the resources you have—books, the web, locals, farmers, experts, scientists, the animals—and any other source you can learn from. Hopefully, this is a good resource and a start on a lifelong journey of learning that will never end as long as you live. Thank you and happy foraging!

Foreword

I first became friends with Doug Boudreau through our mutual interest in wild edibles and our mutual respect for Green Deane and his excellent videos, blogs, and website (eattheweeds. com). I was a newcomer to living in Florida, and I was amazed at how much I didn't know. Decades of study in edible and medicinal plants seemed insufficient for the diversity of flora and fauna in the unique terrain found in the peninsula of Florida.

I found many North American plants and Central American tropical plants that seemed to have come together with other international transplants to make seemingly entirely new sub-species, and it made me unsure about many of the plants that now surrounded me.

This is where Doug came into my life. As a native country boy, he grew up learning, being taught, studying, and seeking knowledge on all these special Florida plants. As such, he had a great many trials and errors, and his efforts included a lot of research and querying of other experts. Doug has put in a great deal of painstaking and sometimes just painful work into learning all he could.

Now, Mr. Boudreau has compiled all his years of work and learning into this great book and combined it with my knowledge from living, traveling, and studying all over the world, learning ancient knowledge from local experts over decades of time. And, much in the ways of the Native American traditions, of learning and handing knowledge down to be built on and passed on to the next generation, the knowledge here is neither perfect nor complete. However, it is vast, well done, and a great place for anyone to begin learning about the amazing, useful plants that surround them.

Consider this book a resource of good country knowledge. Learn, study, build on and pass on this knowledge, as it is sure to be helpful.

—Mykel Hawke

1
Special Rules

One of the most important rules of eating plants is proper research. Read all you can in books and online. Learn from experts, others with real, local, learned, tried and tested knowledge. For example, let's say your grandmother may not know much about farming, but she may have been taught by her grandmother that a certain plant is edible. If she grew up eating it, then she has decades of real experience, and if she demonstrates this to you and then you repeat a few times with no ill effects, then that is real knowledge, regardless of books, science, and experts.

Also, be sure to look at as many photos as possible, especially of the plants in different seasons, soils, and regions. Look at videos if you can and also look at images for all the stages of growth. In short, do your utmost to properly and positively identify any plant before you consume it.

Advice on the Learning Approach

Next, start with plants that are near you and with which you are very familiar— for example, dandelions, wild onions, and clovers. Most folks have seen these all their lives and if they spent any time at all playing outside, have likely nibbled on a few of these. Once you get comfortable with the fact you are now foraging on your own for wild edibles, then slowly expand into other plants.

Always start slow and small. Eat a little nibble and wait a long while. Sometimes, folks have reactions to even normal everyday foods. And there are always unforeseeable factors like soil, animal excrement, pesticides, and allergens that could impact anyone at any time. So, exercise caution and common sense, always.

Thoughts on Medicinal Plants

It is far beyond the scope of this book, or any one book, to even begin on such a weighty topic. Some believe, like I do, that everything on this planet has a purpose and a use, even if we haven't found it yet. Whether you believe in God, as I do, and that all of these plants are gifts for us to figure out, or whether you're purely scientific, we find new things every single day in science that we didn't understand the day before.

As such, with almost 400,000 plants we know of on the planet, we only use about 40,000 of them, or 10 percent. That says a lot, that there's much we still don't know and are learning. And when you consider that most of the folks studying plants for medicine are mostly doctors with a decade of school and a decade of practice dedicated just to studying medicinal plants, it's far too much to mix medicinal with edible plants in any comprehensive way in any one book, especially for laymen.

Therefore we may touch on some of the more common, practical, and safer known herbal remedies, but as a Special Forces medic, paramedic, and medical service officer with a Bachelor of Science degree in pre-med biology, I strongly recommend using modern medicine over herbal medicine, since most modern pharmaceuticals are based on herbal remedies but are more concentrated in labs, making them a better bet for treatment and survival. But do consider learning some basics for emergencies when those run out or if you're stranded without. The more you know, the more you live!

Thoughts on Poisonous Plants

It is absolutely impossible to learn all the poisonous plants in the world. Even if you dedicated your entire life to this purpose, you would never be able to do it. So, the best thing to focus on learning are general rules that help you determine edible from non-edible plants. When we speak of poison, it's a generic term to cover anything that isn't edible for us as humans. Some things may just taste awful, some may cause unpleasant reactions, some may make you sick, and some may actually be so toxic that they kill you.

The main thing to know is this: Either it's edible or not edible, and if you're not sure, then it's not edible, and that makes it poisonous. A good general guideline is to make sure you err on the side of going hungry before getting dead.

There are a few key things I teach as a global survivalist that differ from my Florida specialist brother Boudreau. I teach that there are a few plants which are found all over America and are plentiful, so they make for good eats, and as such, would be a shame to waste. However, they do have poisonous look-alike plants. For those, you absolutely must know your rules to differentiate the edible from the poisonous plants. That is a choice you must make, a study you must commit to, and attributes you must memorize. For most folks, this is fine when doing it for practice. But when you're sick, tired, hurt, hungry, and surviving, you may not remember correctly. So, back to the basic rule: only eat what you know.

90/10 vs 10/90 Rule

I made this up as a general guide for my survival students, to help put things in perspective and to help them remember when they are tired, sick, hungry, and surviving. Most of the animals on the planet are edible. There are a very few that are poisonous to eat if they're not prepared properly. Most plants are not edible.

So, use the 90/10 rule. We can eat 90 percent of the animals on the planet and only 10 percent of the plants. The purpose of this book is to help you learn how to identify as many of those edible plants as possible. The good news is that with animals and plants added together you get 100 percent. I find this comforting. Add to that the bit of bug info we provide and that bugs by themselves are a 100 percent nutritious food source, then you're well on your way to ensuring you have the best chance of surviving. One key thing I have emphasized in all my years of survival teaching is that hope is the most important human factor to espouse. Keep your faith strong and your hope alive; when all else fails, those could make or break you.

General Berry Guides

I'll cover these in detail later in the book, but since many folks like to think of berries as the most obvious form of edibles next to roots, it's good to have an easy guide to help you in your learning. This very simple rhyme can help.

Black through blue are good for you.

Yellow and white, it isn't right.

Rules for Red are 50/50—could be good, could be dead.

I'll elaborate more in later sections. For now, let that bounce around your brain a spell.

Universal Edibility Guides

There are a handful of these tests out there meant to help you when you have to resort to the guessing game The military has had its own version of the Universal Edibility Test (UET) for decades, but I debunked that myth with my large survival manual a decade ago. In short, it simply took too long and was impractical.

I came up with my own, which I'll cover later in the book. Doug also addresses the same issue and comes to a similar conclusion. His suggestion is similar to mine and based on tried-and-true trial and tribulation. Simply, if it doesn't look right or smell right, then it isn't right. If it does look right and you touch it or taste it and it burns or is bitter, it's a quitter. Get rid of it.

The only time to even consider using a taste test is when you find yourself staring at a large supply source of something and you know, if you can determine its edibility, that you could survive for a good while off it. For example, you're lost in a swamp and you find this swamp apple tree. You've never seen it or eaten its fruit. But it's a tree in season, with hundreds of potential meals. Then it might be worth the inherent risk of putting it to the taste test.

There are some trees, like the manchineel, that are deadly poisonous. They do look different to a trained eye, but to a novice they might look similar. So, there is always a potentially fatal risk inherent with eating anything unknown to you.

Make sure the risk is worth it if it pays off. Going through the risk of eating something poisonous when there is only one or a few of them doesn't pass the common sense test. Make sure there is "P" for plenty to eat before taking any chances.

My guidelines for learning any plants that you intend to eat for survival are:

Available. Make sure they are found all over to increase chances of finding it.

Identifiable. Make sure they have some absolute features to 100 percent identification. Also know that they have no poisonous look-alikes.

Plentiful. Choose plants that, when you find them, provide abundance.

Seasonal Considerations

One thing I found to be disappointing and difficult when I began foraging was finding food in the off seasons. Most of the country goes through four seasons that have a heavy impact on plant life cycles. In my home state of Florida, we almost have two springs, with warm weather and plentiful rain and sunshine. For the rest of the country, we must adapt to nature's cycles and learn how to forage successfully even in the dead of winter. That is extremely important when you consider that winter is when it's hardest to get any food, whether it is plant or animal, and survival can be the hardest, too.

For that reason, I encourage folks to start slowly, and focus on ten big plants for the region they live in. Start with three, but make sure you master ten plants. Know those plants inside and out, especially in all four seasons. Some plants have vines that have a unique shape, and while the leaves, flowers, and fruit of them may all be hidden in the dead of winter, knowing the shape of the vine can lead to the tuber or root, that can be dug up and eaten, providing a solid meal of life-sustaining starch. So learn to identify your core plants in all four seasons and your chances of survival are increased greatly.

Mushrooms

Doug and I agree on mushrooms: they can be tasty, and they can be plentiful, but they have so very many variations that even the experts make mistakes and die from eating the wrong mushrooms.

Some of the special problems that mushrooms present is that many of the spores and tox-ins that are poisonous to humans are not killed by fire, heat, or boiling. These heat-resistant spores can still kill once consumed.

Another problem unique to mushrooms is that once they're consumed, there is no way to stop the process. You can't vomit it out or take a neutralizing agent or take any form of antidote. Once they have entered the body, the toxins begin doing the damage and death, usually due to liver damage, is unavoidable. There are only a couple of deaths each year, and not all mushrooms have this absolute finality, but the risk is simply too high for any amateur forager to risk.

That said, I have done a lot of study and practice with mushrooms and, as such, I teach a handful that are very easy to identify and have no poisonous look-alikes that we know of. Science does have limits and life evolves, adapts, and mutates, so there are no absolutes, which is critical to keep in mind, especially with mushrooms. I only teach these special mushrooms to my advanced students, and not for a book, as it would be a shame to go hungry with such a safe prospect. But again, it is always a real risk of death, and until recently there weren't a lot of known nutritional value in mushrooms, according to the FDA. However, science has advanced, and there are now sources that state that mushrooms have a lot of nutritional value. So, if you want to make mushrooms a part of your foraging experience, you need to consider that a specialty skill and make it a special study.

A note on science, plants, and change. When I first became a Special Forces medic, I had an unusual experience in Korea with ginseng. I was quite amazed by the effects, as I had absolutely no belief in its claimed beneficial properties. After all, according to western medicine it was primarily placebo and an old wives tales. However, the plant has been revered around the world for millennia, including at home in America by the natives, and it didn't seem to make sense that is was not legitimately beneficial in some way. Fast forward two decades and with advances in scientific methods to analyze micro-nutrients of gin-seng, it now is considered to have well over a dozen potentially beneficial medically useful components.

Warnings

Finally, we have to stress that eating wild edibles can be dangerous, and that death is a very real possibility when eating unknown things. We, as humans, are simultaneously incredibly strong and resilient, but also very fragile and delicate. A small piece of paper can cut us. A small dose of poison can kill us. So be smart, use caution in all you do when it comes to for-aging for wild edibles.

I encourage folks to find things around them and then try those things at home where you have access to a phone and can get medical care fast if necessary. Hopefully, applying all the guidance we give, using common and known plants that are easy to identify, and which have no poisonous look-alikes, you'll have only good, safe experiences and your knowledge and confidence will grow with your experience.

But it's important to understand that anytime you eat something unknown, you take your life into your own hands. No one but you puts that plant into your mouth, and in that moment you assume all responsibility for your action. Mostly, you should be fine; we don't want to scare anyone, but the warnings must be said. Now, they have been. So, be safe, be smart, and have fun.

Last Tip from Your Uncle Myke: Bleach

While we left out a lot about poisonous plants as there are just too many to cover, I feel it would be a very useful thing to pass on this old country doctor's remedy for poison oak, ivy, and sumac.

Before you go foraging, be sure you're familiar with whichever of these you have in your area. I won't dwell on what they look like, how they work and how skin reacts to them. That's a chapter all by itself. What I will share is a small anecdote about how I came to learn this cure.

I was on a Special Forces patrol in California. I was new to the region, and wasn't familiar with poison sumac. We were on a night patrol breaking through serious brush all night long. By daylight, we saw we had been wading through a sea of poison sumac. And I learned I was highly allergic and my arms swelled up like Popeye. The Military Doctors game me shots, pills, creams, and all to no good effect. I had towels wrapped around my arms to absorb the ooze. I suffered like this for about a week and then ran into a country doctor. He told me to use bleach. I scoffed at him as a Special Forces Medic—if that worked, I would have been taught it! He smiled and said, suit yourself. That night, at 3 a.m. in total misery, I tried it. I'll be darned—it was cleared up right then and there. I did it once more the next day and I was cured. Ever since then, I have used it dozens of times and taught and treated hundreds of folks, always with 100 percent success and no ill effects.

So, the chances are, you're going to bump into some in your foraging. When you get home, get naked, in the shower, take a white wash cloth, pour bleach all over and wipe yourself down. Let It set one minute, then rinse and shower like normal. Problem solved. I now do it after each trip and never got it again. It seems to help with ticks and chiggers, too

2
Wild Food History and Weeds

Long before the human inhabitants of North America purchased practically all of their food through the market economy of commerce, they subsisted almost exclusively on what they could grow themselves and forage from their environments. Even today, people look forward to the seasons that produce the favored wild food of their regions. In New England, they look to the spring for the unfurled ferns they call "fiddleheads," which are edible in most of those northern species after cooking, and then look forward to the autumn for delicious wild blueberries. In West Virginia, it's a wild member of the Allium genus—the group that includes onions, garlics, and leeks that the locals call "ramps" or "wild leeks."

Here in Florida there once was a prized wild food that comes from the native *Sabal palmetto,* or sabal palm, swamp cabbage, and cabbage palm—the heart of the palm—which is now supposedly protected by law, a state statute, and very difficult to harvest anyway without much of a caloric pay-off.

Most modern Americans have been taught that the Native Americans, inappropriately called Indians and appropriately called First Peoples and First Nations, lived strictly off of animal flesh while raising corn, squash, and beans. However, that could not be further from the truth. They were very much dependent upon a plant-based diet of wild food. For example, they anxiously awaited the beginning of the spring in all climates for the spring greens of wild edible plants that pop up after a winter of eating mostly roots, breads, preserved meat, and other food, with the occasional fresh-killed meat. As settlers came here from around the world, they brought with them a wide variety of other wild edibles.

Many of the spring greens are leafy, like a wild lettuce, spinach, and mustards. Other plants can provide edible roots—starchy and loaded with carbohydrates—or combinations of edible greens and roots. Some of the plants are edible from the ground up—all aboveground parts are edible one way or another. Many edible plants, particularly from grassy plants and edible greens, also produce seeds that can be used as a grain for a gruel, meal, or flour. Many wild food recipes consist of specific parts of specific wild plants that can be used together with conventional foodstuffs as well as with parts of other wild plants.

I call a survival stew any soup or stew that can be put together with wild plants (even with edible insects), with or without conventional ingredients added. There are many kinds of edible wild berries—some absolutely delicious—in practically every region of the North American continent and beyond.

Most of the edible wild plants that grow in your area can be raised easily in your garden or scattered around your property. When you turn over and loosen the soil as you would to begin a garden, you can produce wild edible plants by either scattering seeds collected and dried from other locations or simply by not planting anything after tilling the soil and waiting to see what comes up. Seeds from past plants can lay dormant for centuries. There is no need to fertilize—although a little might help—and there is no need to pull any weeds, because most of the plants that are the most common wild edibles actually are those weeds. This wild food garden requires little to no tending and no mowing at all.

Many of these plants followed populations of natives, pioneers, and homesteaders around the country. Even today, when I see a new construction project where there were woods, fields, or crops, I know that the soil will be disturbed, chewed up, loosened, and packed before something new is built there. As soon as the work is nearly done, new plant growth appears in bare spots. Up through the new sod, almost like magic, spring plant types that may or may not have been there before the construction began. Many of those plants are considered invasive weeds, yet most are useful to humans in one way or another.

Natives, early pioneers, and immigrants knew how to use their favorite plants (mostly herbaceous)—many of which were brought here as seeds from around the world—to cultivate and manipulate for optimal growth and to influence the fertility of through hybridization. It created specialized varieties that could spread and grow quickly. And the abundant seeds got attached to birds, animals, horses, buggies, trains, cars, trucks, cycles, ATVs, pedestrians, and hikers and quickly spread to other areas. Over the last few centuries, many of these plants were brought here from around the world. Some were useful for food and medicine, but are now considered noxious and unwanted, and so are being sprayed with poisons that will ultimately harm all living things to some extent.

When I walk into a patch of woods along well-used hiking trails and dirt roads, I see many of those plants at the trailhead and then see fewer of them the deeper into the woods I go. It is evidence that many edible wild plants follow us wherever we go as if they were purposely designed to do so. Most of those plants that we call weeds were once food and medicine that our ancestors designed to grow that way—invasive and widespread.

And that's not all. All of the plant based food that you eat every day was once wild before people started cultivating, breeding, and manipulating them for our benefit. In the future, when food shortages, economic collapse, and political upheavals occur, the best emergency food will be those weeds that you allow to grow in clean, wholesome soil—assuming there is wholesome soil left.

Over a century ago when people had to forage and farm exclusively to survive, the kind of food that they lacked and needed the most was the kind that they craved and wanted the most; the fats, sweets, and salts. We now have these in abundance and yet we still crave them the most because of our past. The result of that is the adverse health effects of having too many fats, sweets, and salts in our present diets.

At the onset of a survival situation, your first impulse may be to trap, snare, or hunt an animal for food. Second impulse might be to find grubs and insect larvae. What you may not realize is that many edible plants provide protein, carbohydrates, and fats in small but easily obtainable amounts. And by easy, I mean you don't have to snare, trap, hunt, or dig for them, they're right out in the open. They will not put up much of a fight to live or to protect their leaves, seeds, tubers, and flowers. However, making a positive identification is virtually imperative. Never assume something is edible unless you know absolutely positively that it is. Here in central Florida, I have documented edible subtropical and temperate zone plants as comprehensively (but not perfectly) as I could.

Some survival guidebooks attempt to instruct you on wild edibles with generalizations. They might say that most roots, bulbs, and tubers are safe and that blue and black berries are usually safe to eat and then present just a short list of certain plants that are found in specific places around the world. They might even say to watch the animals to see what they eat. All of those generalizations are dangerous. To be prepared for a survival/doomsday/famine situation someday in your region of the world—wherever that may be—just do your homework ahead of time: study, study, study, and study some more.

As I started learning about edible plants long ago, I became much more observant of the plant life around me. As you become more familiar with them, you'll find yourself looking for them practically everywhere you go. Learning this subject suddenly instills in you a self-sufficiency of which you couldn't imagine before. We know that survival requires four priorities: shelter, water, fire, and food. Shelter can be provided in a variety of ways. Water can be a challenge, but ultimately, a water source and purification of it is not impossible to find in most temperate regions of the world. Fire can be needed basically for warmth, light, purifying water, and cooking. Trees, coal, some plants, mosses, sunlight (solar-cooking, reflective material), and other sources can be obtained for the benefits that fire provides. Then, what about food? Once you have a wide-ranging knowledge of wild edibles, from plants to animals to insects, then you have all the knowledge necessary to be completely self-sufficient if you have to be. For a life-form as fragile and vulnerable as we are, that is a huge advantage over others and a great confidence builder.

However, most people will refuse to learn about wild edibles. They refuse to consider a plant that is not cultivated in mass quantity for commercial sale in their own country as potential food. Even though insects are food for people all over the world, many Americans refuse to even consider it. They will refuse to eat the weeds no matter how much information you can provide them on their edibility and palatability. It is ridiculous that so many Americans weed their gardens and spray poisons around their dwellings to kill perfectly good food. Most popular landscape plants are poisonous or simply toxic. Commonly used landscape grasses are not edible either. It figures that the hated crabgrass has edible uses. The seeds can be harvested as a grain.

Today's lawn-care methods include chemicals that can make us sick or at least increase the risk of cancers. So, people kill all potential food-sources around them and spray poisons that contaminate the soil itself, making it unfit to forage from for virtually years.

I began to study all the aspects of survival skills and decided to focus my energy on foraging. If survival essentials are shelter, water, fire, and food, the forager is much more prepared for a survival scenario, however it happens, than most. Even the average well-armed doomsday prepper is not as prepared and self-sufficient as the forager. Especially when you can't eat bullets and when you consider that many people would refuse to eat a weed unless their lives depended on it. However, if their lives actually did depend on it, and they don't know what they can safely eat, they're dead. This subject fascinated me so much that I obsessed over sharing it with people who might be interested. Unfortunately, most people aren't very interested because they just assume that their food will always be there for them—even in emergencies—picked, preserved, packed, and paid for.

So, if you take this subject seriously, you can become as self-sufficient as one can be.

3
Warning Signs

Here are a few warning signs to know when foraging for edible wild plants. I would state here, right off the bat, that making a mistake on a wild plant can either cause no harm, be mildly unpleasant, make you sick, or can kill you. The photo at right shows a very toxic butterweed (*Senecio glabellus*) that could be mistaken for a wild mustard or wild lettuce species. Be sure of what you forage!

Highly toxic butterweed

There are many varieties of *Lattuca* and *Sonchus* plants that are similar and edible—especially after cooking. You may be 90 percent sure that you have identified a *Sonchus* genus and take the chance of boiling the leaves for greens (if you must) and you'll probably be okay. Or you could mistake a very toxic butterweed for a *Sonchus* or *Lattuca*. The possible symptoms of butterweed poisoning are "abdominal pain, vomiting, diarrhea, enlarged liver, bloody vomiting, ascites, followed by death." (Julia F. Morton, *Plants Poisonous to People in Florida*.)

In Florida, the poisonous butterweed comes up in January and grows away by May, about the same time of year as our *Sonchus*. It can also fool people into thinking it is a wild mustard species, many of which grow in the Southeast at the same time and are edible. One of the best indicators of a toxic plant is a burning, hot sensation in the mouth as soon as you bite into it. That's right, a spicy-hotness sensation in the wild is not a good sign. Another warning sign is extreme bitterness or rank flavor that makes you want to spit it out. My advice, no matter how hungry you are, is that if something is so bitter or rank flavored that you feel the impulse to spit it out immediately, then spit it out immediately. As you can see from the effects of butterweed, it's better to be safe than sick—or dead. That's not the only plant in Florida that can kill. There are plenty.

As you learn about edible wild plants, you'll realize that most of them taste very good or acceptable when all the precautions and prescribed methods of preparation are met.

I read where a survival "expert" says to study the woodland critters' food sources to tell whether a plant is edible to people. It is a huge mistake to assume that we can eat something that an animal can eat. The fact is that many things are edible to certain animals that are not edible to us and vice-versa.

Know your plants. Learn how to identify them, and know what times of year they grow. Know the environment where you're likely to find them, and always be sure that you know the proper method of preparation for each plant—whether you can eat it raw, or if it must be boiled. Some plants need to be soaked in water or wood-ash for several hours or days. A plant can have tiny hairs on the leaves and/or stems that might be filled with formic acid, which can sting you like a bee when you touch it, as in stinging nettles and spurge nettles. The effects can be similar to ant bites or bee stings. Wild plants with pole-bean-type seedpods are more often toxic than edible. Don't assume that something is edible just because it might look like a familiar fruit or vegetable or something you have learned is edible. Be positive that it is edible before consuming!

Another warning sign is a soapy scent or flavor. A toxic substance in some plants, such as in the roots of the *Yucca filamentosa* and other yucca species, is called saponin. It is not just a soapy taste; it can be used like a soap to produce suds for cleaning. Do not mistake the root vegetable at your store that is called yucca for the ones that actually grow in Florida. They are not the same. When you shave or scrape off tiny pieces of the root of our local yucca species into water and agitate the water, you can produce soapy suds for cleaning anything that might need cleaning. It will not disinfect anything but will break up oil, dirt, and dead-skin particles for extracting in water. This substance is toxic if consumed in large amounts or high concentrations. Sometimes a plant can have a tiny amount in it that is edible but not the roots of our local yucca species.

A milky, white sap or white, liquid substance from plants is sometimes a warning sign to indicate that something is not edible, but not always. Sometimes, for specific plants, they just need to be boiled. It is called a latex, and is either a sign to steer clear—as in any cactus—or a sign that something should be boiled if it is of a green-vegetable type. Dandelions, *Sonchus*, milkweed, milkweed vine, and groundnut come to mind as being wild edibles with a white sap that is usually too bitter to eat raw (some are toxic raw), but mellows down or eliminates the toxicity and bitterness after boiling. The edible parts of the northern common milkweed, *Asclepias syriaca* and *A. speciosa* (not included in this book) must be boiled to be edible (some people can eat the young tops raw without harm). There are no edible species of milkweed (*Asclepias species)* growing in Florida. Some people might be sensitive to a plant with latex, causing an allergenic reaction, but probably not many. An aroma that is described as bitter almonds on any plant part is also a warning sign and indication of cyanide-causing constituents.

Also, avoid using any seeds that contain a purplish, pink, or black discoloration or spur. This is particularly so if the discoloration appears in the form of a spur on a grass or herb seed when observed closely with a magnifying glass. It may turn out to be a very dangerous fungal infection called Ergot. All seeds of grassy plants are susceptible to fungal growths that must be diligently scoured and purged from the potential grain that most of the grassy plants provide. I don't include the plants called yellow sweetclover, *Melilotus officinalis* and white sweetclover, *M. alba* as edible in any way because it is reportedly very susceptible to ergot.

A few guidebooks on edible plants and survival-guides suggest or encourage using what is called the Edibility Test. It is intended to be an emergency procedure for testing whether an unknown plant's part is edible or not. I've only seen one guidebook on edible plants suggest it as a viable option. Many survival-guides suggest it if one comes across a large enough amount of a particular unknown fruit or plant to feed oneself sufficiently for days if necessary. The concept uses many varying methods, a step-by-step process of elimination—starting with rubbing the leaf or fruit of an unidentified plant to your skin (usually on your arm) and wait to see if any kind of adverse reaction occurs; which includes an itching or rash—but any reaction out of the ordinary. The concept requires waiting a sufficient amount of time for a reaction. If no reaction occurs, you move to the next step. The next step can involve touching the object to your lips, followed immediately by licking your lips. Picture this as one kissing the object and then licking your lips. Again, wait for a sufficient amount of time for a reaction. This reaction could include a burning sensation, even a spicy hot one, or any unusual physical manifestation. In the wild, a burning taste is not a good sign at all. Highly toxic chemicals can consist of acids that can severely burn your insides if you consume it. If no reaction occurs, it's on to the next step. Put a leaf into your mouth and hold it there for ten to twenty minutes or more before spitting it out. Wait a sufficient amount of time again. The next step after that is usually the last one to determine edibility, eating a small amount of the object and waiting anywhere from six to twenty-four hours to see if anything bad happens. I suggest that this Edibility Test methodology is only good as a last resort for those who do not know what is edible. This is why knowing your environment and what is edible there is so important. Don't take the chance if you don't have to!

Our bodies are very good at going for a few days without any nourishment and not cause severe limitations to your strength and energy. Water is different. Your bodies require water every day—I would estimate a half-gallon per day as the average goal for water in a survival situation when not experiencing extreme conditions or activities. And while there is plenty of very edible wild green food that you could harvest and forage on, the need for protein, carbs, and fat is paramount in a survival situation. There are also the cultivated garden-variety fruits and vegetables that sometimes can be found in the oddest of places. There are insects that are perfectly edible after cooking (to kill parasites) with legs, wings, shells, and head/guts removed and many forms of lichen moss that are edible after properly preparing (soaking in changes of water with wood ash or baking soda for days). Taking a chance on just the nutrition one can get from some unknown plant in the Edibility Test is hardly worth the risk of putting something toxic into the stomach of someone in a desperate situation. What you'll need the most if undernourished is cooked edible animal flesh or nuts, roots, and seeds—then green plants and fruits to round out the needs of the body. Pine tree cambium tastes bland but has carbohydrates. Pine tree needles can be used to make a tea—using warm water not hot—for the vitamin C content. Hot water destroys vitamin C. However, one leaf of water hemlock can make one very, very sick. If someone is already malnourished when eating a toxic or poisonous plant part, it could kill even if medical attention becomes available soon after symptoms appear.

I once conducted an experiment on a plant with questionable edibility. The black night-shade aka common nightshade, *Solanum americanum* and belladonna contains a tropane alkaloid, solanum, a toxic chemical. The ripe, shiny, totally black berries are barely edible (for a particular species) but okay in moderate amounts and the leaves are said by some to be edible after two or three boils, but some say that the entire plant is not edible no matter what. I ate one leaf raw and experienced a mild nausea after about twenty minutes that lasted about twenty minutes. That one leaf only gave me a very mild case of nausea but could be devastating to someone that is in a stage of starvation.

Another important warning is foraging from contaminated soil. While many wild edible plants grow close to roads, busy roads provide extremely bad places to forage. Along a busy highway and/or downhill from one is the worst place to forage, even if there may be lots of good edible plants, berries, nuts, or especially roots. Roots will be the more contaminated of any other part of a plant when it sits in toxic soil. The plants closest to busy roads have been sitting in exhaust their whole lives. Choose places uphill or several dozen feet (but not downhill) from busy roads, factories, mines, animal farms, and railroad tracks. Sometimes apartment complexes and business centers use reclaimed water for watering their landscape plants and grass. Many edible plants grow right up through sodded grass or along the perimeter. Be wary of herbicides and pesticides (like the weed killer, Roundup).

Although you can eat edible plants that are watered with reclaimed water it is important to sufficiently boil such plants regardless of whether boiling is necessary or not. You should also be aware of edges of fences that might have also been sprayed with herbicides. Many landscapers and lawn-maintenance workers and homeowners use them to cut down on, or eliminate, the need for weed-whacking. The weed killer sprays wear off after a few months or so but the plants that come up where previously sprayed with chemicals will contain at least trace amounts of those chemicals for quite some time.

This is a grasshopper species that I would not eat even if an expert said that it is edible because of the general rule of no bright colors. Even though that yellow color is a dull yellow I would still hesitate to eat this kind. Mykel would eat it, but all grasshoppers and crickets need to be cooked as they can carry parasites. Once cooked, most toxins are neutralized as well.

Driveways accumulate amounts of gas, grease, rubber, and oils—which contaminate the soil along its perimeter when the rain washes it from the concrete or asphalt. Where you decide to forage depends mainly on how hungry you might be at that time and dependent upon the circumstances of the situation. The chemicals and heavy-metal contamination mentioned above can make one nauseous and sick to some extent, especially if already weakened by fatigue and malnutrition.

4
Doug's Thoughts

Our consumerism is wasting and polluting the earth's resources. It's just a matter of time, and sooner than you probably think, until the sheer number of humans on Earth will pollute/deplete all available resources and over-stretch Earth's ability to support us all. The effects of this are growing in intensity exponentially. You are looking at the adverse effects of this becoming painfully clear to everyone in a matter of decades, not centuries. What will the starving masses eat when civilization collapses under the weight of increasing heat waves, massive drought, and the increasing floods of climate change; the burgeoning populations, continuous war, depletion of wild fish and animals, economic collapse, and chemical contamination of all resources by reckless, profit-driven industries?

My guess is that it will be the wild foods that past generations depended on almost exclusively in tough times. Today's generations are clueless and indifferent about it. From upper-class to lower, and from filthy-rich to filth-poor, most of humanity (particularly Americans) couldn't care less about the wild food found in those "weeds" that invade the landscapes of virtually every region of the world.

For obvious reasons, I must warn you not to eat any wild plant unless you are as sure as you can be of what it is, that it is edible, what parts of it are edible, that it comes from mostly clean, wholesome soil, and how to prepare it if required. However, this book has been written for the purpose of telling you and your descendants what you can eat if you have to. The soil might be questionable and you might not be absolutely sure of identification of plants in a survival situation. These things are left to each individual to risk if he/she has to and be as prepared mentally for the challenges ahead as one can reasonably be.

Check as many sources of information as possible online and in bookstores and ask locals among your populations who might know something about the wild plants around you before you make the decision to actually eat any of it. However, I'm focusing this book on plentiful and nutritious wild plant food in my neck of the woods to aid in one's survival, should it come to that, not for the purpose of supplementing wild food into your present diet. I advise experimentation to some extent with wild food now as you prepare yourself with a critical subject involving the knowledge of absolute self-sufficiency.

I've noticed some very different species of foraging plants here on the eastern half of the US from those on the western side. Because of this, I've had to focus on plants available through parts, or most of, the Eastern United States. In particular, my home state of Florida is where my focus has been the most. I've done my best to provide accurate and helpful information here. All guidebooks disagree somewhat on some things and no guidebook is perfect, including mine. Some edible plants here have close relatives elsewhere that are not edible and which may be dependent upon a particular region. Our Spiderwort here is very edible, but other species exist elsewhere that are not edible.

Beware of common names. Many different plants can have the same common names. To be sure, always check the scientific name. Even then, scientific names can change over time.

Be sure of the method of preparation if it requires it. Some plants, for example, must be boiled, and some must be boiled multiple times while changing the water each time. All but two of the more than twenty thousand kinds of lichen are edible after soaking out the acid content. Some guide books might dismiss lichen as a viable resource because of the extensive leeching process necessary to remove the acid and make it edible. Adding wood ash or baking soda to the water will speed up the process that can take up three or four days. Soak it for days at a time in clean water mixed with clean wood ashes and/or baking soda. After every half-day, dump the water and add more with more ash and/or soda. This must be repeated for a few days to leech out the acidic contents of the lichen, if it can be leeched out. The results are very, very high in carbohydrates. Only two kinds are toxic—the sulfur colored one and a yellowish-green one. Some lichens, like reindeer moss (*Claydonia spp.*) and bearded lichen (*Usnea spp.*) can be found in Florida and the Southeastern US but others are strictly northern species. I didn't address lichen in this book because of my lack of actual experience with it and because of negative information some sources report on concerning it. Do some homework on lichens for a potentially plentiful and nutritious food source. Early explorers depended heavily on it for emergencies.

Focus on the edible plants that are the most common and plentiful in your area. Some plant parts will just require soaking in water to make edible for anywhere from an hour, a few hours, a few days, and even a few weeks (shelled acorns, if boiling is not an option). I decided not to address acorns for three reasons. One, I don't have any real experience with them. Two, there's plenty of info already out there on that subject. And three, I've been questioning some of the info I've accumulated on it, like the best/easiest method for shelling them and the extent of how much our local live oak, of the white oaks, needs to be leeched of tannin. However, Mykel addresses this subject later in the book.

Some plants that require extensive boiling procedures might lack in nutrition once properly prepared for human consumption. I've excluded some of the green plants that require multiple boils. I've excluded plants like taro which require too much preparation and is reportedly too toxic to make edible in the Florida wild. Our wild taro is quite different from most cultivated and escaped species. I advise staying away from it in Florida. Maybe not in other parts of the world, but definitely here in Florida.

There are many edible plants that I did not mention for various reasons. For example, they just don't grow wild in Florida at all, like Jerusalem artichoke (*Helianthus tuberosus),* or they are difficult to make edible, or I just haven't had the opportunity to study them, like some of the edible plants that only grow in the Everglades and the southernmost portion of Florida.

Seaweeds and coastal plants have many edible and nutritious species but I don't live close enough to any and so many have salt that might mess with my blood pressure. Besides, in a future doomsday/famine/survival scenario, the shorelines of any country will be where most people will go for fishing, cooling from the summer heat, and for turning saltwater into potable freshwater with distillation or desalination devices. It will be crowded there. Mykel covers seaweeds and seashore plants later in the book.

Sometimes edible wild plants turn bitter and rank with age, which is alleviated to some extent with boiling. But if you don't mind a little bitterness, in those cases, only boil as much as you need to in order to get as much nutrition as you can from it. Too much bitterness in a plant is a sign that it might cause nausea and/or vomiting. It may also be a sign that you have the wrong plant. If it tastes so bitter that you feel compelled to spit it out, just spit it out.

I learned long, long ago that I needed to know about this subject. I've been unskilled, homeless, hungry, unemployed, underpaid, or under-employed, and lacking in resources for the vast majority of my adult life. Hungry, homeless individuals struggle to be fed even in a country of such plenty. I know that from my own experiences. I never weighed more than 135 pounds (six-feet tall) until I began to receive government food assistance a few years ago at the age of fifty-seven. Before you judge me falsely, I've never been a drinker of alcoholic beverages or drug abuser. Being unskilled, physically weak, generally not cheerful, and relatively unhealthy and homely, I was forced into the outcasts of our society and never found a viable career at anything that paid even close to a living wage.

I once vomited while living in New Hampshire woods, surviving extreme poverty, after eating what I thought was just boiled dandelions and plantain (a plant, not the fruit). The nausea came on fast after about fifteen minutes or one-half hour of eating and the moment I vomited it up I felt better. I was very young and still quite new to foraging. I knew I had been overconfident and a little careless while gathering the plants. While a possible reason for my reaction to what I ate could have been plants that were too old and bitter to be consumed on an empty stomach even though I boiled it, I believed at the time that the cause was some leaf or leaves from a toxic plant had mixed in with the ones I collected that day. This is why harvesting, gathering, foraging, whatever one wishes to call it, must be done carefully. I was lucky it wasn't the leaf of a plant with the name hemlock in it. That could have been the end of me right then and there.

This is a vital survival point here: Even if a plant is universally edible and 100 percent positively identified, a person never knows if they might just have an allergic reaction to that plant. And allergic reactions can develop for any one at any time, even after years of eating a plant without issue. Hence, we both reiterate repeatedly: be cautious, prudent, judicious, and wise in your foraging.

I remember how much it scared me. As soon as the nausea came on fast and hard I started hiking (late in the evening) toward a payphone at a closed convenience store on the nearest road a mile away. I didn't get a hundred feet away from camp when I threw it up. I remember how relieved I was when I realized that getting it out stopped the nausea immediately. I knew how lucky I was that night.

I hope to impress upon the reader just exactly how important a subject this is going to be in the not-too-distant future. The world is finally becoming aware of the need to teach this knowledge to the millions of less fortunate and starving around the world. Why hasn't it been a priority? Because wild food is free food. The world is consumed by the consumer-market economy. Food charities are big business. Our culture does not teach people anything that is not somehow profitable in the form of monetary currency. It is a pathological culture driven by apathy, distractions, delusions, competition, self-absorption, and greed. It is not sustainable in the long run, and is clearly unhealthy in the short-term at every level for the individual, the community, and the Earth.

5
Doug's Bugs, Slugs, and Grubs

Don't eat ticks, flies, fleas, or mosquitoes; they are disease carriers.

In modern America and Western Civilization in general the main source of protein comes from animals, yet, in developing countries it is not unusual for human inhabitants to trap and harvest bugs, slugs, grubs, and snails for their regular fat and protein consumption. The term for the consumption of insects is entomophagy.

The Bible regards grasshopper species like locusts as clean for human consumption. However, not all of them are edible. The main reason that modern humans associate bugs as unclean is because we associate them with the deadly microbes, pathogens, parasites, and diseases that many of them carry. Aside from those disease carriers listed above, many insects can be cleansed or purged of toxic substances and/or simply cooked to rid them of parasites and pathogens. Even our foul-looking palmetto bugs (large roaches) can be purged clean by putting them into containers that they can't escape from (with pin-holes for air) with fruits and vegetables (or edible wild plants). The process for roaches takes forty-eight hours. After that, removing the legs and the hard shell before thorough cooking is still required to insure edibility. I would not try this with roaches or palmetto bugs except if being faced with critical stages of starvation and absolutely nothing else to eat. That's not likely to happen to me. There are better creepy crawlers to choose from. Snails, slugs, grubs, crickets, and edible hopper species would be my preferred choice of creepy-crawler cuisine—even dragonflies.

Slugs and snails are best handled with gloves until thoroughly cooked. Boiling snails in their shells makes it easier to remove them from the shell. Always purge them (put into a container with edibles for a period of time first) in a cool, dark place for the purging process. Same goes for slugs. For slugs and snails, a twenty-four-hour period of purging is acceptable. Mykel just boils or cooks them and kills most everything that can be harmful. But it is vital to cook snails and slugs as they can carry parasites that can kill.

There are at least two general rules to entomophagy. Rule number one is that plant-eating insects are able to eat plants which are toxic to us and therefore should be purged to be safe for us to eat. There is even the possibility that some insects consume edible plants but build up a substance from it that becomes toxic to us in concentrated amounts. This is a good general rule to be safe, but most of the time, boiling or cooking neutralizes most of any potentially negative side effects.

In Florida, the most abundant of edible plants to use for purging consists of green vegetation. I would use any one of our delicious year-round or seasonal wild, green, edible plants to put into the container with the edible critters. The exception for purging could be when finding snails, slugs, grubs, etc. that you find are eating plants that you already know are safe. There will be a 99 percent chance that it is safe to eat. Grubs that are not hairy or with tiny legs all along their bodies are probably safe to purge, cook, and eat. Some grubs will have a few legs in the front of their bodies. If they have substantial legs throughout their bodies and/or they are hairy, they are caterpillars and are better left alone in Florida. I know that there is at least one kind of hairy caterpillar in Florida that is very toxic. When they fall out of a tree and land on my bare shoulder they sting me with the toxins in their hairs. Although many of these insects have their sting neutralized when boiled, but it's easier to just leave them be and find others.

Edible insects contain a storehouse of nutrients that the survivor will need—including fat and protein. Earthworms are edible as well. However, it is their skin that we need most, not their guts. Purging them is not necessary, just squeeze out their guts and dry the skins in the sun until they have the texture of a crusty powder. Add this powder to your survival-stew and it should be safe and valuable for consumption.

A Survivor Stew, as I call it, is your best method of obtaining nutrition in the wild or in any doomsday/famine/survival situation. Roasting over the fire burns the outer portion of whatever you are roasting in order to cook it through thoroughly. Boiling something thoroughly kills all pathogens and parasites (as it does in making water potable) while retaining all of the potential nutrition in the portion being cooked and in the broth. Having a fairly large canteen cup or small stainless-steel pot (not aluminum) packed away in your survival gear is a survival essential for making potable water from groundwater/surface-water sources. It will double its value as a method for cooking survival stew.

If no edible plants are available to purge edible critters with, you can still purge them of toxic contents by simply stashing them away in a container for at least a twenty-four-hour period without anything for them to eat. A few drops of potable water placed in with them should help the process.

The second rule of entomophagy is that brightly colored, multi-colored, or slow-moving insects can be very toxic and even deadly poisonous no matter what you do. In nature, a sign of a poisonous species is usually (always for insects) bright colors like reds, yellows, and orange. Very many plants used in landscaping are completely toxic to humans, often being brightly colored. Practically all lilies and defi-

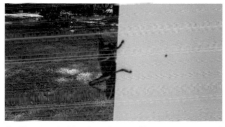

Southeastern Lubber Grasshopper (*Romalea microptera*).

nitely all iris species are toxic/poisonous even though the colorful roses and hibiscus plants have very edible parts, as well as other colorful flowers. So, for plants it is a generalization but not a rule. For insects, however, it is very much a rule.

In Florida we have large, slow-moving, multi-colored grasshoppers called lubbers, or southeastern lubber grasshopper (*Romalea microptera*) with yellow and black markings and reddish stripes on the fore-wings. The young lubbers are mostly black with yellow stripes. It can emit a foul-smelling secretion when disturbed or threatened. This grasshopper is reported to contain two toxic chemicals that cannot be leeched or purged by any means. It is toxic to consume by all standards of the rule. Slow-moving—because they know that most birds and other predators will not attack them (nature usually knows better but not always), brightly colored—the red stripe on adults and yellow stripes on the young ones are a kind of STOP sign in nature. And, emitting a foul smell to repulse any would-be predator is another warning sign. With almost any potential edible in Florida, if it doesn't smell good you probably shouldn't eat it, papaya fruit and Skunkvine being exceptions.

However, the most edible hoppers include shades of earth tones, like a green broad-winged katydid (*Microcentrum rhombifolium*) which is found in Florida woods and fields, or the green cone-headed grasshopper (*Neoconocephalus species*) with its long, slender body and cone-shaped head. These hoppers make distinctive sounds that can tip off a survivor to their presence. To be safe though, wings and legs of all flying insects should be removed—as they have the potential to scrape the tissue of your digestive tract with sharp and indigestible fibers.

Broad-winged katydid *(Microcentrum rhombifolium).*

There are brightly-colored, tropical frogs that have deadly poison in their skin and toads with toxic glands that should be avoided. I'll save the frogs, salamanders, and lizards for another book but the rules are basically the same. Suffice it to state here that the edible ones must be cooked thoroughly as well and in many cases the skin should be discarded by picking the meat out with your teeth and fingers or peeling off the skin before cooking, especially if boiling. Remove the skin of any amphibian or reptile beforehand if you intend to boil it, just to be on the safe side. Otherwise, roast it over the fire and then pick the meat off of the skin. To some survivalists out there, some of these precautions will seem a bit extreme. However, some have trained themselves with the knowledge of how to deal with a few days in the wild before getting back to civilization. My focus is to deal with long-term survival in the event of civilization becoming uncivilized and breaking down completely for an indefinite period of time. In that case, there will not be a doctor or hospital that one can get to any time soon. One must be extra cautious in those circumstances.

Insects that are edible should always be cooked first somehow before consuming—or just stun them, place them into a glass or clear-plastic container, and leave it in the sun for a dozen hours or so to cook solar-style. Tapeworm parasites are a common threat when eating insects, particularly for all hopper species. Whether you roast, bake, or boil them, be very sure that you've cooked them evenly and thoroughly.

A grub is a weevil or beetle larva. If the grub has legs all along its body it is a moth or butterfly larva, a caterpillar, not always edible. Grubs will generally be found in rotting wood or in the soil itself. Look for them in black, dark, rich, and fairly dry soil. If any larva has hair it is a sign of possible toxicity and best left alone. With so much wild food in places where caterpillars live why take the chance? The edibility of insect larvae is a wide and varied subject. Many kinds of insect larvae are edible, but not all.

My rule is to choose only those that are found in rotting wood or soil without hair and with no bright colors. I don't know how foolproof that method is; my research indicates that it's your best bet but you should do more research on that category. Acorns can contain edible grubs and can be harvested by placing the acorns in a container of water. The acorns with possible grubs will float on the surface as the ones without grubs will sink to the bottom. Then those that float are placed in a colander (or improvised container/basket with holes) and placed on newspaper, concrete, or very large leaves. The grubs will crawl out of the acorns and try to get to the ground. Make sure you collect only grubs. Scoop them up to boil, bake, or fry. Do not place grubs in hot oil or they might explode. You can also find acorns with grubs by looking for holes in the nuts themselves. These grubs are also good fish bait. Just remember: hairy ones can be used for bait, but cook them first if you want to eat them. You can eat grubs raw.

Suffice it to state, in my opinion, that a skill in the science of survival is less about how to perform the physical tasks of building a debris hut or starting a campfire with a bow drill or hand drill—it is much more about knowledge and attitude. The knowledge of survival goes way beyond the physical tasks—one must know exactly what to do and then you can take confidence in knowing that you can improvise, adapt, and overcome obstacles no matter what your situation might be, within reason, because you did your homework.

The last thing you want to happen in any survival scenario is to get sick from something you've eaten. Sure, you can go for days at a time with no food as long as you have potable water, shelter, and warmth, but why weaken yourself by purposely going hungry because you lack the knowledge of wild edibles or because you must maintain the modern American and somewhat natural aversion to eating insects?

The kinds of edible insects available to the survivor depends on the kinds in your region and present season. Edible hopper species and insects in general, including crickets, (crickets are edible cooked but be sure they have no colorful striping) are recognizable by their actions when you approach them. Toxic ones aren't very afraid of us, even though they will try to avoid close contact with you. The ones that flee quickly as you approach, with no bright colors, are usually safe to cook and eat. Florida has a slightly yellowish beige–colored hopper that was reported to me as toxic from a non-accredited source. I cannot confirm it at this time. It would be wise to avoid them as well, even though they flee from any living thing that approaches them and the colors are relatively light earth-tones. Catching enough hoppers or dragonflies to add to a survival stew will mean using some clever methods. A net of some kind, like a cast-net for bait or any mesh material that can be fashioned into a cast-net, will work best. A piece of screen from a porch or mosquito-netting from a tent (or pieces from several old tents sewn together) can work well also. If you approach a colony of crickets near a body of water you can corral them into the water, then just picking them out of the water one by one. Beetles are reported to be edible cooked as well. However, the hard shell and legs must be removed, leaving very little meat. If an insect is acting out of character and erratic, it might be sick and should be left alone.

Some ants are edible while others are either toxic or simply not worth the effort. Large black carpenter ants that often live in rotting logs are best. Frying their rear portions is best. However, Florida does not normally have carpenter ants. Boiling a few ants in with a survival stew is good. Fire ants are toxic and best left alone. Small black sugar-ants are plentiful in Florida, don't bite, and are edible as far as I know. Ant larvae is edible cooked, maybe even raw. You should check other sources of information. Termites are edible cooked, and hot water kills them easily. If you catch a handful of them alive, drop them into very hot water That should kill them almost immediately. Then pick them out and pull off wings and as many legs as is reasonable at the time before boiling or frying. They should be sun-dried and winnowed of legs (large ones) and wings (if winged). They are reported to be very tasty when fried and mixed with rice. The larvae of many insects are a prized edible to many around the world.

As much as it would take a great deal of effort to de-wing and remove hard parts of june bugs and boil in salted water, they are reported to be very edible. In some parts of the world they are eaten whole after baking and covering with chocolate or sauce. If you need to be extra safe, large grubs should be soaked overnight in salt-water, then the head removed and squeezed from tail to head of their guts before boiling or baking for consumption. Eating them whole after cooking without purging can be done but will not rid them of possible toxins from what they've eaten. This is why taking the time to purge them is so worth it. Remove wings and legs from dragonflies before cooking. Any of the fly species other than dragonflies are literally off the table. Houseflies carry as much as a hundred pathogens. Maggots can be edible, containing more than 50 percent protein, but they are obviously composed of what they eat and should be cooked. However, they don't consume rancid meat. Flies lay the eggs that produce the maggots in freshly killed animal flesh, not in flesh that has spoiled. That is why maggots are fairly safe to eat, even raw. If you find maggots on feces, leave it be. Scorpions and some spiders are supposedly safe to eat after cooking under certain conditions but my rule in survival-grub is to not try to catch something that could sting or injure me unless the reward is great. I've read somewhere that bees are edible after removing the stinger and cooking but I don't advise it and won't suggest it. The same goes for spiders. Mykel notes that large spiders and all scorpions are edible, but you must remove the hair from spiders over fire and cut the stingers off scorpions.

However, with all this being said, just as there are edible plants that are edible but nearly unpalatable, the same goes for insects. Simply put, in a real survival or famine situation anything goes, within reason, as long as you are over 90 percent certain that what you are eating is edible and safe. Or, 100 percent sure, if you don't want to risk it. It will always be a judgment call based on your knowledge and need.

MYKEL'S GENERAL GUIDELINE RULES

HUMANS CAN EAT 90 PERCENT OF THE ANIMALS ON THE PLANET.
Since we get more energy from meat, it's usually a better survival option for work-to-food ratio.

HUMANS CAN EAT 10 PERCENT OF THE PLANTS ON THE PLANET.
Since a lot of vegetation isn't digestible for us, we need to be sure what we DO eat, is good.

HUMANS CAN EAT 50 PERCENT OF THE BUGS AND 50 percent OF THE BERRIES.
For bugs the general color rule that helps is: bright isn't right, but bland is just grand.

If they sting or have vivid bright colors, it's best to avoid, that's nature's warning sign, but the earth tones and bland colors meant to blend is usually a good sign they are okay to eat. Over all, bugs have more nutrition than both plants and animals, but the main issue is if you can find enough to make a meal worthwhile. As Doug points out, they are great additions to a survival stew and for survival, stews are your best, safest bet as they're easiest to make, you make most food safe, and you get lots of nutrients, sustenance, and hydration all in one go.

Since berries can be tricky, you must be sure to correctly ID them.

Yellow and white, in general isn't right.

Black through blue, in general are good for you.

Red is 50/50, could be good, could be dead.

If the red berries are singletons or tight packs, they're usually good.

If they are singles on a stem but in a cluster, they're generally not good.

There are exceptions for every one of these.

So study them well before you eat and as Doug says, if they're bitter or burn, spit them out.

6
Foraging 101

The most plentiful edible plants you may find have been following people for centuries. People carry pollen and seeds from plants as they travel around the world. Pioneers purposely brought dried seeds of edible and medicinal plants here from Europe and elsewhere and spread them out over time, either by planting it wherever they stayed or inadvertently spreading the seeds around that stuck to their clothes, packs, horses, carts, wagons, trains, cars, trucks, etc. The locations where the soil has been disturbed in some way is the usual spots that these edible wild plants grow. A study that was recently released found that wild fruits and vegetables had more nutrition than the farm-produced kind because of a depletion of nutrients in the soils of farms.

Location

While locations that are very close to roads and buildings provide many kinds of wild edible plants, they aren't safe to eat in large quantity. They are, however, a great place to learn about them because of so many growing there. The swamps, woods, marshes, mountains, and fields of the Eastern US supplies a variety of edible plants as well, just not as prolific in the kinds and uses of edibles in disturbed ground. In any average town in America, toxic and carcinogenic chemicals are spread around by emissions and leaks of mechanical fluids like oil and gas as well as rubber and plastic's toxic fumes. As an emergency survival food, these edible plants are perfect as long as you forage as far from busy roads and parking lots as you can find them, then wash them off thoroughly. Rain washes heavy metals and toxic chemicals from the roads. Roots that are edible in polluted soil has the highest concentrations of heavy metals and chemicals, but the leafy greens there have much less contaminants. Eating weeds that grow too close to the road can make one ill. The biggest problem now in foraging is estimating how much potential pollutants are in the soil at any given location.

Identification

Identification of edibles is paramount—incredibly important! In a survival situation, your survival depends on providing what I call the Four Essentials—shelter, water, fire, and food. A shelter can be found, made, or provided by a tent (with extra tarp). Water can be filtered and purified from standing fresh water and rain or other sources in areas unpolluted by factory-farms or industrialization. Fire is not always necessary, depending on weather and the need to cook food or boil water. Fire can be made in survival situations with fire-starting tools (matches, lighters, flint sticks, etc.) and other implements with dead and dry wood, mosses, shrubs, and other materials. Then there's food. The food packed into survival kits and bug-out-bags will not last very long or provide the fresh vitamins and minerals that provide us with optimum health. Knowing the differences between toxic and edible plants is the main ingredient in a perfect survival plan. There are lots of plants in the world. However, positive identification requires years of study and field experience. Guide books use complicated botanical terms, crude sketches and drawings or sub-standard photography (with the exception of a book by John Kallas, PhD called *Edible Wild Plants: Wild Foods from Dirt to Plate*), along with a limited number of specific plants usually dependent upon the region where the author lives.

Learn by Experience

I learned over time that the key to foraging is learning to identify plants from the experience of positive identification in the field. Whenever I positively identified a specific plant for the first time I saw what it looked like in the reality of three dimensions rather than just pictures and sketches in books. Once I knew what it was, I started finding it in other places. I started to know when and where I could find it, what it looks like as a sprout, as it ages, and its variations. I could then focus on how it could be used, what parts are edible, cooking and preparation requirements, and other uses. I also began to know what many of them taste like and the possible variations in how to use them. While I learned about some minor medicinal uses, I was focusing on edibility so much (and discovered so many plants) that I decided to restrict my focus to only learning about what I could eat and how. Mushrooms are the most dangerous subject in foraging. Many, if not all, edible mushrooms can look similar to toxic or poisonous ones. So, I decided to forsake the study of wild mushrooms as well. The nutritional content in mushrooms is not very high anyway. I decided to describe the things that can make you mildly sick or carcinogenic as toxic and the deadly ones as poisonous in order to differentiate the two, even though there is sometimes a fine line between something that can make you a little upset in the tummy and what can kill.

Thank You

I enjoy teaching to others what I've learned about this subject. I really don't consider myself much of an expert. There is so much more that I can learn. I suggest taking notes whenever studying foraging. It helps one retain memory better that way. I don't want to charge anyone for what I teach. I believe strongly in sharing this wealth of knowledge with anyone interested completely free of charge. In any survival situation, the last thing one wants to see happen is getting sick from something that was eaten. No survival expert is truly an expert unless he knows the art

Eureka Ultralight Spitfire tent.

and science of foraging. You may never need to know about the wild food around you, but you never know exactly what the future has in store for us, or whether there will even BE a store. I teach about a particular form of survival that utilizes mostly invasive species of plants which also requires leaving some for animals, insects, and seed production—as well as for other people and future foragers. Simply put, every living thing is connected in a dependence upon each other. If humanity insists on careless and selfish damage to their own environment they will eventually cause a mass extinction event—leading to the demise of the human race (or near demise/extinction). Sharing resources will be crucial to our survival (both now and later) so I start by not charging for lessons while explaining that we must share our resources if we want to really survive. If we cannot share, we will all die. The human race will eventually become extinct if greed and self-absorption continues to rule, unchecked, over our countries and cultures.

7
Snug as a Doug Bug, Part 1

As I ended my career of poverty wages in dog-racing, there were no job opportunities suited to this battered-and-bruised by age and wear-and-tear, untalented, unskilled laborer; so I drifted away. The tent is a Eureka Ultralight Spitfire that was stripped of its covering—leaving just this coffin-shaped structure of mosquito-mesh and one pole stationed near the middle but toward the head of the tent. Being able to sit up completely, even in that one spot, in any solo-ultralight tent is a huge benefit. I roll up the tent, its five stakes, and the pole section taken apart, and place it in that large backpack with a large tarp, a lightweight but thick comforter (for winter journeys), and other provisions. In cool or cold weather, I untie the tarp and let it lay over the entire tent. The comforter is very lightweight but very thick, making it ideal for someone who can't use a sleeping bag because of restless-leg syndrome. The original pole of the tent was left behind in Vermont several years ago. The original cover was thrown away years ago due to mildew. I tried pitching the tent without the pole under the limbs of trees that hung low enough to tie three or four corners of the top of the tent to. Then I discovered trashed, old tents and poles that are frequently left to rot in hobo-camps—tent cities as they are often called—and I could scavenge the poles I needed to use for my little solo-tent. In a pinch, I can use a bamboo cane or willow branch bent over to shape the tent-pole.

Also in an abandoned hobo-camp, I found a small outside-use, patio-style mattress with a canvas covering. As I unzipped the mildewing canvas cover, I could see the three inch-thick foam rubber underneath was in perfect condition. I stripped off the canvas and cut the foam-rubber to a size just big enough to rest my upper-body and head down to my knees. This made its dimensions about 2 feet wide by 4.5 feet long, which I roll up and stuff into the backpack as well. This leaves very little room in the backpack for other necessities, but the comfort level at night is worth it. When it is hot at night, as Florida frequently is, the only thing between me and the breeze is mosquito mesh material. The three-inch-thick foam rubber mattress makes sleeping on the hard ground perfect, while it separates me from the cold ground in winter, and the comforter works better for me in cold weather than any sleeping bag. Thickness, not weight, is the key to insulation.

My campsite in Pennsylvania while homeless. Behind the trees is an interstate overpass.

Now that I've studied survival skills and edible wild plants for most of my sixty-plus years I feel pretty confident that I could repeat the homeless experiences of the past—setting up a camp for myself with no campfire (if necessary) in the middle of any large or small patch of trees and weeds like the interstate on-ramp in Pennsylvania where I stayed for a week (photo on opposite page) snug as a bug in a rug. My closest neighbors were chipmunks and the passing vehicles getting on and off the interstate. It worked so well, for one who focuses only on survival when necessary, I could easily maintain this existence indefinitely.

Just as long as the FOUR ESSENTIALS of survival (shelter/water/food/fire) are managed, which they were then, one lone survivalist/hermit could remain in that situation for quite some time.

8
Snug as a Doug Bug, Part 2

The four essentials of survival are shelter, water, fire, and food. The fire is not always necessary, as long as warmth from cold temperatures are managed and cooking with a campfire is not required. It was important for me to stay undetected and discreet. I would otherwise easily be forced off by law enforcement. Even a small fire, whether day or night, would have got me evicted from the area. This campsite was in the middle of a small patch of weeds and trees at an interstate on-ramp, I-81 near Hazelton, Pennsylvania. No one knew I was there during the entire seven days that I stayed (no trash was left behind). For light cooking I used Sterno, since it is lightweight and cheap. It doesn't give off smoke and I don't use it at night. By walking a half-mile to a convenience store I could buy food that did not require heating to supplement foraging and use water faucets at the store for my canteen.

Staying close to civilization without being detected is important for a homeless transient. Periods I spent miles away from anything were tough just to find and process potable water. The springtime in the Northeast and Pennsylvania produces a wide variety of edibles along the trails and backroads that are safe to forage.

Staying away from other homeless people is important as well. Many of them bring their various addictions like alcoholism and drug abuse into secluded campsites and it is always a recipe for failure. I feel strongly that the best way to be successfully homeless in America is in complete seclusion from other homeless people. Obtaining water from stores and gas station's bathrooms or water fountains and any outside faucet is easy enough if you are close enough to it. Drinking even purified water from any given stream, creek, pond, river, or lake these days is risky considering the level of chemicals and heavy metals now present in practically all ground/surface water sources along most city, rural, and suburban America.

Take it from me, you don't see people living under the overpass of interstates these days except maybe in some very large cities where it is tolerated out of necessity. Law enforcement officers frequently chase away homeless people with threats of imprisonment if they try to squat (sleep or loiter) in places where they can be seen by the public. That is why some unused, vacant patch of woods is frequently used by homeless people without being evicted or harassed (unless breaking the law some other way) by police. If the landowners don't care, the law and the residents of the community will often allow homeless people to gather in groups in tents at designated spots of thickly-forested empty lots away from public view. These sites always end up with discarded trash (mostly beer cans and bottles) laying all over the place. I don't camp anywhere near them. The majority of those sites are patrolled by law enforcement and the homeless people are evicted on a semi-regular basis.

If food stamps can be maintained while working odd jobs and pay-by-day labor for laundry money and toiletries and the occasional visits to food banks and charities, one could maintain such an existence indefinitely—as long as the focus is on the *needs of one's survival* only. Solitude and stealth is the key to diverting attention from oneself in this type of survival situation. Other homeless people will bring their problems to you or try to rob you of anything you might have that they want. It's best to stay away from them. I don't suffer from their addictions. The first thing I did when I quit my career in dog-racing was quit smoking. I used my asthmatic problems to convince myself that I could no longer smoke and breathe at the same time—so I had to choose breathing.

And knowing what one can eat from the weeds and trees of the lawns and landscapes of one's terrain is an added advantage that should be of high value to anyone conscious of life's vulnerabilities, even the lifestyles of the semi-rich and somewhat-famous. As I like to repeat, no one really knows what the future has in store for us, or whether there will even be a future.

9
Mykel on US Survival Plants

If I haven't made it plain and clear before, let me do so now: Eating unknown plants can be deadly! It's just plain dangerous to rely on plants as a food source if you do not know the plants you're trying to eat.

The other harsh fact is that plants simply don't give you enough bang for the buck. They do have nutrients in terms of vitamins, minerals, fiber, and maybe some starch and carbohydrate action, too. Such nutrition for the survivor is a secondary concern, whereas real energy in the form of calories is critical to the survivor and that comes best in the form of meat, plain and simple. But, if you find a lot of something, and it looks like it might yield a large amount of food, then the taste test comes into play. Of course, this might warrant the ultimate risk factor—death.

Use all of your experience and common sense in trying to assess not only the quantity and quality of the potential food-source plant, but also its danger criteria. Use what you know to be good, and only after a taste test.

Does it look like anything you've seen in the store or restaurant before?

Does it look like any food source you've heard of or seen pictures of?

Maybe there was something like it in that crazy local market you visited the day before you got stranded out in the bush; maybe you saw the picture on a menu last week in that Asian restaurant. Bring it all to bear in evaluating the next steps, as it might save your life, or end it. Now let's talk about the UET.

The Universal Edibility Test

Okay, the first thing to understand is that there is no failsafe universal test to see if something is edible or not. For example, there are plants that are fine when raw but kill if cooked, and vice versa. Likewise, there are exceptions for every rule out there for plants that are safe.

It is important to understand that the Universal Edibility Test (UET) really should be called the Edibility Test Universally Applied. That is its intended purpose and why it was designed by the military. They recognized that wars happen all over the globe and that it was not uncommon for soldiers, sailors, and airmen to get separated during the course of warfare and become isolated in remote regions where they might need to rely on the land for food.

So the military designed a universal edibility test as a guide for soldiers to use to test unfamiliar local plant life and see if it was safe to eat or not. It's not infallible, nor is it the only way to go about it. Remember, humans have been trying foods forever and a day since the beginning of time, and that's really what it all comes down to—observation, common sense, and a calculated risk. So, let's look at some parameters to help you reduce the risk in the first place and then we'll discuss the UET by the book and its alternatives.

Understand that many people die every year from eating poisonous plants. It begins to border on unintelligent if you have animals around and the ability to catch and eat them. Almost all land animals are safe to eat, and once skinned and cooked, all of them are!

But let's say there are no animals around, or you haven't caught any lately. When do you start eyeballing plants to eat? Well, start eyeballing them right away. ALWAYS be on the lookout for chow!

First, look for anything familiar. If you know what something is for sure, or you find a plant that looks a whole lot like something you know is edible, then there is a chance it might be of the same family or a local variation of that edible plant. So, that's a good candidate for starters.

Next, make sure there's lots of it. This is really important! No point in taking all that risk, and making all that effort, to get a handful of nibbles. If there aren't a whole lot of little things, or a few really big things, then it might not be worth the risk.

In general: Things that stink, sting, burn, or are barbed are usually not good candidates for a taste test. Exception: Prickly pears on cacti have mighty mean tiny spines but taste great and are very nutritious. Thistles are tricky ones, too, as are some of the crazier tropical fruits which have heavy hornage but juicy innards. Try to pay attention to all the exotic fruits and veggies in your grocers and markets to make a study of what some of these look like. The first time I saw papaya in the wild, I had no idea what it was, though I had eaten it plenty before that time.

The taro leaf, for example, is a food staple for many indigenous folks in the oceanic areas, but it's a poisonous plant because it has oxalate crystals which look like barbed spikes under a microscope. However, boiling takes all that out and makes a yummy meal of it. So, there are tons of exceptions. That's why the "universal" part of the edibility test isn't universal.

Alright then, let's look at some of the classic indicators for perilous plants.

Plants to Avoid

Mushrooms. These are tasty and they do have some (albeit very little according to the FDA) nutritional value, while new sources claim mushrooms have recently been found to have a great deal of nutritional value, but the bottom line is that the risks of eating any mushroom out in the wild is borderline suicidal! There are experts with years of study who still die from eating the wrong mushroom every year. For the survivor, mushrooms are simply OTL—Off the List!

Now, I know some good-to-eat mushrooms well, and when I've found them, I've eaten them because I found a large quantity and I could 100 percent identify them. But I never teach mushroom class to my students, because it doesn't pass the common sense test. You'll usually simply not find enough, and even if you do, they don't provide any nutritional value. So, do not risk eating mushrooms. I do teach a specialized edible mushroom class for my advanced students, but even in that class, I only teach those mushrooms for which there are no poisonous look alikes.

And here's the kicker for mushrooms; The things can taste fine and you think you're all good and they turn around and kill you twenty-four hours or even days later when it's way too late to do anything about it. If you're going to try and eat the things anyway, then do try and cook them. But know this: many fungal toxins are resistant even to high heat, and so cooking the mushrooms will not always kill the toxins!

Shiny-leaved plants are generally taboo, but not shiny like banana leaves; we mean shiny when they look like they have a sheen from a light coat of oil. In some of these plants, the oils can remain on clothing, or anything they come in contact with long after the plant is gone Not trying to instill paranoia, just the skill of observation.

Yellow and white berries are almost always bad juju, though there are exceptions. But for this book: if it's yellow, white, or even green, stay off it! (While we're on berries, the upside is that 90 percent of berries that are purple, blue, and black are good to go. Also, raspberries and similar cluster or aggregate berries are 99 percent safe.)

The rules for red berries are tricky. We all know strawberries and cherries are yummy as are cranberries, raspberries, salmonberries, lingonberries, etc. However, many red berries are poisonous, so the guide here is like for mushrooms—if you don't know it, don't eat it. Holly berries are red and juicy but these are toxic, whereas Hawthorne berries are dry but healthy. Yes, I know the birds eat holly berries! But that doesn't make them any less toxic to humans. In general, if the critters can eat it, so can you. BUT that is not the rule because some animals have immunities to these toxins.

Umbrella-shaped flowers are bad.

Plants with three-leafed growth patterns are bad. Some of these are also poisonous to the touch, such as poison ivy.

Milky or discolored sap is usually bad. One of the notable exceptions is coconut milk. There are others such as dandelion, which is one of the few I would recommend because it is such an easily identifiable plant and grows in great abundance. Even with dandelion though, it needs a cooking to become palatable as it ages.

Beans, seeds, and pods are generally best avoided unless you know them. You must know them pretty well, and positive ID is essential. Even the most edible ones need some sort of processing, if for no other reason than the presence of phytic acid, a compound common in so many foods that unless neutralized to some degree by boiling, roasting, or sprouting, inhibits the body from extracting nutrition from the plant. A person could in fact starve by eating a diet too high in this substance.

Grains are just tricky anyway because often it takes too many and too much work to be worthwhile, and if you find any heads with a pink, purple, or black spur just leave them well enough alone.

Plants with a soapy or bitter taste are best left alone.

Fine hairs, spines, or thorns are signs of plants to avoid, except in the cases of some cacti, stinging nettles, and thistles where these sticky parts can be removed either by cutting them off, burning them off, or in the case of something like stinging nettles, neutralized by cooking or drying.

Plants that look like dill, parsley, carrot, and parsnip are often very poisonous, and that's a shame because they sure smell like the real deal. If you're truly desperate and have many of these roots staring at you as a potential food source, then risk the taste test at your own peril as the poison in the plant that resembles the edible persuasion is none other than the deadly hemlock—which can kill you in a hurry. Don't go there.

An almond smell in plants in general almost always indicates it's poisonous. Some chemical and biological weapons, like cyanide, also smell like almonds. Unless it's an almond, anything almond-smelling should be considered poisonous. Even if the almond smell is on the leaves and/or woody parts—skip it! (The counter to this is the general rule that plants smelling of onions and garlic are usually safe to try.)

Mind the mangoes and cashews if you're highly sensitive to poison ivy and sumacs, as these have similar properties on their surfaces that can cause a bad reaction.

Don't eat plants with worms in them as they are decayed—instead, eat the worms!

Burn, boil, wash, and peel! Try to peel everything first, wash everything you can't peel, and cook everything! Some plants from the water have giardia, and anything from the soil can have bacteria, fungus, and other parasites. So use these simple methods to best prepare your food for safe consumption. Hygiene is the greatest concern in a survival situation, because you are often at the mercy of the elements, compounding even the most minor situation into a medical emergency, or worse, a coroner's report.

Some plants, like acorns, are highly bitter due to tannin concentrations, but with a few boils and water changes, are excellent to eat. So, it's a bit of work and a learning game when it comes to plant selection and preparation. If you can't get fire, try rinsing in water and drying in the sun. Practice your survival skills before they become a necessity. Knowledge and experience is power, and could save your life.

Now let's dig into the Universal Edibility Test. Below, I cover the official US Army procedure and my comments and observations based on experience and application. Ultimately, it will be up to you to decide what you do and how you do it.

Universal Edibles

Fruits, nuts, and berries are found all over the planet. Even in the arctic it is possible to dig up berries from under the snow. The problem is that they come in so many shapes and sizes and colors. So, all one can do is to be on the lookout for anything that looks like these things, and then apply the rules of the UET:

- Amount: Are there lots to eat, or are they big enough to make a real meal from a few?
- About: Do they look like something you know or have seen before?
- In Doubt: Do any warning signs—smell, touch, taste, look—call it into doubt?
- If in doubt, throw it out!

Also keep an eye out for the critters around you. Are they nibbling on something? Could be a nut or berry. Are there lots of insects about? They could be attracted to some fruit. Look on the ground; I've often found fruit and nuts not because I knew what their trees and leaves looked like, but only because I saw some on the ground and looked up—they couldn't have fallen too far from the tree! When doing this, carry a probing stick with you to search with. You never know what might be competing for that morsel of food you're after; most snakes aren't particularly out to get you, but if you happen to reach down for a tasty bite, and end up receiving a nasty bite instead, don't say I didn't warn you.

Berry Rules

- PB&B (like the acronym for Peanut Butter and Jelly, but replace jelly with "Berry") means Purple, Black, and Blue Are Good for You (90 percent good to go!)
- Yellow, Green, and White Mean Death by Night (90 percent deadly to know)
- Red can be good for the head, or . . .
- Red can mean you'll soon be dead (50/50 is the red way)

10

Hawke's Handy Helpers for American Wild Edibles

Roots, tubers, and other stuff to dig up. Anything you dig up should be cooked if at all possible. Not only is there concern about ground bacteria, fungi, and other evil spores, but the real deal is that roots are a concentrate of everything that's in the plant as its storage facility. So, boiling or cooking can neutralize any toxins or otherwise strong concentrations that might cause you some grief. Remember too that roots concentrate all their goodness, or evil as a plant dies back which compounds the situation. Learn and track plants through their season so you can know them no matter when you are looking for a meal.

Secondly, it's real hard to just arbitrarily go around digging stuff up. That takes time and energy. So, try to have an idea what to look or smell for, and only commence to digging if you're pretty sure or, if there are so many of a plant sprouting up that if it does have an edible root or tuber, you'll be in a good stock for a while. Remember that if you expend more energy going after something than you get in return, it kind of defeats the purpose of exhausting all that energy. This is like going job hunting and taking the job that pays the least, yet requires the most amount of labor, and the least satisfaction.

Again, look at the ground for signs of disturbance to see if any animals have been rooting around trying to dig up and eat some yummy grubs. Chances are, if they dug, they got it and ate it, so study the plant stalk they left behind. Look for more of those and try digging one up and see if it's good. It helps to have a digging stick for this sort of task. Keep in mind, though, that if you see an animal eating something, it doesn't mean it will be good for you. A good example of this is that deer eat poison ivy. Need I say more?

Grass, greens, shoots, stems, and all in between. Many plants that grow in and around water are edible. Also, people can eat grasses—not a lot, and they should only be the brightest green, newly fresh grasses, but they can be eaten—they are not dangerous and have some nutritional value. People do not have the enzymes needed to break down grass and get the nutrients out of it the way animals can, but a little grass in the diet can help a bit. Try chewing the grasses, swallow the juice, and spit out the indigestible fibers. We require some fiber in our diets, but to get clogged up with indigestible clumps of fiber is not only very uncomfortable, but dangerous as well. A lot of nutrition and even protein can be found in the seeds of many grasses. Those seeds can be sprouted, boiled, ground into flour or, if done in small quantities, eaten raw. Be very careful with grains and don't consume any that have mold, pink, or dark growths mixed in or on them. This could mean the presence of Ergot, a black fungus that grows on rye and other grains which is very toxic.

Make sure when eating grasses, or any food for that matter, that it isn't contaminated with either chemical or organic substances. You could get parasites or other illnesses if your food has been exposed to animals, such as livestock, cats, dogs, or any animals for that matter. Always wash foods as best as possible with fresh clean water, or cook them well done.

Remember though that cooking won't get rid of chemical contaminants. Just be mindful and very careful when foraging, wherever you are.

Many plants are edible when in their very early stages as shoots. Even these may have to be cooked in one or more changes of boiling water. Plants such as poke, and many fern fiddleheads among others fall into that category. Many plants are fine in their early stages of growth, but produce toxins as they mature.

Roots contain their most potent elements, good or bad, during fall, winter, and spring when all the energy is in their underground roots. In summer the above ground parts are utilizing the most energy.

Keep in mind that different parts of a plant can have different properties. Come to know all those parts equally well, and in all seasons as best as you can. This way you will be prepared when you need them.

Many trees have brand new stems that are edible, or, when small saplings are coming up out of the ground, they are often edible as well. The same rules apply here as with other plants. Make sure you are eating from a safe tree, free of toxins such as maple, beech, birch, and pine, and many others. Avoid toxic trees such as yew and cherry, among others. Do as much homework as you can ahead of time, and always apply the UET.

Eating trees! One thing that really makes me happy is trees. In combat, I go into the trees and have my moment in the quiet before the storm. But the main reason they make me happy is all the good things that they mean. They mean life! They provide shelter, weapons, tools, lookout points, fire, and transport in the form of boats or litters, and medicine as well. They also mean food. Not only do animals live and rest in them, providing you a hunting ground and source of meat, but you can actually eat a good many trees!

For example, the spruce tree buds, needles, and stems can all be eaten raw, but they're better cooked. Many fresh baby sproutlings can be nibbled on from a lot of trees like the evergreen (green year round) coniferous (plants with cones) pines.

Birch trees have an inner bark that is edible, as do pine trees, too. See the list of edible plants by region for a better idea, but many hard woods do have some sort of edible inner bark, and many winter trees have nuts, and many spring trees have edible shoots. As you view the natural world as an integral part rather than separate from it, things make more sense, and it becomes easier to see how nature provides for your needs. All you have to know is how to see and understand the bounty that is lay in wait.

It's not ideal and certainly not a complete survival diet to go around nibbling on trees, but if you have an idea of which ones in general offer a food source, apply what you know, all your common sense and the good old fashioned taste test and you'll likely be alright and find something you can eat. With all that said and you're still looking for food to eat other than killing critters. Let's take a general look at some of the most common plant food found in abundance in each of the world's regions.

American Deserts

Cacti are all over most deserts and they're mostly edible. If you chop into them and they're green, they're good to go! If they have a white sap, don't rule them out right away—smell, finger-touch, lip-touch, and/or tongue-touch the sap. If no bad smell or burn, go easy at first; but figure it's likely okay. But if it doesn't look right, forget it.

One cactus comes to mind that makes an excellent survival food is prickly pear. It so common in many parts of the world that it is a staple in many of those areas. Unlike most cacti, it is found outside desert areas, even in such unlikely areas as the Appalachian mountains of the eastern US. It is easy to identify, easy to prepare, is nutritious, and large paddles from the plant can be fashioned into a container for holding and purifying water by means of boiling with hot rocks. More on that another time.

You gotta prepare both the big round parts of the cactus, sometimes called paddles, available in spring and summer, and the delicious fruit that appears later in the summer. Let's talk about paddles first as they appear first. Select a nice healthy one that looks nice and green, and has few blemishes, as well as the least amount of thorns and fine hairs. Use either gloves, or fashion tongs of some sort, and a knife to harvest both paddles and fruits. Steadying the paddle, cut it off right where the neck meets the big round part. With the back of your knife, if you are so fortunate to have one, scrape as many prickly parts as you can, then just trim off the edges of the rest of the paddle. At this point you really should have a good fire going. Singe the remaining sticker parts off in the fire, then roast or grill over the fire for around ten minutes on each side, or until soft. Cut into narrow strips, and season if you can as it is rather bland, and eat, either solo, or mixed with other food.

The fruit, which appears later in the summer, can be green, turning red as it ripens. It is harvested by cutting or twisting it off the edge of the paddles, the hairs singed off in the fire, then, by cutting both ends off and making a cut from end to end, peeled, and the juicy fruit eaten as is. Be careful not to break a tooth on the many hard seeds inside. They are not toxic, so you can eat them too, but they are very hard.

Other cacti are good too, but some are not edible, so use care, and don't get stuck with bad luck. Oh yeah, be careful when harvesting your cactus ents as snakes often hide out in their shade.

Agave and yucca flower stalks are good to eat and provide a decent meal. Cut off about three feet of the bud and stalk (which looks like a huge asparagus tip), peel the hard outside, and eat raw, or any way you please. The flowers of both are edible raw, but cooked is better as the yucca flower tastes soapy (in fact, it can be used to make soap).

The fruit of both can be eaten as well, and it's best to eat while white inside. You can cut the agave down to its middle section and dig a hole that fills with water. After drinking, cut it off and cook it for a few hours—the agave is like a big potato, and the yucca roots are also just like potatoes.

Yucca flowers appearing in early summer are creamy white with tulip-like blossoms. They are crisp and really good raw with edible berries, wild blueberries or huckleberries, for example. Start slow with yucca blossoms as some people get a little queasy from eating them, but if you can eat them, they are mighty tasty.

Incidentally, dried yucca stalks make some of the best hand drills for starting friction fires, and fibers processed from the leaves can be used to make excellent cordage.

Date palm is a good find. They look like the obvious palm tree but instead of large nuts, you'll see clusters of small round fruit. The best way to get at them is to cut the tree down. If you should happen upon these fruits—which are like coconuts and bananas—in the jungle, you'll know what to do and enjoy.

Acacia are those little trees with the thorny spines and nice yellow flowers that smell good. These trees are all over the world in good quantities, and the best part is, a tree can feed you a whole meal as the flowers, the buds, and the young leaves are all good to eat. There is a little confusion between the Acacia trees that grow in the warm southern states from California to Florida, which have yellow flowers, are evergreen, and bloom naturally from winter into spring, and the very similar mimosa trees with feathery, fragrant, pink flowers that bloom from spring to mid-summer depending on how warm it gets. The confusion lies in that there is an Acacia variety that is referred to as a mimosa. Confused yet?

Both of these trees have edible parts, but the mimosa with pink blossoms that bloom in spring and summer have blossoms that are edible, and the young leaves can be boiled and eaten. The seed pods may NOT be edible, so are best left alone. The true evergreen Acacias found in the south, as well as warm climates throughout the world have more edible parts including the seedpods, edible raw or cooked.

Amaranth is found all over the world as well. It is full of vitamins and minerals, and when found, it is usually in abundance. It can be eaten raw or cooked. It is also known in:

- Africa: Vegetable for all, or yoruba.
- Asia: Different names all over, but the Chinese call it yin choi.
- Latin America and Caribbean: Here it's called callalou.
- US: Chinese spinach.
- I'm a fan because it is easy to identify, plentiful, and has lots of protein in the seeds. It grows in any areas where it is drier in climate.

Sea

America is fortunate to have two oceans on our coasts and a gulf to the south and great lakes to the North, so anywhere there is salt water there are plant food sources for humans.

Seaweeds, kelp, samphire, and pretty much anything green from the sea or near the sea can be eaten. The seaweeds and kelps can be eaten raw in a pinch, but only take small amounts unless or until you can cook or boil them. Many of the harder shoreline plants are also edible, but best boiled. In general, most sea greens are fairly safe to munch—just make sure they're healthy and still anchored in somewhere. The only poisonous one you might encounter looks feathery, not leafy. Do not eat any sea plants that are colorful. Ideally you'll want to boil your sea greens to reduce the salt, kill any bacteria and parasites, and generally make them more palatable. If you don't have fire, try rinsing well in fresh water if available and letting it dry in the sun. They can cause a laxative effect if too much is eaten without anything else in the stomach. Remember any effort is better than no effort at all when in a dire situation Never give up, and don't get lazy when it comes to taking care of yourself.

Arctic or the Cold Regions of America

Green stuff here is generally hard to come by, but it is there. Most of the mosses that you find on trees or the ground, and the lichens you find growing on rock, are all edible. In a pinch, these can be eaten raw, but are best boiled—a few times, in fact—to get out the bitterness and rinse them clean. These have been used in hard times as a food source by Inuit. They even dry them out after boiling, and then beat them into a powder to make a nice starchy flour for bread. Many of these sorts of foods are often called famine foods, and while they may not be the best, they might get you through another day.

Arctic willow is a plant that you pretty much will only get to chow on its tender little sprouts in spring. If you're there in spring, enjoy!

All pines and spruce are edible, and the same rules for eating apply to both. The needles are edible and make fine, nutritious tea. The inner bark is edible, as are the baby cones, as well as the pine nut seeds from young cones in spring. Most parts are almost always better boiled just because it's cold and you need the warmth and the liquids. These too have been used by Native American Indians of the Northern Tribes, who found hunting difficult after some longer harsh winters. As did the Intuits; they would also eat these raw, boiled, or roasted, or dry the bark out to crush and use as a flour to make a nice carbohydrate bread source. (See notes on pines in the section below on oaks, pines, and beechwood.")

The fern is a fine plant for eating. But only eat the freshly sprouted tips that look like their nickname: fiddle heads. These can be eaten raw, but are also better and safer to eat any quantity after boiling. They often grow in batches, so chances are you'll be able to get a whole meal out of them. They are starchy and high in vitamin C. The roots can be dried, then boiled and mashed to get the more than 50 percent starchy pulp out so as to be able to separate from the fibers that are also in the root.

Fiddleheads are a tricky lot, and there is argument as to which varieties are edible, and which contain toxins. The most edible variety seems to be the unfurled ostrich fern which is found in the northeast US. Even those are considered suspect by some, but the tradition remains, and as long as you get an edible variety at the right time, and preferably boil it, you should be okay. This is one of those things I would recommend a serious edibility test, and some in-depth study of ferns, and even better, an outing with someone experienced in the fiddleheads of the area.

I imagine there are edible fiddleheads in most regions, but it would be unwise to forage for them without knowing how, when, where, and what to look for. When you do find them, even though some say you can eat them raw, boil them always, as this may help neutralize any toxic element. A taste of it raw may be fine, but not in quantity. Exercise moderation even once you do know what you are doing, and all should be okay.

American Forests and Mountains

Lots of green stuff is out there, in volume, easy to identify, and safe to eat.

Oaks, pines, and beechwood all have edible inner bark, and for all the evergreens (except the yew, which has flat needles instead of round ones) you can eat the raw needles, baby cones, and seeds from the cones. The deal for eating bark is to peel off the brown stuff from the tree, then find a thin layer of slightly slimy but meaty bark, kind of like an inner skin known as the cambium layer—this is what you peel and eat. Not the dry outer bark, and not the hard wood inside. It will always taste funny—it's a tree! But it is edible and nutritious and filling. When harvesting this layer, avoid taking too much from a single tree, and try not to remove anything from the entire circumference or the tree will die. Collect a little from many trees if you can. Of course, in a survival situation, all bets are off so do whatever is necessary to survive. It is harsh on the trees, but that is survival.

Oaks

The *Quercus* family provide acorns, nuts of many shapes and sizes as well as edibility. Most need to be processed in order to be made edible. This is done by collecting, shelling, pounding or grinding into a fine mealy texture, then soaking in either constantly running water such as a stream or river, or if that's not available, many changes of the cleanest water you can find to remove the tannins, the part that makes them bitter, and then the resulting mush is ready to be dried, made into breads, cooked into soups, or any number of things. You can also leach the tannic acid by boiling in numerous changes of boiling water. Each process yields slightly different, but equally good results depending on what you want. The cold water process takes longer, but the resulting mush binds better for making breads and such. If you want to get at the good oil from the nut, you must go through the boiling process and skim the oil off the top of the water. White oaks tend to be milder than, say, red oaks, and some such as the chestnut oak sometimes need no processing at all. Always make sure to use fully ripened acorns, and not green ones. Sometimes they will fall off the trees prematurely which could mean a grub infestation, or some other problem with the nut. Explore and experiment with the many varieties of this major wild food source. You will be glad you did.

Pine

Pinaceae has so many useful elements it's hard to find a place to start. As food goes, the inner cambium layer, the slimy soft, stringy part between the dry crumbly outer bark, and the hard wood inside. The needles can either be chewed and the juice sucked from them, or boiled into a nutritious tea very high in vitamin C among other things. All pines are edible, or have edible parts, however, NOT ALL EVERGREEN TREES ARE! I emphasize that because one such evergreen often mistaken for a type of pine, is deadly toxic. That is the yew. Yew or taxus are used extensively as an ornamental shrub and as little as fifty needles eaten from a yew can stop a human heart. One identifying feature of yew is it has flat needles. Another is the presence of soft red slimy berries with a single black seed in it.

Getting back to pines. The pollen heads are nutritious, mostly as a nibble, or mixed with flours and baked into breads. The unopened cones of pines can be laid beside a good fire, until they open exposing the very nutritious and delicious pine nuts. The best part of the pine tree.

Spruce

The *Picea* family of evergreens has the same edibility profile as pine, with the exception of maybe chewing the needles, so any further discussion is somewhat redundant. The differences are in their needles. Spruce needles tend to be shorter and definitely stiffer than Pine needles, which is why chewing them would be an issue except with very young, tender ones. There are other differences in the cones, and the bark. These differences are physical only. Edibility is the same. For the sake of simplicity of identification, we will stick with the needles.

American Beech

Fagus grandifolia has an inner bark or cambium that is edible as are young leaves and buds in the spring, and taste good while they are soft with a slight citrus quality. There is a slightly toxic element called fagin found in the skin of the nut, but this can be easily rubbed off when roasted. The sweet seeds can be crushed, boiled, and made into a nourishing drink. Although I haven't tried it, the seeds can be ground up and added to cornmeal and berries to make bread. In times of famine and scarcity, beech sawdust has been mixed with flour to extend it when making bread. As with all nuts, raw nuts should only be eaten in moderation. I am a fan of roasting all nuts due to levels of phytic acid and other possible toxic elements that are often neutralized by roasting.

Other Abundant Plant Foods

Plants like burdock, plantain, cattail, arrowroot, dandelion, sorrel, and sassafras are all good finds as food sources. These plants offer food in abundance, are easy to identify, and have multiple edible parts.

Burdock

Arctium lappa has a first year taproot that while a little hard to dig can be boiled, baked, fried, and thinly sliced and dried for future use when you have those hard-to-harvest days. A favorite way to eat burdock is slow roasted beside a hot fire, turning it from time to time until it is soft, much like a potato. This long, slow cooking process also brings out a pleasant sweetness to the plant. Second-year burdock roots become woody and inedible for the most part. This second year of the biennial burdock (a plant that's lifespan is two years) allows the above-ground portion of the plant to have its glory. This is apparent as the first-year burdock is a low lying basal rosette because all the energy is in the root. The second year, the plant will often grow to over six feet in height This is when the edible parts are the leaves, stems, and seeds. A little preparation is necessary to make this plant palatable. The leaves have little hairs on them that can make your mouth numb and very uncomfortable for a couple of days, but this can be neutralized by blanching it in boiling water for no more than two minutes so as to preserve their nutrients. At this point you can eat it somewhat raw, boiled with other veggies, fried if you have the luxury of cooking oil of some sort, or you can use the large leaves to wrap other food in for further cooking and eating. Fish is particularly good when wrapped in burdock leaves and baked underground in an earth oven.

Plantain

Plantago, is among the most common and useful plants around. Not to be confused with the banana-like plant also called plantain, this one is considered a common weed wherever you go. The two most common varieties are broadleaf and narrow leaf plantain. Both are edible, either raw or cooked when young, and better cooked when older. The seeds from both are edible either raw, roasted, ground into meal, or sometimes boiled. Broadleaf seeds grow all along a single spike growing from a basal rosette of oval shaped leaves that can get quite large, five or six inches across, and around ten inches long, although usually a third that size and smaller, and have veins that start narrow at the stem, and widen as the stem widens, pretty much following the leaf shape.

One identifying feature is the presence of stretchy fibers in the veins that are apparent if you carefully pull the stem from the leaf. Narrow-leaf plantain has a very distinct stem with an elongated seed head on top surrounded by a halo of tiny flowers. The leaves are long and narrow in a basal rosette as well. Plantain is found in yards, gardens, parks, fields, cracks of sidewalks—everywhere humankind seems to have been.

Aside from being an excellent edible, its medicinal qualities are near miraculous. Only one mentioned here is the ability of the crushed leaves rubbed on insect bites and stings, rashes and other skin issues brings immediate relief. There are no poisonous look-alikes, however, be mindful that this plant is considered a weed, and is commonly sprayed with herbicides to get rid of it by those who don't know or appreciate its powerful nutrition and medicine. Other hazards are either manmade, or brought on by contaminants from animals, so avoid collecting near roads, where it may have been sprayed, or in commercial and industrial areas. Be sure to wash and cook if cleanliness seems suspect. This is one of those plants that can be eaten in quantity and is dense in nutrition.

Sassafras

Sassafras albidum is an aromatic, deciduous tree that can be found from Massachusetts down into Florida, and west to the central US. To call it an edible on its own would be to leave you pretty hungry. The dried, powdered leaves are used traditionally as a defining ingredient in Louisiana mostly, to make file gumbo. The leaves will make a flavorful tea if steeped in boiled water for around ten minutes. A better tea can be made using the roots of young saplings, shoots, and even a handful of bark steeped in hot water for fifteen minutes or so.

There has been quite a bit of controversy surrounding possible carcinogens found in sassafras, but a good hot cup of this fragrant spicy tea won't hurt from time to time, and it does help soothe a sore throat. The leaves dried and powdered can be used to flavor and thicken soups and stew, making your own wild file gumbo of sorts. It is very important to note that the fruit of the sassafras tree is NOT edible in any way. It is a blue berry surrounded by a red outer part.

The sassafras tree is most easily identified by its distinctive spicy root beer–like scent, and the fact that it has three different shaped leaves. They are shaped like both left, and right-handed mittens and also like a mitten with two thumbs. These leaves have smooth edges, and rounded lobes. This is very unique. Mulberry is the only other tree I can think of that has more than one shape of leaf.

Pokeweed

Pokeweed is poisonous if not boiled, but one plant provides a lot of food. When harvesting poke, use only the very young shoots before any red appears in the plant. With poke, red could mean dead, or at least very sick and maybe wishing you were. These young exclusively green shoots, usually no more than six to eight inches tall, are the ONLY edible part of this plant, and must be boiled in at least two or three changes of water to remove the toxins. Make sure not to get even the slightest bit of the root in your harvest, as the root is the most toxic part of the plant. Poke is considered among the best wild edibles, and was even sold commercially and canned until it fell out of favor a few years ago. In Appalachia, some folks say the antidote if you get poisoned from poke is to drink a lot of vinegar and eat a pound of lard. I would venture to say that would clear most everything out of your system, poison parts of poke included.

Purslane

Purslane grows everywhere: open sunny areas, next to creeks in woods, city parks, sidewalk cracks, and probably anywhere it has a chance. It is a thick, fleshy-leaf plant with all parts being edible raw or cooked. It is a staple food in parts of the world, but here, for some reason, it has fallen into the weed category along with so many excellent, nutritious plants. Purslane is highly nutritious, and contains so many dense nutrients not found in garden vegetables. It is one of those of those wild foods that you could really make a meal out of if need be. It has a mild flavor and the seeds add a nutty goodness to balance it out. Most people seem to enjoy it, and it has a unique civilized quality about it. If I find it growing in a safe environment free of toxins and questionable surroundings, I will eat it as I would anything from a garden. Wash it in clean water, and eat as is. Purslane can also be cooked though. Rinse, and cook chopped stems and leaves in just enough water to cover it for a few minutes. Then discard that water, and add just a little bit of water, and cook covered until tender. Season as you like, and eat.

Purslane is a succulent, slightly mucilaginous plant with thick green oval leaves, reddish smooth stems, and small yellow flowers with seeds. It is important to note that purslane has smooth and NOT hairy stems, and the juice, or sap, is clear. It is found year round in warmer climates, and spring and summer elsewhere.

The only toxic look-alike that I know of strongly resembling purslane is spotted spurge. It grows in similar areas, often side by side with purslane, so be very careful not to mix any with your harvest spurge leaves while similar in shape, are not succulent and thick, and it has a lighter coloring to it than purslane. Also, recall the emphasis on purslane having no hairs and clear sap. This is very important because spurge has a milky sap, to be avoided, and hairy stems.

Even though purslane is a commonly eaten plant, start slow, making sure you tolerate it well, and you should be good to go.

Chicory

Cichoium intybus is one of my favorite plants for making field coffee. To do this, roast the roots until dry and dark brown, then crush and use like coffee. Just look for the sky-blue dandelion-like flower on the base of the stem with milky juice. You're in there! Grows all over the world and all parts are edible, too.

Chicory is a common wildflower easily found from May to October. It is a perennial, meaning one that returns in following years, growing up to four feet tall with blue or lavender flowers. Chicory leaves taste best in the spring and fall and can be eaten raw or cooked. Older leaves are best cooked. The roots can also be dug, cleaned, and cooked either by boiling or baking. They can also be chopped, dried, roasted, and ground to be used either as a coffee substitute, or seasoning. The flowers, while edible, are very bitter, so eat them if you like. All in all, chicory is treated similarly to its relative dandelion, which can be prepared in the same ways.

Thistle

Thistle is good when you peel and boil the stalk, and eat the roots raw or cooked. It can usually be found in dry woods. It is an unlikely candidate as a wild edible because of its appearance, and being covered with thousands of spikes and stickers. This reminds me of stinging nettle, which will flat burn you up with its stinging hairs, but when cooked or dried, becomes a nutrient rich edible. Thistles, while they may appear a formidable feast, are excellent, and like many greens, are best when young, but become more bitter with age. (Hmm, sounds like some people I've known.) Young, peeled thistles are good raw, taste and texture much like celery, but are better cooked when they get older. Like dandelion, chicory, and others, the roots can be chopped, roasted, and ground for a good coffee substitute.

All true thistles are edible, however, not all are palatable. This being said, once you know how to spot this very distinctive plant, do a Universal Edibility Test as with any plant, and try whatever variety you like. No poisonous look a likes come to mind either, and they grow commonly in fields, open areas, roadsides, disturbed areas, and are very widespread. As a parting note, older plants can be processed to make cordage.

Alliums

Wild onion and garlic are good for starters. These are found most anywhere in such regions. For the few you might not be so sure about, look them up before you travel as they're very common, and once you know them, you'll always know them. As a rule, if it smells like an onion, it is an onion, and is edible. The entire wild onion plant is edible, but if they don't smell like onion, leave them be. There are numerous plants that may look like wild onions, but may be toxic, so always make sure they have that characteristic onion smell. That goes for a popular wild Appalachian edible called ramps as well. Smells just like onion and is delicious. They are best cooked or mixed with other plants as they are very strong and you can often tell if they are nearby just by their strong scent. There are toxic plants that may look like onions, but they don't smell like them. Like I said, if it doesn't smell like an onion, but still looks like one, best to leave it alone. Wild onions and garlic grow in yards, fields, open sunny areas, and like many other weeds, anywhere man has been. For this reason treat it as you would any other common edible considered a weed. They may be contaminated by herbicides or other chemicals and may have been exposed to animal excrement which could expose you to parasites. Ramps are the exception as they grow mainly in less populated areas. They should all be washed thoroughly or cooked, especially the root parts.

Wild Rose

Wild rose produces rose hips through the colder seasons and the fleshy part of this berry-like plant part is among the highest in vitamin C of any plant found in the wild in America. To eat the rose hips, only eat the fleshy parts which are best gathered after a frost. Avoid the seeds and fine hairs that will make you itch. The best way to do this is to cut them in half and dry the hips enough to separate the fleshy part from the seeds. Some rose hips are quite small, and some get pretty big. The big ones are naturally the best. Experiment with how much drying makes this process easiest. Somewhat of a process, but worth it. Rose petals can be eaten, however the white parts of the petals can be bitter.

Cattails

Cattails are my favorite as they are near almost all swamps and ponds and small stream areas, and they offer so much food in that all of it is edible—raw if you must, but boiled or roasted over the fire, these are great grubs. In early spring, the yellow pollen heads produce a bright yellow, nutritious pollen that can be mixed with other flour, or even the starch leached from the roots of the cattail, and baked on a flat rock by the fire as you might make ash cakes. You can also mix them into a batter and fry them as you would pancakes mixed in with other flours. The young flowerhead when still green, before it starts looking like a corndog, can be eaten either raw or cooked and is eaten much like corn on the cob. The roots and tuber that can be stubbornly pulled from the mud of shallow ponds can be cleaned, and a starch extracted by soaking the tubers in cold water. This leached starch is nutritious, and can be used in many ways. One interesting use is as a binder for wild flours such as dock flour to make bread that can then be baked on a hot rock by the fire, kind of like a pancake. If you are fortunate enough to make some nut oil or any edible oil, you can fry this up into a hearty meal. The stalks can be peeled to reveal a somewhat slimy shoot similar to bamboo shoots that can be eaten raw if your water source is clean. Ponds are always to be held suspect, so cooking anything that comes in contact with the water is best cooked. Above-water parts like pollen and heads are usually okay to eat raw.

Dandelion

Dandelion roots and heads and leaves are good to eat—just discard the stems with their milky white sap (which makes a decent glue). They're good to eat raw or cooked. But try not to eat a lot at one go just because you found a field of them—tummy upset is likely to result if you do. Early spring is the best time to collect the leaves of dandelions, before the heat of summer makes them bitter At that point, they are best cooked as a potherb. The flowers are delicious raw or even baked into a frittata or to top off an omelet from some duck eggs you may happen upon, for example. The roots can be dried, baked until dark brown, and ground into a darn good coffee substitute, as can chicory.

Palms

American jungle–like terrains are primarily in Florida but some parts around the Gulf of Mexico can be a mix of swamp, mangrove, everglade, and jungle. There are no hard and fast rules, when it comes to life; things will grow wherever they can. So learn all that may apply for your needs.

Palms are just wonderful things to find in the jungle. They mean life. Not only in terms of shelters and cordage, but they are a good food source. Cut the tops off and eat the tips, the soft parts, the flowers, the seeds, and the heart of the palm. This is high in fat energy.

Nuts

All nuts you can find are not only a great source of food, but they are excellent travel food as they'll last for months in their shells. So save these up for any journeys being planned. If you do find a lot of nuts, you can squeeze the oils out of them by wrapping them in a strong cloth and beating them and then using something to press the oils out. You can use the oils for your skin, cooking, candles, etc. Also, use the oil cloth as your wick for your oil candle.

When eating nuts in quantity, it is best to neutralize the phytic acid, found in most if not all raw nuts, seed, grains, and other foods. Phytic acid prevents our bodies from absorbing many of the health-giving nutrients found in the food. You want to get as much from your vittles as possible. To do this, crack the nuts, remove the nut meat, and soak them in water overnight. Next, you dry the nuts, sprout, roast, dry, grind up, whatever you wish to further process. Sometimes, you can just roast nuts by the fire, which helps remove phytic acid.

That aside, you can find many varieties of nuts in the woods such as walnuts, hickory nuts, pecans, chestnuts, and many others. Acorns are a nut that requires a more involved process to remove the bitter tannins that often make them seem inedible, but a very worthwhile endeavor that leaves you with a most delicious nutritional product that has many possibilities. Native tribes used acorns as a main staple for thousands of years, so why stop now?

Nuts are usually found in abundance anywhere you find the large variety of trees that produce them, and contain valuable nutrients including protein, minerals, oils, fats, and various vitamins. Any way you look at them, nuts are in good supply, found in the fall and sometimes into winter. Because they are so good, they are in high demand by a lot of other critters. Worth all your efforts if you can get to them first.

All nuts are surrounded by an outer covering known as the hull which often contains self-protective elements in the form of often harsh components. When harvesting nuts, this part has to be removed, but don't automatically throw them away. An extract made from the hulls of the black walnut for example, contains juglan, which can be used to treat skin problems, and taken internally in just the right concoction, will rid the body of parasites such as worms and other nasties. The outer hull of hickory nuts burn very hot, and are good dried and burned in your fire.

Next layer in is the actual shell containing the nutty goodness inside. Some shells are hard to crack so you must smash them in just the right spot, with just the right pressure so as to break the shell and have the nut meat inside remain as intact as possible. Once inside, most nuts should to be washed, soaked, roasted, and sometimes ground into a meal to make them edible. You can eat a few raw, but only a few until you finish the steps to get the most from your cache. Seems like a lot of work, but well worth it because of the valuable, nutrient rich food you get.

Coconuts

Coconuts are simply the gift of the gods in the jungle. They're easy to identify, but not so easy to get. Chop the tree down if you can't climb it, as that will be less risky than trying to climb and taking a fall. If you must climb the tree, coconut trees usually grow on an angle and you can get up it fairly easily. Use bare feet, and wrap a strong cloth or towel around the back of the tree and hold it on either side to create holding pressure, and walk up the tree by scooting the towel up after each few steps. They're not easy to get into, either, but worth the effort. If you don't have a knife, take a sharp rock and just start jabbing into it. Brace the coconut between some other rocks or logs to keep it in place while cutting. Do not use your feet to hold it in place; it's too risky as the cutting rock or knife may miss or slip off the nut and through your foot. Many cultures call the coconut tree the "tree of life" as they have so many uses.

Bananas

Bananas are another great source of food. Easy to access and plenty filling, not to mention a great source of Potassium, a vital element for the human body to function properly. Without enough of it, our muscles cramp up, our heart ceases normal function . . . you get the picture. They'll last a week or so depending on their condition, and the banana tree itself is a fantastic source of water as well. Bananas are already so common in our everyday diet, that there seems little else to be mentioned about them. Some people don't tolerate them well, and typically will experience nausea.

Indian Grass

This is another plant found readily in many warmer climates. There are many varieties, from the less-than-edible types of North America, sometimes called bison grass, to the more desirable types that are sour and often called lemon grass. The key to ID is simple—if you see a field of grass, it is likely bison, or if you see clumps of fat stalked grasses, these are likely to be lemon grasses. Simply pluck one and taste—if sour, it is lemon; if almondy, it is bison. Both can be eaten and are best added to soups.

Papaya

Papayas are super to find because they are so huge that one will fill you up. But like any of the soft fruits in the tropics, they will go bad quickly, so consider slicing them very thinly and drying them in the sun for longer use. These are often confused with the papaw. Papaya is a bit more red and oval, and sweeter. The papaw is more yellow, round, less sweet, and more like a banana in its flavor.

Bamboo

Bamboo is also awesome to find for the absolute all-purpose utility of it. The baby shoots can be eaten raw, although they can be bitter. Boil with a few changes of water to make them a lot nicer-tasting.

Sugar Cane

Sugar cane is not a likely find, but it is all over the tropics as a remnant from failed plantations. Peel the outer hard layer and enjoy, as these are very nutritious.

Taro

Taro is found all over in the tropics, and again, it has to be boiled to neutralize the oxalates. Once that's done, the leaves and the roots provide super tasty greens and starches, and one plant can make a whole meal. The edible part of this plant is the corm which is a potato-like tuber growing underground. The above-ground portion is a large elephant ear–looking green plant. It grows in tropical and subtropical regions and has been a staple in those parts of the world forever. It is making its way into grocery stores in most metropolitan areas though so provides a good source for trying something new without too much effort.

Taro root is higher in calories than potatoes, is a great source of fiber, and is gluten free. These are all positives as a food source goes. One word of caution with Taro is that it does contain oxalic acid so the plant must be cooked in order to be safe to eat. The good news is that cooking renders the plant completely safe to eat. Both the corm and the leafy parts are edible and can be prepared in many ways. The leafy parts are good in soups and stews and the corms can be baked or boiled and used however you choose.

Water Lilies

Water lilies are plentiful and actually tasty, but it's real hard to get out there and actually pull up their tuber roots. Once done, boil or roast, and enjoy. Almost all water lilies—*Nymphaea, Nuphar* species, and *N. tuberosa*—have edible parts that can be gathered most of the year and all have edible tubers, or roots year round. They may be a little mushy, and don't have much flavor during the summer, but can still be eaten; they are dug from the mud and prepared like you would potatoes.

Either bake them like most edible roots beside the hot coal bed of a fire, or maybe even in an earth oven wrapped in burdock leaves. An earth oven is a pit dug a couple of feet deep, and whatever other dimensions you need including the rocks, coals, and dirt required to accommodate what you are cooking. First, line the pit with flat rocks, making sure the rocks you aren't using creek rocks, or any that have absorbed water, as they explode from the moisture from vaporizing and expanding. Next, build a fire using whatever hardwoods possible so as to get the hottest fire you can that will heat the stones to a point they will serve as an oven. Now you have a coal bed with a few inches of hot coals. Then a layer of green grasses, or some sort of non-toxic leafy material is added, and a little water poured over this layer to keep it from igniting. Next, place your food wrapped in burdock leaves, or some nontoxic grasses, or whatever non-toxic material is available on this layer. Wrap your food well enough to prevent burning. Next, cover with large pieces of bark, plywood, animal hide, anything to keep the final layer of dirt from getting through to your food. Now, you cover the remaining part of the pit with about four inches of the dirt you dug from the pit. Go do something else for three hours or so, and when you return and unearth your meal, you should have evenly cooked juicy food. There are many variations on this method to improvise with, so experiment and enjoy the process before you are caught not knowing what to do.)

Getting back to edible water lilies. The young leaves just beginning to open, and unopened buds make a decent potherb, and the seeds can be dried or parched, winnowed, and ground into flour, or toasted further to make an acceptable coffee substitute. Two of the more common edible varieties are the yellow pond lily and the fragrant pond lily. I always recommend cooking everything that comes from a pond thoroughly to avoid any waterborne illness you may encounter by eating raw, even if the plant itself is edible raw. Try to find these and all edible water plants in the most unpolluted sources possible. You will regret it otherwise.

Sops

Sops are some crazy-looking fruit to most Americans. They are mainly in the tropics of Asia and there are two kinds—sweet and sour. They are tasty and plentiful. A variety of this family of plants grows in abundance in Appalachia, and other parts of the Eastern US known as the pawpaw. Although the fruit of the pawpaw tree is edible, you have to get it at just the right stage of ripeness, and then be sure to beat all the other wildlife waiting for the same thing. It is loved by squirrels, opossums, raccoons, foxes, and many others. When ripe, it tastes kind of like a cross between a banana and a mango. It is quite sweet, and has a custard-like texture. It usually has ten to fourteen large bean-like seeds in two rows, and a thin skin, neither of which is edible. The soft fruit inside is the only edible part of this native tree. The fruit itself is about the size of a medium-size baking potato and is oblong with a green to yellowish-brown color. It is best picked when it is soft and just about ready to fall off the tree. It doesn't store well, and should be eaten soon after collection. The fruit ripens during a four-week period between mid-August and into October, depending on environmental conditions, and is quite delicate and thin skinned. When ripe it is soft and lightens in color, sometimes developing dark patches on the skin which doesn't affect the quality of the fruit at all. It should be eaten right away, within a couple of days at most, unless you have the luxury of a freezer where the pulp can be frozen for up to six months. It is high in protein, antioxidants, vitamins A and C, and several essential minerals.

Now that we've looked at the guidelines and overview, let's look at specific plants!

11

American Wild Edibles for Survival Foraging

Location, Location, Location

When it comes to locations for plants, not all of them fit neatly on a map, or in regions, and certainly they don't constrain themselves to state lines. Trying to place them all on a map, by name, number, colors, or other variations just leads to a very messy looking map and then you default to our suggested way below anyway, ha!

So, we found the best way to help you figure out which plants are near you is to go through this list and put a check mark by all the ones that might be found in your area. Then begin your studies and learning the plants around you. If you even think it's in your area, go ahead and check it off. Then use a color code for learning those and another for the next ten and then the rest.

For example, maybe use green for your top ten, yellow for the next ten and blue for all the others in your region. This helps you prioritize and makes the learning less daunting. The key is always going to be dirt time. So, if it's an easy task to tackle, you're a lot more inclined to get out and get learning.

Acorn

Oak—*Quercus* species, more specifically the acorns produced that provide sustenance for so many creatures, from the lowly acorn grub which in itself is edible for humans, to the native tribes who regarded Acorn as a major part of their diet.

There are many varieties of acorns that grow in the US from coast to coast, covering most of the continent, and all acorns from any oak tree are edible once properly prepared. They should be harvested once they turn brown and begin falling from the tree anywhere from late summer till well into fall. Green acorns are not edible, and if they fall from the tree there is likely something wrong with the nut. Once you find a healthy source of nuts, it is a good idea to try a little taste just as it is, unprocessed, to get an idea of which varieties are going to supply the best food with the least amount of processing. Taste can vary even from tree to tree even with acorns from the same species of oak. A tiny sample will reveal the acrid, bitter quality of the unprocessed nut due to the tannin levels contained within. Some will be very bitter, others almost palatable, and the very rare example of a nut that needs almost no processing at all.

As a general rule, the larger the cap on an acorn, the more bitter it will be because of the presence of tannic acid. This is the case most of the time, but not always. Acorns from the white oak family tend to be milder than those from the red or black oaks The leaves of white oaks have more rounded leaves, and the others more pointed ones. Some varieties such as the chestnut oak and live oak, both from the white oak family, are among the mildest of all. Their leaves are more rounded than their relatives, and have either smaller teeth, or as in live oak, no teeth at all. Also of note, is that white oaks fruit every year, whereas red and black oaks every other year. There are so many details that could be covered, but I think once you understand the basics, the sooner you can get to some good food.

For the sake of brevity and simplicity, I will mention how to sort good acorns from bad ones, and then both cold and hot leaching processes. To determine which acorns are good, and which are bad, fill a container with cool water, and dump in your acorns. Simply put, bad ones are floaters, and good ones sink to the bottom. Don't just throw the bad ones away. Chances are they have a grub inside that can be eaten if you like, either raw or cooked. I would recommend cooked. You can also use live ones as an excellent fish bait.

Next, remove the caps. Before shelling them, you will want to dry them out a little either in the sun, away from squirrels and other critters for a few days, or in an oven at a low temperature around 150° F for about fifteen minutes. You don't want to cook them yet. This will allow the nut inside to shrink slightly making them easier to shell. Next shell them, and grind the good nuts into a fairly course meal. If you find bad places in the nuts, just cut them out if you can, and grind the rest. Once ground, you can leach the tannins with hot or cold water. A third method is to bury them, but that takes a couple of years, so we will stick with just these two other methods here.

The cold water method preserves the oils in the nut, and allows us to use them ground even finer into a flour to make bread, eat plain, mixed into other foods, or made into a sort of acorn gel that can be eaten as is, or cut into strips and cooked like noodles. To leach the ground meal you want to soak it in many changes of water never allowing it to get over 150° F, until the water is clear. This can take several days to do depending on the level of tannins. Once leached, you can grind this meal further and use it however you like. If you want to extract oil at some point, just take cold leached meal and boil it. The oil will rise to the top and you can skim it off and use accordingly. This oil is valuable for cooking, oil lamps, and a variety of other things. Having any edible oil in a survival scenario is priceless.

The hot water method is quicker, but a bit more involved. You must leach in several changes of boiling water until the water stays clear. The key, is you have to change from one container of already boiling water to another container of already boiling water, repeating this process until clear. Make sure not to let the acorns cool down between changes of water either, or that will spoil them as well. If you transfer the unfinished acorn meal into cold water and boil them, you will permanently seal in the tannins leaving you with unusable acorn meal. When using the hot water method, the acorns also release their oil.

The biggest difference I can see in hot and cold leaching methods is that the cold method, keeping the temperature at below 165° F, doesn't cook the starch, thereby allowing it to be used as a thickener for soups and stew, as well as allowing it to bind better when making bread. In other words, acorn meal that has been leached cold makes bread that holds together, whereas that which is boiled to process cannot make bread or a thickener. If you are going to leach and roast whole for snacking then boiling is fine. If you are going to use the acorn for flour it should be cold processed, or you will have to add a binder. Boiling takes a few hours, whereas the cold process can take up to a couple of weeks to do. How you process your acorns will depend on your situation.

Acorns provide a tremendous amount of nourishment, and this writing is only the tip of the iceberg regarding the use of acorns. There are many medicinal and other practical uses for acorns, but that is another day, and another story. For now, you got some good grub, or grubs, depending on how far up the food chain you wish to go here.

Acorns are quite nutritious. For example, the nutritional breakdown of acorns from the white oak is 50.4 percent carbohydrates, 34.7 percent water, 4.7 percent fat, 4.4 percent protein, 4.2 percent fiber, 1.6 percent ash. A pound of shelled acorns provide 1,265 calories.

ALOE: Not for Dinner

I know what you might be thinking: Aloe is not a wild plant and not edible. You would be right and wrong. First, there are species of aloe that grow wild here, if just escaped from cultivation. Second, several drops of the highly mucilaginous gel into a glass of water when constipation threatens can help keep one regular and their bowels covered by a protective coating—an advantage for sure in any survival situation. If you look around in grocery stores you might find a commercial beverage of water with aloe. However, one should discontinue internal use of aloe in cases of chronic constipation, presence of hemorrhoids, or chronic renal disease. The laxative effect of aloe taken internally (with water) should occur within eight hours. Aloe is effective for healing the gut lining and is safe for children but should be avoided for internal use by pregnant women.

Many herbalists consider it to be the best external healing plant, particularly for burns of all kinds—including radiation. If foraging for survival means dealing with a campfire (and everything which that involves) you can't have a much better plant nearby to treat cuts, scraps, burns, stings and bites. A wild plant that comes to mind for that would also be plantain, *Plantago species*.

There are reports of speeding up the healing of burns from radiation with aloe, technically described as "accelerated healing." However, there is also conflicting evidence on the effectiveness of aloe for applications in cancer patients receiving radiation therapy. Suffice to say that it is most likely better to use than a hydrocortisone cream. The overall use of aloe as a healing enhancement has been sufficiently proven to be effective, yet, the pharmaceutical industry would prefer that you not know about that. There is also growing evidence that aloe can be an effective means of preventing the spread of skin cancers and possible effectiveness in treating psoriasis, peptic ulcers (internal use), and for veterinary uses. A report states that a tablespoon of aloe gel consumed twice daily might help reduce insulin resistance in diabetics, lowering their blood glucose levels significantly.

The word "forage" means, "to search for provisions." The absolute minimum necessities to support human life; shelter, water, fire, and food—in a prolonged survival situation will require subsisting on edible roots, berries, grubs, and so-forth for nutrition and seeking out OTHER provisions as they become necessary. Aloe is a plant that might well be a necessity to find.

For internal use when constipation becomes a problem, consuming any amounts of aloe gel (no skin or yellow substance) with water (a few drops of gel per glass), avoid a yellowish film that frequently lies just beneath the skin of the aloe's flesh. That substance may cause a heightened laxative effect. And discontinue use if the constipation becomes a constant problem. The aloe might either cause unintended consequences from internal over-use or have no effect at all. These plants can be grown throughout the southern half of the continent outside but kept in a greenhouse northward. That can also be said for most of the plants in this book. Aloe is presently reported growing wild or introduced in California, Texas, and Florida.

AMARANTH, *Amaranthus retroflexus*

This "weed" is a plant that I read about some forty years ago now (give or take) but was never absolutely sure of its identification till recent years. I saw the plant that I thought it might be over the years, but wasn't sure it was. If you're not 100 percent sure of what it is don't assume anything. It took this long until enough sources indicated that the plant (weed) that I thought was a variety of amaranth really was an amaranth. Most of the books I studied in the past either showed a full healthy vibrant grain-version of it and some bad photos or sketches and drawings with complicated botanical descriptions. To say that it likes to grow in disturbed ground is an understatement.

Native to Central America, it has been used for food by humanity for ages. It is a well-known grain to those who know their heritage grains. Two main types of amaranth exist here. The most common, short, weedy, vegetable version, is that noxious leafy weed to many people which only grows up to a few feet high on a reddish stalk, or the less common grain version cultivated with its thick, strong stalk that can grow to six feet high for abundant grain production.

You can use the young leaves of either in a salad, older leaves in the pot, and winnow the mature seeds for grain on either. Here's a simple way to winnow the seeds, "Indian-style," on a slightly breezy day—but just a light breeze. Sit on the ground with a sheet or large bowl in your lap of freshly picked and dried mature reddish-brown seeds. Take handfuls of them and hold them fairly high above your lap as you rub them together with both hands. The chaff will get blown away from you by the breeze as the grain falls into your lap. The seeds can then be ground into a flour.

This is one edible plant that you can rely on for a healthy wild green or grain provided you have the right plant and that it's not being harvested from too close to a busy road or otherwise contaminated soil. It absorbs heavy metals, chemicals, and nitrates from the soil as well as many nutrients. Try to find this one in open fields and away from traffic or otherwise contaminated land. The grain was used extensively

Prominent veins on the underside of the Amaranth.

by the Aztec. It can be ground into flour or just roast it. You can also sprout it or fry it. It's high in protein, amino-acids, and fiber, and contains calcium, iron, vitamin A, potassium, vitamin C, and more.

One thing that struck me on identifying them is the leaves. When you turn a leaf over, the underside is a silvery light green with very numerous bulging veins that seem to want to pop out of the leaf. Botanists call that "heavily veined" and "prominent veins." There is also new leaf and flower growth coming out of the joints (called "nodes") on the stems and stalk where the stems connect with their main stems or stalk.

There is a thorny variety of amaranth that I stumbled upon many years ago, *Amaranthus spinosus*, commonly known as spiny amaranth. The sharp spikes grow from the nodes on the stems alongside the growth of new stem and leaf production. I found it along the Florida Trail near Dade City. I thought that it looked like the plant that I thought (at the time) might be amaranth but it stuck me with one of its thorns when I touched the stalk to take a close look at the nodes. Little did I know at the time that the plant that I had suspected was amaranth really was amaranth and that I had just found its spiny cousin. Well, actually, that's exactly what I figured it was at the time, didn't know for sure, and turned out to be right. Another identifying trait is the five-sided stalk.

This plant starts popping up here and there throughout most of the year here. It's one of our few wild greens that doesn't mind the heat of central Florida.

From Southern Canada to the southern-most of the temperate region of South America and nearly all over the world one can find the *Amaranthus* species.

AMERICAN LOTUS, *Nclumbo lutea*

Also called lotus lily and lotus, the edible cylindrical-shaped rhizome roots are hard to find which requires digging around in water and mud. They aren't just found underneath those flower stalks or leaf stalks; one must start by digging around in the mud to find the root system first and then follow them to a rhizome. They are connected by an underground root system that leads into the large potato-shaped to banana-shaped rhizome, or tuber. These are chopped and soaked in water first to remove any bitterness they might have. Then they can be boiled or baked. The mature seeds are edible cooked too, removing any green sprouts beforehand. This aquatic vegetation is another staple food of our ancestors. There are other edible parts and uses to it. The main use was the roots and seeds.

From the bottom up: Roots, peeled and baked or boiled; young stems peeled and boiled (twice if bitter), mature stems used as a straw; very young unfurled leaves still underwater can be boiled (maybe twice) and a mature leaf used as bowl or wrapping food for baking in hot-ashes of fire; dried petals edible (just try cooking them), dried stamens for tea; soak and

boil green seeds until soft or roast/bake and grind mature seeds into flour. It is the largest flower in North America besides the sunflower.

The seeds form inside of the strange-looking showerhead-like seedpods. The unripe pea-sized seeds can be soaked and boiled, just boiled, or peeled and eaten raw. When they mature, they become hard and are only good for cracking, roasting, and grinding into a flour additive. I took the accompanying photos at a pond near Dade City, Florida. For much more information see the section on lily pads below.

APPLE-DRAGON FRUIT, *Cereus* species

There is a large variety of this species around the world and some are escaped and introduced locally but many are now endangered in south Florida. This particular cactus (most likely a cultivated species that was planted here years ago) has six protrusions from the center, looking like an asterisk when viewed from above. Some varieties have been naturalized up the coast to central Florida and planted inland from there. There are many of these cacti here and they're around my present home in Zephyrhills, Florida.

Cousins of these cacti are the mighty saguaro cactus and the pitahaya of the desert southwest. The Saguaro is protected because of its edible uses and limited range. The fruits of all these cacti species are edible as long as one is absolutely sure that the plant does not have a white sap. Any cactus with white sap is very poisonous. A species in Africa can kill us just by inhaling the smoke when one is burning.

The ripe pulp is an off-white color which has the texture of a soft watermelon, sweetish, and the numerous, small, black seeds are super soft in this species but not in the species of opuntia cactus, aka prickly pear. The seeds of prickly pear are very, very hard but edible.

These cactus stalks grow straight up, sometimes twisting and turning among trees, to as high as thirty feet. The scientific name of the genus, *Cereus*, changed recently among the varieties and is pronounced like "See-rious." It blooms and fruits locally this time of year in late summer, through fall, and gone by December. Every place that I saw these in the third week of September has ripe fruit on them. The fruit is best eaten chilled and then cut in half lengthwise to eat the pulp, as is, with a spoon. The pulp can be made into preserves, the entire fruit into a syrup, and the seeds made into flour. The related fruit called dragon fruit that you can buy in some grocery stores in the fall looks exactly the same on the inside but has a papery, loose skin on the outside. The fruit of the wild plant here is much sweeter than its store-bought cousin, probably because mine went from the cactus to my fridge and then consumed soon after.

The fruits are mostly water with a little fat, carbohydrates, fiber, and even some protein.

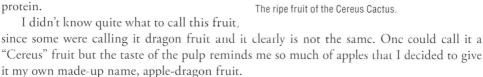

The ripe fruit of the Cereus Cactus.

I didn't know quite what to call this fruit, since some were calling it dragon fruit and it clearly is not the same. One could call it a "Cereus" fruit but the taste of the pulp reminds me so much of apples that I decided to give it my own made-up name, apple-dragon fruit.

ARROWHEAD, DUCK POTATOES, *Sagittaria* species

The flower stalks are all the same: clusters of three flowers along the top portion of the stalk with three delicate, white petals surrounding a large, ball-shaped pollen-bearing center.

The most plentiful *Sagittaria* species in my neck of the woods does not grow the egg-shaped tubers like the arrowhead-shaped leaves of the well-known foraging *Sagittaria* commonly called arrowhead and duck potatoes. Many foraging books have that one but most of them (if not all) don't mention the other species of the genus—ones with these wide or thin lance-shaped to spaded leaves (see photos above). The *Sagittaria lancifolia* has leaves like a spear-point and there is a grass-shaped leafed species. All three have the same kind of flower stalk. However, while they don't all have the egg-shaped potatoes (in some places only marble sized), what our species does have is growths on the ends of the rhizomes with edible cores of starch (carbs). There is starch in the lower stem and the rhizome itself which can be baked in the hot ashes of the fire and chewed off of the fibers. Also, the young leaf stalk and flower stalk can be boiled. The flower's white petals are edible raw. There are plenty to harvest around Florida ponds, lakes and mudholes.

Other common names of the arrowhead/duck potatoes are katniss, swamp potato, wappato, wapato, and wapati. Wappato was the name that the northwestern Native Americans gave to the arrowhead-leafed species. I've been looking for the well-known Arrowhead species, *Sagittaria latifolia*, for some forty years now (not actively searching for, just keeping an eye out for it in the back of my mind). The leaf-shape is very much an arrowhead with three points, looking similar to a taro or elephant ear plant. Part of the problem was the guidebooks that I studied years ago. They did not adequately include certain details. They did not take into account the very different climate and environment Florida has from the rest of the country. It was as if they excluded our state. Most of those books were geared toward the northern half of the eastern United States or just focused on the areas where the authors lived. In recent years, I've been able to study authors who focused on Florida's edible wild plants like Green Deane, Julia F. Morton, Peggy Sias Lantz, and Mariam Van Atta.

If it is recipes you are looking for try: *Wild Harvest: An Outdoorsman's Guide to Edible Wild Plants in North America* by Alyson Hart Knap (1975). Her book has recipes for arrowhead corms (tubers) as well as another book, *A Naturalist's Guide to Cooking with Wild Plants* by Connie & Arnold Krochmal (1974) which has recipes for Buttered Arrowhead, Creamed Arrowhead, and Baked Arrowhead. They all seem to report about the arrowhead species (that name is based on the shape of the leaves), but nothing on the other species of the genus. I've come to the conclusion that the species with large potatoes and really arrowhead-shaped leaves does not grow in Florida. Or, at least not anywhere in central Florida.

The guidebooks all report these facts about the tuberous *Sagittaria latifolia*, the arrowhead; that the tubers (corms) grow away from the center of the plants as much as a few feet in a clockwise fashion on the underground (under-water and/or under-mud) rhizome runners, they are reportedly unpleasant tasting raw but edible, they travel well (not getting stale fast or rotting quickly), and are best cooked with their "jackets," or skin, still on and then removing the skin before consuming. Kind of like a baked potato—but the edibility of the skin is questionable since they all suggest removing it after cooking. Also, you can't harvest the tubers by pulling up on the plant's flower stalk or leafstalks (or in combination) but you can, in some cases, loosen them with a garden rake or your toes if there is enough water for them to float up to the surface.

Again, the species of *Sagittaria* here in the Deep South does not produce the tubers that the species is well known for. I have searched the muddy undergrowth of ponds, marshes, and mud holes where the lance-leaved species grow in abundance around here—without luck.

Do not mistake the plant arrow arum for the arrowhead *Sagittaria*. Those leaves are too long and you won't see that unique flower stalk. Always LOOK FOR THOSE FLOWERS! arrow arum is very toxic and plentiful in Florida. The Seminole here knew how to make the roots of arrow arum edible by a long process that no modern forager should attempt.

Also called tuckahoe, arrow arum (*Peltandra virginca*) grows frequently along the same kinds of places where *Sagittaria* grows—along the margins of fresh-water swamps, marshes, lakes, and stream banks throughout Florida and much of the eastern United States (*Florida Wildflowers and Roadside Plants* by C. Ritchie Bell & Bryan J. Taylor 1982, 1992, 1998).

And, as always, you should be sure that you are not harvesting edibles from polluted waters. You should look for signs of pollution: greasy, shiny surfaces or cloudy, white and/or foamy surfaces. Notice how much aquatic vegetation is around (a good sign if plentiful) and then weigh the risk versus the reward. If a root tastes bitter, spit it out. Boil it some more in fresh water. If it is still bitter, spit it out and move on. Greens are different; a little bitterness can often be expected for some wild plants and is fine to consume in small amounts or accompanied by a variety of other foods. If any roots are bitter, they are best avoided.

Survival requires a full and complete knowledge of what you need to know when you need it. If you don't know information that is critical to your survival you can't risk it. Better to be safe than sick, or dead.

BANANAS: Food, Water, and Shelter

As a survival food, water, shelter, and fire-starter, the coconut tree is king. But did you know that the banana tree can provide not just edible fruit, but many other uses like; two vegetables, potable water, and shelter material? And did you know that the banana tree is not really a tree? It is actually a very large weed, the tallest grassy plant in the world.

Fruit

The banana plants (trees) with the edible fruit that we all know is actually a mutation of wild bananas. Our common store-bought banana is being threatened by a disease. Eventually, we may end up with store-bought bananas that look more like the small wild ones—but not the plantains, just a different mutation of the species of the banana tree (plant).

Most people with banana trees have small bananas that are edible, although more triangular in shape than round. However, most species of banana trees in the world have fruit that does not have edible pulp—just seeds that can be used to grind into a flour additive or substitute.

That present store-bought kind does not have seeds, just that edible pulp we're all familiar with, but that species is threatened worldwide by a fungus epidemic.

I once picked a small yellowing banana from a tree and began to peel it. When I saw large seeds surrounded by a hard plastic-looking substance (not looking like pulp or anything remotely edible), I was perplexed. How does a banana have seeds and no edible pulp? I thought. Turns out, most wild bananas are just like that.

If your banana tree's fruit are the kind that has the edible pulp and they are green, you can wait for them to turn yellow or they can be made edible while still green. To use green bananas, cut into sections, and boil until the peel starts to peel itself from the pulp. Remove from heat. Carefully (not getting burned) remove the peel from the pulp (I use two forks to maneuver the hot peel off of the hot pulp). Then continue boiling the peel-less pulp in fresh water until it is soft enough to mash with butter, salt, and pepper (or as you would prepare mashed potatoes) or slice and fry. It's really quite good, especially when you're hungry. Otherwise, you can wait for a stalk to show a few yellow fruits on it and cut the whole stalk off and hang it in a cool and dry place. One by one the fruit will turn its ripening yellow color. However, you must not cut off the fruiting bunch while they are all green if you want them to ripen. Save the flower bud, it is edible too.

Flower Bud Vegetable

Chop off the large, dark red flower; peel off the thick outer layers until you have the core of it. This can be eaten raw but it is reportedly better when chopped and cooked by steaming or frying or both with added other vegetables. Whether boiled, steamed, fried, or however you choose to prepare it, the taste and texture reminds me of a bland cabbage. Some people soak the flower bud overnight or a day before boiling to reduce any possible rank or bitter taste.

Cabbage Vegetable

After I cut down a six- to seven-foot tree I start pulling off its outer layers by pulling off the large leaves that are attached to each layer. This strips off the layers one at a time down to the core—showing the thin, green, rolled-up cabbage very near the center of the stalk. I unroll it to display a thin, paper-like substance. This must be boiled pretty extensively to soften the somewhat fibrous nature of it. The resulting substance had the texture of a slightly chewy, bland cabbage—which I topped with butter, salt, and pepper. It would blend in well in some survival stew with assorted other edibles.

Water

First, a banana tree is cut down, which is easier than you might think—my machete sliced through it fairly easily. I cut it to within several inches from the ground with a fairly clean horizontal cut. I then dug out a hole in the center of the trunk by cutting out some of the core of the stump. The water seeped into the center as I sucked out the clear sappy water with a straw (keeping a straw in your survival kit can come in handy). The first mouthfuls of water are very bitter. I spat them out. After that the water will taste better. As you take water from it, more will enter, somewhat slowly though. No need to purify it; the roots that push water up from the ground into the trunk filters it. This method of collecting water can last for days according to some survival experts. I don't know, but I'm not looking forward to a situation where I would have to find out.

Shelter

The leaves are good for shelter building material for roofs, for covering a firewood stash, for collecting rain water, for bedding material, for cordage, and for wrapping up food to be cooked within the hot-ashes and coals of a campfire. The trick is to surround the wrapped food with enough ashes to keep the hot coals from actually touching the food wrapped in the banana leaves. The sap of the tree along the trunk is somewhat sticky and the sap closer to the top (especially around the fruit) is like glue.

Many banana plants have escaped cultivation in all parts of the world where the climates hardly ever experience hard freezes or snow—like most of Florida. While I have seen them in vacant lots, I don't expect to see them while hiking Florida's wilderness. But, you never know, they could be right around the corner when you need them to be.

BEAUTYBERRY, *Callicarpa americana*

Beautyberry, aka French mulberry and beautybush, the name of the genus, *Callicarpa* comes from the Latin for "pretty seed" and includes about 140 species worldwide.

While the berries are edible and used to make jelly, their taste raw is mealy and bland and can cause a kind of dry mouth that forces you to salivate (produce saliva). The sugar that is always added to make jelly sweetens the flavor and the cooking eliminates the mouth-watering effect. The jelly is reported to be very good. The berries are ripe when they become a bright pink or magenta, sometimes even light purple.

As for the leaves, while not edible they contain a natural bug-repellent that repels ants, ticks, and mosquitoes (maybe not chiggers). I rub the leaves on my skin and clothing; it does not give off any strong or unpleasant odor. The mosquitoes don't bite for a few hours, provided you don't sweat profusely, and the process can be repeated over and over. Beautyberry plants can be very abundant in deep central Florida woods of partial to heavy shade as well as open spaces.

A good campsite in the summer here (where beautyberry, heat, rain, and mosquitoes are prevalent) is along high ground, under medium-size trees (the tall ones attract the lightning more)

with healthy limbs and branches overhead, on the edge of a field facing the prevailing wind, and with beautyberry all around. Beautyberry ranges from about Maryland, south to Florida, over to Texas and across parts of the Midwest.

There are edible differences and medicinal uses for the plants in the *Callicarpa* genus. I only know about those berries for emergency food, a trail nibble, or jelly and the insect repellent in the leaves. I once took a day-hike through my favorite local hiking trails in summer without store-bought insect repellent by rubbing the beautyberry leaves all over me, putting some in my pockets and placing some under my hat. I hiked for four hours without getting bit by any mosquitoes even though they frequently buzzed around me. However, I did get chiggers around my feet that itched for days where I didn't rub any leaves on. Next time during the chigger season I'll put the leaves in my socks and see if that helps prevent the summer chiggers from attaching themselves to my feet.

At this point I'll assume that it won't stop them. Chiggers are summer pests that are too small to see and dig under the skin, mostly around ankles and somewhat up the legs to the waist. I'm getting very positive reports concerning the effectiveness of repelling mosquitoes by rubbing Beautyberry leaves on your skin and clothing. Some natural insect repellents are using it now as an ingredient.

BITTER GOURD, BALSAM PEAR, *Momordica charantia*

The gourds ideally should be completely green with a little white at the bottom to be edible, and only after boiling at least once. The small bumpy vegetables are boiled separately from other food for the first boil and while still green. Then it can be added to ingredients for cooking in stews and soups. PREGNANT WOMEN MUST NOT

EAT any part of this plant as it could cause an abortion or miscarriage. People who are hypo-glycemic or suffer from a condition called Fauvism should limit the amount they eat, if any. The gourds are very poisonous to dogs, possibly even causing death. I chop the little gourds in half and give them a thorough boiling, dumping the water, and then either adding to ingredients in a stew or soup or cooking them some more with less water and with butter, salt, and pepper. ALWAYS DUMP THE WATER FROM THAT FIRST INITIAL BOIL. I have been told that the yellow gourds are also edible but that was from the cultivated species from Asia. The wild un-domesticated species that grows here is like the precursor of the cultivated species. While it is true that the yellowing gourds of the cultivated species is perfectly edible after cooking, the original wild version is not.

There are other edible uses for other parts of the plant but only as famine food. It is a delicacy in the Far East, one that tastes a little bitter, but good enough for me. You can't get the bitterness completely out, but that is okay. As long as the little gourds are still completely green with a shade of white on the bottom they can be harvested and boiled for a passable food. As soon as any yellow begins to appear on it, it might become toxic. It is invasive, which is beneficial in case of a famine-related disaster. The best famine foods are the most invasive plants that are also edible. If all hell was to break loose and the more you know the less you need, the invasive edible plants are the ones to know. For famine food, the leaves and shoots can be boiled twice with a change of water to be safe enough to eat by anyone other than the restrictions listed above.

The deep bright red colored, sticky, fleshy substance on the mature seeds is edible as long as the seed itself or the plastic-like casing between the flesh and seed is not consumed. That sticky red flesh is called an aril and is reported to consist of more than 90 percent lycopene. Lycopene is the red pigment in red colored vegetables that is reportedly very healthy. I put one seed at a time into my mouth and gently, slowly, suck off the red, gooey, flesh from the seed.

BLACKBERRY, *Rubus* species

This is one of my favorite wild edibles to find growing in deep Florida woods. The original natives of North America—known these days as First Peoples or First Nations—used black-berry leaf tea for inflammation and infusions of the blackberry rhizome (crawling root system) was used as an eye wash, cold remedy, and gen-eral tonic.

It is also reported that they used a tea from the roots to fight dysen-tery—which in layman's terms is a bad case of explosive diarrhea that can drain a person of fluids to the point of death. It is also reported that blackberry juice, wine, and cordials are used as a remedy for diar-rhea, nausea, and other digestive issues.

For processing the berries, they can be cleaned and cranked through a food mill processor. Then jelly, jam, syrup, wine, and medicinal preparations can be prepared without the tiny hard seeds. The berries can also be mashed and strained through wet muslin or cheese-cloth to make a tart, refreshing drink. When un-sugared, it was used by some to stew meat and can also be made into a blackberry vinegar that can also be diluted with sugar added to make a cold, refreshing blackberry nectar. It is also reported that the blackberries don't dry well, recommending that the berries be made into a fruit leather instead. Blackberries grow on thorny canes that grow straight up until its own weight causes it to lie down and crawl. The leaf-pattern resembles a poison ivy with thorns, which poison ivy does not have.

The very close relative and edible look-a-like dewberry looks the same but is a thinner stalk—more of a thinner vine than blackberry—which always crawls along the ground from sprout to maturity. The taste, texture, color, and shape of the dewberry is so much like the blackberry that very little separates them. The blackberry canes rarely produce fruit during their first year, sometimes produce during their second year, and always during the third year before dying off. Dewberries produce every year. When harvesting from a patch, it would be best to leave plenty for the woodland creatures and for propagating future yields.

Leaves must be dried for making tea, fermenting them improves the flavor. As a famine food, young shoots of sprouting blackberry canes can be eaten if peeled and boiled in one or more changes of water. My favorite use for the berries when I have been able to find a large patch maturing is with cereal or just gorging myself on them right then and there. The seeds are reported to contain essential fatty acids. I've found both kinds reported here miles into the woods along my favorite hiking trails.

BLACK CHERRY, *Prunus serotina*

This fruiting tree has a similar appearance to the northern species, *Prunus virginiana*, called chokecherry, which doesn't grow this far south. Our little cherry tree grows throughout most of the eastern half of North America down toward the desert southwest into Mexico and elsewhere.

These mature leaves will have fuzz along the midrib underneath the leaf, starting out blond when young then turning rust colored and blackish when old. These leaves can also resemble another wild cherry species called pin cherry, *Prunus pennsylvania*, which also doesn't grow this far south. So, in my central Florida home, a wild cherry tree like this is most likely the black cherry species. There is a toxic species that resembles this tree called cherry laurel, and the best identifier of the edible one is that hairy rust-colored substance along the midrib underneath the leaves (not all leaves will have it) and a dimple on the bottom of the berries.

The inner bark (cambium) of this tree was used for centuries to make a cough syrup. The fruit is of particular interest to many birds and animals. The leaves are a favorite of our white-tailed deer. However, the twigs, bark, seeds, and leaves are all poisonous to at least horses, cattle, and humans due to cyanide. If you saw a deer eating the leaves and thought that people can eat it too because of the deer you would be deadly wrong.

Because of the cyanide content in all cherry trees you can break a twig and get the aroma of almonds, a warning sign to the presence of potential cyanide. The seed is not edible, also containing cyanide potential. If trying to eat the berries off of the tree, only consume one at a time to focus on spitting out the one seed, or stone, so as not to swallow one—just to be on the safe side. Try not to actually chew the berry with your teeth. Swallowing a whole seed or two un-chewed will probably just pass through you without harm. Once removing the seeds, the ripe black fruit can be made into jelly, jam, pies, etc. The whole stones can be cooked with the fruit for berry recipes but must be removed (sifting out the seeds) after the cooking process. A gum can be made from the resin or dried sap and dissolved in alcohol for putting on your throat to ease a sore throat and quell a cough. A tea is made from the bark to ease diarrhea and calm a nervous stomach. However, I don't suggest it. As the name implies, the black berries are the ripe ones.

BLACK NIGHTSHADE, *Solanum americanum*

I like to see the reaction of my students when I introduce this plant to them with its shiny black berries and say, "This is called black nightshade, aka common nightshade, and also called deadly nightshade," and on that note I pull off one of the ripe shiny-black berries and eat it. The look I sometimes get can range from shock to amusement to perplexed.

But the truth is, if you are unfamiliar with this plant you should leave it alone. For every species of this plant (that I know of) the green berries can kill. That should be reason enough to keep it away from homes that have children or livestock (various forms of livestock can die from it too). However, many of our North American species are edible in two ways. The leaves can be boiled twice (with a change of water) as famine greens that are high in vitamin A or the ripe, shiny-black berries are edible raw or cooked by most (if not all) credible reports. There is also a species with dull black berries, not shiny, that might also be edible but I'm not sure about those. The leaves of all the species are probably fine as a cooked green (boiled twice, to be sure) during a famine/doomsday/survival event but with so many other species of wild greens usually available in Florida (and beyond) I would not need to try boiling the leaves. If the boiled product tastes at all bitter I would spit it out and dump it. Forget about boiling it a third time, no viable nutrition would remain. This plant's genus was named after a common toxic alkaloid called solanum which is deadly in large, or concentrated amounts. I do not eat more than a small handful of the ripe shiny-black berries at a time and the flavor can range from slightly rank and musty to sweet and tasty. It is related to the tomato plant.

I experimented with this plant years ago after reading mixed reports on the edibility of it by eating one leaf raw and waiting to see what happens. I'm not sure why I decided to eat the leaf and not the berry because it was the ripe berries that are reported edible raw rather than the leaves. I knew of reports that the leaves were edible boiled but not about boiling them twice. Any plant that requires boiling twice is one that absolutely should not be eaten raw at all. It was a mistake to assume that eating one leaf raw would have no effect. I felt a tiny bit of nausea come on about twenty minutes later which lasted for a few minutes and went away. And that was just one small leaf!

BURDOCK, *Arctium lappa*

This is one of those plants that has accompanied me since childhood. It is easily recognized as a rugged biennial plant with large rough leaves growing to over a foot in size with slightly wave and toothed edges, and hollow leaf stalks, one of its identifying features, that can grow to over feet feet tall with burr laden stalks in their second year that stick to clothing, animals, and everything in its path There is a good reason burdock was the inspiration for the invention of Velcro; at least that's what is said. One thing is certain, burdock thrives, and is easy to spot because of these features.

In its first year, and the beginning of its second, burdock has no stem and grows only as a basal rosette of leaves that stays close to the ground It is the first-year roots that run deep and hard to dig up, but the effort pays off in this case They are best and most edible either raw, baked, boiled, or dried. The leaves of the first-year burdock can be eaten, but you have to like bitter foods, and they are best when blanched for no more than two minutes before preparing them further. As the roots age they become more bitter and woody, particularly in their second year when the leaves come into their prime as food. The peeled burdock stems in the second year are also edible, and not as bitter as the leaves. Burdock is in the same family as daisies, chicory, thistles and dandelions, and there are at least three species of burdock in North America, all edible. Second-year flowering stalk, with large spade to heart-shaped leaves that are hairy and lighter in color underneath, with hollow leafstalks and purple flower head clusters about .5 to 1.25 inches across, bloom between June and October later turning into burrs are the mark of this majestic plant that also can reach heights of greater than four feet. The edible parts of burdock as mentioned are primarily second-year leaves, stalks, and sprouted seeds, and first-year roots.

Because first year roots are the best, the edibility discussion will begin with them. Dig the roots up and leave the dirt on till ready to slice thin for cooking, and don't peel the root before cooking. These roots, like most all root's should be dug in the fall of the first year or even in the early spring of the second year if you know where to dig first-year roots, and second-year stems can be cooked by boiling for about half an hour, possibly in more than one change of water depending on the bitterness factor. The cleaned taproots are best, I think, baked slowly beside the heat of a cook fire with a deep bed of hot coals, and not too much flame. I have had the roots baked with skins on, and they were quite good. Slow cooking, and rotating the roots like you would bake a potato in the most primitive way beside the fire brings out a sweetness to the roots. They are done when they become soft; I suggest going by feel. Very young roots can be eaten raw, but older roots are best cooked. I am a bit leery of raw roots because of possible parasites, bacteria, and the like in the soil the roots came from. Old and very long roots are likely to become woody at the core and are reserved for starvation situations. When like that, boiling or perhaps thin slicing and drying may be your best resort. While not so flavorful by itself, the root will take on other flavors. Young roots have a mild flavor becoming stronger as it gets older raw or cooked. The stems should be peeled, and roots scrubbed or peeled if boiled to remove the bitter skin. These roots, at the end of the first season, are tender, nutritious, and tasty. These hard-to-dig tap roots are best harvested in the fall of first-year plants. You can boil them by cutting burdock root into thick slices and boiling either alone or with other edibles until tender. Thinly sliced burdock root can be fried and are similar to a potato chip from what I understand. I've not had them that way. Probably best if you can do so in oil, and add salt. Lastly, thinly sliced dried burdock root is to make tea, or to preserve it for later use. Slice it as thin as possible and dry it in the sun. This method seems very valuable as you can easily rehydrate the root slices when you may need them the most.

As the second year approaches, we turn to the above ground parts of burdock. There are a couple of risks involved with eating young burdock leaves. Foremost, make sure not to mistake them for foxglove, which is poisonous. One difference is foxglove leaves have a blue-green coloration to them. Secondly, even though young burdock leaves are edible raw. They have to be washed with clean water to remove the tiny hairs that while not toxic, can cause numbness and general irritation to mucous membranes, your mouth for starters. For this reason, I recommend blanching them for a couple of minutes at the most so as not to cook all the nutrition out of this wonderful edible. At this point, you can add them to other vegetables or eat them by themselves. You can harvest and eat burdock leaves at any time of the year, assuming you can find them, even if they are a bit bitter. Young shoots can be boiled until tender, more if bitter. Second year, stems can be peeled before flowering and boiled twenty minutes. Seeds should be sprouted to make them edible. Young flower stalks may be collected in late spring, before flowers appear; their taste is likened to that of artichoke. Also leaves can be wilted by fire then used for wrapping food; I have wrapped fish in burdock leaves and cooked them in an underground earth oven and it was perfect. Look for instructions on making one for cooking. It is well worth it. After blanching the leaves you can also fry them in whatever oil you can manage, if possible. Whatever you do, don't overcook the leaves as it further destroys valuable nutrients. Because of their size, burdock leaves make good vessel parts for carrying water, and helping a shelter better shed water. Be creative, and most of all be careful. Follow that old Edibility Test and track this plant before you are in a situation where doing so would be difficult.

Burdock is very nutritious. The young leaves contain about 3.5 percent protein, 1.8 percent fat, 19.4 percent carbohydrate, and 8.8 percent ash, calcium, magnesium, phosphate, potassium, folate, vitamin C and K consisting primarily of carbohydrates, volatile oils, plant sterols, tannins, and fatty oils. The root is white but discolors rapidly when exposed to the air. They contain about 2.5 percent protein, 0.14 percent fat, 14.5 percent carbohydrate, 1.17 percent ash, and contains about 45 percent inulin, a starch that passes straight through the body undigested. Inulin can be converted into a sweetener that is suitable for diabetics to eat.

Burdock looks a bit like rhubarb, which has toxic elements in their leaves, as mentioned before, but the underside of a burdock leaf will be hairy whereas a rhubarb plant will not be. Also, the stem of burdock will be hollow, while rhubarb's solid young leaves resemble foxglove leaves, which are toxic. Other than those, I can think of no other toxic look-alikes. Make sure you can add burdock to your diet. You know the drill. Stick to it.

Burdock grows well along river banks, disturbed habitats, roadsides, vacant lots, and fields. It grows throughout southern Canada and northern US, but not in the deep south. I have seen this distinctive plant my entire life and used it as food from time to time.

Burdock roots are dark, or nearly black on the outside, and light inside. The basal rosette of leaves stays close to the ground the first year and the beginning of the second and can be up to three feet across.

The tender pith of the root and the leaf stalks when young, before the stem has begun to lengthen, boiled in two waters (with a little soda in the first water, to break the tough fibers, salt in the second water), make a really palatable and unusual potherb.

The young stems, which are often an inch or more in diameter, are gathered before the flower heads are well formed, in late spring or early summer, and carefully peeled, great care being taken to remove every shred of the tough, strong-smelling and bitter rind. The remaining pith is a half-inch or more thick, tender, and succulent and, when cooked in two or more changes of water to remove the strong taste, makes a superior vegetable, in flavor like salsify—another way I plan to try it when I get a chance.

As a side note, the long straight stems when dried make an excellent hand or bow drill.

BULL THISTLE, *Cirsium species*

Many guidebooks on this subject include this plant, calling it bull thistle. I've noticed a few over the years growing around my Central Florida area in the winter. I couldn't imagine harvesting anything from it until recent years. The spines are hard and sharp and cover the entire plant.

It starts out as the rosette you see here during its first year and then a stalk with purple flowering buds (all spiny) pops up the middle in the second year or sometimes both in the same year. There are several ways to harvest food from it, which all require dealing with the sharp spines. If you cut off one of those spiny leaves from the rosette and hold the thick end with pliers, tongs, or gloves you can gently peel all of the spines off the leaf with a sharp knife until all you have left is the bare mid-rib, that whitish center down the leaf. After rinsing or rubbing off any foreign particles, you can then eat it raw like a skinny stalk of celery or chop and boil it. You can do the same with the young stalks. Cut, peel, and eat the thick core raw or cooked when it has a core and boil the rest. The older stalk becomes too woody and tough and most stalks are hollow inside, no edible starchy core.

Even though the first-year root is edible, I wouldn't bother trying to harvest it unless it was a very large plant (revealing a large root) and if I was in dire straits. Even then, it would require a very large root to be worth the hassle of digging it up, removing the spines around it, and peeling most of the skin off before boiling. With my luck, it would turn out too woody to eat. That happens sometimes with edible roots of certain plants. The trick might be to find a large one that is not too old yet. I can't be sure about the root's edibility. It just doesn't seem to be worth the hassle.

However, when the young stalk comes up the middle early in the second-year of its life cycle before the stalk becomes erect (stands straight up), the center core of the stalk sometimes has a chewy white core that taste fine to me raw, although somewhat bland, and doesn't require much hassle to harvest. I've eaten it raw on the spot. It can also be added to soups and stews. I cut off the stalk at the rosette and slice down the middle lengthwise while peeling it back just enough to expose the fleshy core. By prying out the core with the knife, the whole process did not require holding the spiny stalk with my other hand. I used a stick to hold the stalk down with my other hand while slicing and prying the edible core out of the stalk. You can also just cut the stalk off at the rosette and place it along the campfire on the hot ashes and let it cook. Once sizzling hot, you can then take it off the campfire, let it cool a little, then cut sections of it and squeeze out the flesh. Most of the time the stalk grows straight up, without the thick chewy core. It becomes hollow soon after it begins to grow unless it has the thick core.

Some people claim to have dropped them into a blender with added healthy ingredients. I suppose you could also use a juicer to extract the nutrients and drink without experiencing a stabbing pain from small spines. That blender trick though, I don't know . . . the one main characteristic of all true thistles is that they can make you bleed.

If you use gloves to harvest this plant, make sure they are very thick or very strong leather gloves. The plant called sow thistle is not really a thistle. Only the plants from the *Cirsium* and *Carduus* genus are true thistles.

I've seen these thistles on street-corners, in pastures, along woods of access roads in our local parks, and even along the main hiking trails outside of town miles into the woods.

There are reports of eating the core of the flower bud, but I haven't tried that either and would hesitate to try it unless very hungry. Even then, I'd prefer to have someone show me how to do it first. The young stalks and leaves, once all spines are scraped, peeled, or burned off, is fine raw or cooked.

NOTE: I've noticed something: The thistle stalks that grow straight up don't contain the thick edible core as the ones that start out growing limp. I've seen several of them growing over the years here and there in which the stalk was lying down and flexible, as much as 2½ feet long. When I cut into the core of those I find the thick white starchy substance in the middle (tasted really good raw). When I cut into the completely erect stalks of other thistles they are always hollow, even when young. I peel off the spines and skin until all I have is just light green and smooth. It is good raw or cooked.

CABBAGE PALM, "*Sabal palmetto*"

In any survival situation, the amount of energy you burn to prepare a meal must not exceed the number of calories you'll ingest from it. The cores of most palms are edible and some are even cultivated and canned as heart of palm. As a survival food, however, it is important to note the fact that Florida's native tribes did not harvest the heart of this palm, *Sabal palmetto* or sabal palm, swamp cabbage, and cabbage palm, until European explorers and settlers gave the natives metal axes. The metal axes made it possible for natives to harvest these palms without losing a bunch of calories in the process.

Even with axes, these palm hearts—rich in carbs, fiber, but not protein—might not be practical to harvest by one or two individuals doing all the work. The general rule in survival here is to minimize burning calories by improvising methods and actions which will accomplish a given task without burning lots of calories in the process.

For example: The relatively small piece of tarpaulin that I use to cover my firewood pile at campsites has a rope attached to two of the corners. As I'm out collecting firewood, I drag the tarp along by pulling the rope as I go from one dead, dry branch or log to another, placing the wood on the tarp instead of carrying small amounts back to camp several times by hand. I just have to be aware of any sharp objects on the ground which might cut the tarp and maneuver around them. To have a large pile of firewood, I just make several trips—being careful not to weigh down the tarp so much that it becomes difficult to drag along. By doing it this way, I don't expend as much energy in the process as I would if carrying firewood back to camp by hand.

The cabbage palm is native to the southeastern US and west Bahamas and the State of Florida has designated it the State Tree—even though it is botanically not a tree—and they may or may not have also designated it a protected species. The jury is still out on that question, no matter what field guides say, as far as I know. Taking the core of one kills it, so until all hell breaks loose and TSHTF, harvesting one without a permit of some kind might be illegal.

To harvest the palm-heart, cut off the top three or four feet (preferably from the plants/trees that are not too tall), then discard the top ½ foot (or so) of that where the fronds extend up from the top and then strip off and cut off the outer portions until only the starchy white core remains. It can then be sliced and boiled or chopped up into a slaw and eaten raw. Some people soak the slaw in fresh water for about an hour before draining and mixing in other ingredients (like making coleslaw) and then serving. I don't know why they soak it, unless it is specifically cold water to give the slaw that cool, refrigerated state or soaking reduces any bitterness.

Although called swamp cabbage, it is reported to have a flavor similar to the starchy center core of cattail and sawgrass stalks—which makes sense because most palms are much more related to grasses than to trees or cabbage.

The round, ripe, black berry has paper-thin pulp surrounding the hard, round seed when the seed is ripe. If you squeeze the berry and it crumbles the seed inside into dust the outer pulp and seed is overripe, no longer useful, and the thin outer layer of pulp is now rank tasting. The seed itself is rock-hard when the paper-thin pulp is black and ripe for eating. The pulp is literally paper-thin. The pulp's flavor when ripe is reported to be similar to prunes but my reaction to eating the ripe pulp off the seed—by simply popping them into my mouth and gently chewing off the pulp—is the flavor of licorice and prunes at the same time. I say, gently chew, because the seed when ripe is not just hard as a rock, but harder than most rocks. Some field-guides report that the seeds can be ground into a flour additive or alternative. That is true, but the hardness of the seed makes that very difficult unless one has a sledge-hammer. Once the pulp of the berries has been removed from the seeds these seeds can be roasted at about 350° F for about twenty minutes to make a coffee-like, non-caffeinated drink. Roasting makes the seeds easier to grind into a powder.

In survival situations, the fronds can be used to make shelter and the dead, dry, woody straps stripped apart of the old decaying fronds which wrap around the palm tree is crumbled into a good fire tinder and kindling. It is important to note that palms don't grow in standing water—making any of them that you see in a swampy environment, which is an indication of a least somewhat high-ground.

While hiking and camping out, I have used the fronds to make small lean-to shelters over my campfire-circle when not using it if I saw rain clouds coming. I constructed a wall from bamboo and palm-fronds to form a kind of shower stall at a campsite which has only one trail leading through the woods to it. By showering behind this make-shift wall I can feel comfortable that no one will approach my campsite from the trail and see me in my birthday suit. I bring plastic gallon jugs, filled with water from the nearest water hose or water source, purify the water chemically if it needs it, and place the jugs in direct sunlight for a few hours to heat up the water. I then take my showers by pouring that warm water over me with the jug.

When looking for combustible material that will flame up a campfire, use dead, dry palm-fronds that have turned that beige color that they get as they decay. It is also important to note that wasps and hornets like to nest on the bottom side of fronds on the trees and on the ground. Also, edible insect larvae (grubs) can be procured from damaged, deformed, and old palms.

Another common southern palm I have used for food, shelter, and fire is saw palmetto, (*Seronoa repens*), which is not illegal to use, for sure, and of which I will save for another lesson. For now, you should know that the stalk of each frond of saw palmetto is sharp, finely toothed, like a hacksaw, while the cabbage palm (*Sabal palmetto*) is not toothed but may have a few long spines and the berries of saw palmettos are larger, thicker pulped, and taste very different—almost unpalatable—but edible. If the palm has razor sharp, large spikes close together like a wood-saw you don't have a cabbage palm. Most palms have an edible core, some don't. The ones that don't are generally not native and only used for landscaping. You are likely to find only the edible kind in the Florida wild.

CAESAR WEED, *Urena lobata*

When Caesar weed was used commercially to make cordage it was considered a cash crop and emergency famine food. Now, it is only known as a noxious weed. It grows profusely wherever the clay, silt, sand, and organic matter combine with periodical rains to make healthy soil in subtropical and tropical climates. They are remarkable survivors where conditions are less than ideal. The definition of the word, noxious, is "something physically harmful or destructive to living things." You know, like human beings.

Noxious, invasive weeds spread so quickly and thickly that they prevent other plants from receiving sunlight—virtually choking the smaller, delicate plants. Being a member of the mallow family, it is likely to have edible quality to some extent.

It does have documented medicinal quality, but as a food, only the youngest of leaves, flowers, calyces (the usually green outer whorl of a flower consisting of sepals), and burr-like seeds are supposedly edible and all must be cooked. I'm not sure how to eat the seeds. The flowers and calyces can be eaten raw in very small quantities but preferably boiled. The small, youngest, emerging leaves must be boiled twice with a change of water. Use only the small youngest leaves. We should put this one on the emergency survival-food list, not for prime foraging.

The fuzzy texture of the leaves and medicinal properties within the whole plant can make some people queasy while others might prefer to spit it out. If you can, and you need to, mix just a little in with other greens after the first boil. Always dump that first water, or use it for cleaning things. To preppers, this is a good plant in tropic and sub-tropic areas to investigate for its medicinal uses, preparations, doses, etc. Every 100 grams contains protein, fat, carbohydrates, fiber, calcium, and phosphorus. With that kind of nutrition, one must consider it a potential food source in spite of the off-putting fuzzy texture.

CAMPHOR, *Cinnamomum camphora*

WARNING: No part of this tree should be used by pregnant women.

This is a tree that can grow as high as seventy feet tall with a trunk as much as six-plus feet thick. You can use the wood safely to smoke food as you would with oak and hickory unless you have a pregnant member of the group. The youngest leaves have a pink color to them which appears more prominently in the spring. These young pink leaves can be boiled for famine-food greens in moderate amounts. You might want to boil twice, replacing the water. The tree produces thousands of berries with seeds, NOT EDIBLE, which fall to the ground producing seedlings where they land. These seedling roots produce a very pleasant root-beer tasting, non-caffeinated tea. I'll get to that preparation technique shortly.

Camphor seedlings.

To identify the seedlings and the camphor trees themselves, crush the leaves and take a whiff; it will have a sweet aromatic fragrance similar to sassafras, wintergreen, or root beer. Once you become familiar with the unique fragrance, you can always identify it. I even use the leaves in a potpourri. Native to Asia—and escaping cultivation—the berries are not edible. Oil from the wood can be used in herbal medicine. A little camphor tea on a regular basis is said to help prevent one from catching the common cold. The tea is also reported to calm a nervous/queasy stomach.

To make a cup of tea, use a few sprouts. For stronger tea, use many sprouts. Pull up the 1-inch high (to as high as a few inches high) sprouts from the ground—be sure to include the root of the sprout. Wipe off the dirt and remove any leaves, the seed, and the green part down to about one inch from the root. What you'll end up with is the root of the sprout with about an inch of the aboveground, green stem. If you twist the stem a little you can smell the fragrance to be sure you have a camphor sprout. However, once you get the fragrant oil on your fingers, every sprout you pull up will smell the same. After the first two sprouts, use your best judgment to be sure you have a camphor sprout. The leaves are distinctive.

To ease a sore throat and nasal congestion you can put the older leaves in boiling water and inhale the steam. It really does help. Never overuse this plant for internal methods as it can adversely affect the central nervous system. I frequently harvest the sprouts for a root beer flavored tea, which I prefer to make into an ice tea with a root beer flavor. Simply steep the seedlings in a cup as you would any tea and then put into the fridge to cool and then add ice. It needs no sweetening or dilution.

CATTAILS, *Typha latifolia* and *angustifolia*

No, this is not called a corndog plant. One of the most recognizable of all aquatic plants (plants that specifically grow out of water) is the common cattail. Pretty much anywhere in the world that you can find fresh water you might find cattails. I've even seen it growing where puddles consistently form in mostly dry fields.

The cattail has two distinct types growing in the US. The common cattail (*Typha latifolia*) covers the southern reaches of the continent up to and including southern Canada. The other is called narrow-leaved cattail (*Typha angustifolia*), and only covers most of the eastern half of the US (east of the Mississippi River), with the exception of the Appalachian Mountains, and grows in a few sparse sections of the west. That includes a patch along the Bitterroot Range in Montana/Idaho and the coastal area of the Pacific Northwest into a snippet of the British Colombian coast. The narrow-leaved cattail appears to be virtually the same as the more common species but with its long linear leaves half as thin. There is hardly a better known edible plant among foragers than cattails. It has been used by species of humans for conceivably a million years and beyond.

While there are a number of edible parts to the cattail for you to learn about, the ones that have most interested me are the bottom white core of the stalk, the rootlets growing off the rhizome root, and the immature green flower buds that form at the top of the spikes in early spring all wrapped up in the long green leaves. The orange-yellow pollen that replaces the top flower spike in the fall is rich in protein and plentiful. It can be used as flour; however, I haven't tried that yet.

There is a small window of opportunity for the immature flowering spike. After the leaves expose the early edible, green, fleshy spike, its edibility doesn't last much longer. While both the upper and lower parts (male and female) are still green, before turning even a little brown, that very young, thin, and green corndog is edible by boiling. Even though I like the white starchy and crunchy core at the bottom of the early shoots and later stalks (which reminds me of the taste of cucumbers), nothing beats the cooked, immature, corn-flavored, spike-buds dabbed with butter and sprinkled with salt. You even have to chew the cooked flesh off of a hard but thin center spike, like a very thin corn cob. It reminds me of eating corn on the cob somewhat anyway. I cut the fleshy green spikes off the stalks, and then further cut them into four- to-five inch sections to fit my pot. Simmered for ten-plus minutes or boiled rapidly for a few minutes, the cooked flesh is chewed easily off of the solid thin spike. They should be prepared right after cutting off from the stalks which grow up the middle of each plant. Wrapped in a damp cloth

or placed in a chilled cooler, they will otherwise start to spoil almost immediately. Turning brown on the ends at first, they will begin to turn brown all over and spoil within several minutes if not chilled. This part of the cattail must go straight from the field to the pot. Don't try to carry them around in your backpack and expect them to stay green and delicious. I made that mistake once.

There is a particularly poisonous plant that, when both are young, resembles the cattail. After the cattail forms its long green spike which turns into the brown corndog-like fruit and the poisonous plant produces its flower the differences are easily seen. The poisonous one comes from the genus *Iris*, both the yellow flag and blue flag and other species. First you must look around for signs of past cattail stalks. The previous year's growth, even though quite dead, is usually still standing around with some of the fluffy pollen still hanging on at the tops of the spikes. But most importantly, the shape of the bottom of the stalks, even at the earliest stage, is quite different between cattails and iris. The shape of the iris stalk is very flat, somewhat resembling an unfurling Asian hand fan. The cattail stalks have an oval shape to them, not flat or resembling a hand fan. The difference can sometimes be fairly subtle. To harvest the cucumber-tasting inner core of the cattail shoot, grab the shoot near the bottom between the outer leaves and pull up. Not the whole plant, just the inner stalk. Being careful not to grip the outer leaves around the stalk, just pull the inner core. The bottom white core is quite edible and loaded with carbohydrates. It has a pleasant cucumber taste to it. If it is at all bitter, spit it out immediately. You must have the wrong plant if it tastes bitter. I've been eating them this way since my youth and I've never tasted a bitter one. I've never made a mistake in identification of cattails. No one should make the mistake of consuming an iris shoot instead of the cattail. The cattail is very mildly cucumber flavored. The iris is bitter.

While there are ways to eat the roots, the simplest, quickest part of the root to use is the rootlets. Any nub-like protrusion growing off the main rhizome root can be eaten raw or boiled and the stringy little rootlets growing off the rhizome root is edible raw but better boiled.

First check the water for signs of contamination from chemical or petroleum products. A greasy film or sheen from the surface, or a white, cloudy substance is a bad sign. The darkness of the water is not usually the issue. Dark water is usually a sign of tannin from the trees and plants, (particularly if surrounded by lots of trees and plants) a natural and bitter substance that is consumable in small amounts if diluted by water. That water is not harmful if filtered and purified. How far is the water source from any kind of factory, mining-operation, or mill? Is there a heavily traveled highway nearby? Is the highway at a higher elevation, causing rain runoff into the water source? Be cautious of these things when looking at a water source for any of your foraging needs. Cattails grow in water (hopefully wholesome enough to make potable) or seasonably wet mud or puddles. The leaves can be used as cordage, shelter material, for making baskets, and even for bedding. The dry pollen is a fair fire-starting tinder in non-humid conditions.

There are ways to use the roots themselves for making flour by crushing them in water to extract the fibrous material and then dry it all into a powder for flour. The rhizome roots can also be placed into the hot-ashes of the fire to cook overnight (or for several hours) preferably wrapped in aluminum foil or cattail leaves. Once thoroughly cooked, you can chew the sweet starchy goo off of the fibers. The uses of the cattail for survival are varied and many, from the water, to shelter material, to fire-tinder (the pollen), to food.

Chicory, *Cichorium intybus*

This is a common wildflower easily found from May to October. It is a perennial plant, meaning one that returns in following years, growing up to four feet tall with blue or lavender flowers. The entire plant is edible, just like its relative the dandelion, although unlike dandelion flowers, chicory flowers can be quite bitter, and the roots can either be eaten raw, boiled, or roasted until dark brown and brittle, then ground into a nutritious coffee substitute. Chicory leaves taste best in the spring and fall and can be eaten raw or cooked. Older leaves are best cooked Similar to dandelions and many other edibles, the summer heat makes them bitter. You may want to boil them in a change or two of water to make them more palatable, but they are still edible. Mix them in with other edibles to make them taste better if you like chicory, when flowering from around July till October is easy to spot, mainly because of its bright blue flowers that open up on sunny days, and its long sparsely leafed stems it grows in disturbed areas open fields, and along roadsides mostly. Avoid those along the side of the road as toxins from passing

vehicles render them inedible. Many plants leach the heavy metals found in car exhaust along with road runoff and God knows what else passing traffic leaves behind. Also avoid plants of any sort that may have been exposed to herbicides, pesticides, fertilizers, or too much agricultural activity. I see chicory almost everywhere in the East Central US, and I suspect many other areas as well. You will see this mentioned for a lot of plants found in disturbed areas, urban areas, or anywhere man has managed to control the land.

Chicory leaves look a lot like dandelion leaves, only they're bigger. You'll want to harvest the leaves when it's cool either late spring or early autumn, and at least blanch them for a couple of minutes to make them less bitter. Your options with chicory leaves are, raw, boiled, and fried. Chicory leaves can be eaten raw if they're young enough, or if it's an emergency. Younger leaves are not quite as bitter and can be added to salads and mixed with other greens. As a rule, it is good to have a variety of foods in your diet whether in a survival situation, or just day to day anyway.

The best time to harvest chicory root is after it flowers. The older the plant, the longer the root which is a good thing considering you'll need a lot of it to make chicory coffee. Chicory root is only prepared one way that I know of, and that is to dig the root, clean it, chop it up, and roast it spread out near a hot fire until the roots are a crisp dark brown. The roots are then ground to a ground coffee consistence, and brewed like you would coffee. You can stretch regular coffee by adding prepared chicory root to regular coffee and brew. I personally love it that way. You can do the same thing with dandelion roots and numerous other roots as well. You can also sun dry chicory root like I do with many roots and other plants in a car sitting in the sun with the windows rolled up. Spread the finely chopped or shredded roots cleaned, with as much of the skin left on the root as possible on a piece of metal, or the closest thing you have to a cookie sheet, set it on the dashboard of your car in direct sun with the windows rolled up, and you have an instant mobile food dehydrator.

The nutritional value of chicory is excellent. The leaves contain vitamins A, B complex, C, E, and K and also potassium, calcium, phosphorus, copper, zinc, and magnesium. Chicory root contains vitamin C and inulin, which aids in the absorption of calcium and magnesium making it great for strong bones and teeth.

As with any wild edible, use the edibility test to make sure it agrees with you. Some people get a rash from handling this plant. Although chicory has no poisonous look-alikes, and is edible in all seasons, it is still important to establish a positive ID. It can be hard to identify in winter so it is a good idea to track the plant through an entire year making notes, taking photos, and drawing sketches. This way you cultivate an intimate relationship with the plants you are introducing into your life. I recommend this with all plants, adding new ones all the time.

CHICKWEED, *Stellaria* species

The common name, chickweed, stems from how much chickens enjoy consuming it. I've pulled up bunches of it to feed to chickens, ducks, and turkeys. It can also be used as a kind of spring tonic for rabbits and a wide variety of animals—both wild and farm-raised. The genus *Stellaria* is attributed to the less common name of starwort.

Chickweed. Note the accompanying sorrel.

While flower petals appear at some distance to be ten very small, white, thin petals, they actually sit on five green sepals, deeply cleft twins of five petals. The shape of the tiny, twin petals has been described as bunny ears. The stems have the tiniest of fine, harmless hairs extending down the stem in a row that changes its position on the stem from node to node. That main stem of this crawling and climbing little herb has as its most identifying feature that single row of hairs along it, interchanging from one side to the other between each node of opposite leaves. Look closely at a stem and you can't miss it. The leaves are oval, entire margins, and pointed tips.

Some experts report that the whole plant above ground is edible while some exclude the slightly elastic nature of the main stems. At the inner core of these stems is a thin but sturdy little cord with a definite elastic nature to it—another identifying trait.

Chickweed is full of nutrients, many of which are not available to foragers in the winters of cold climates, making it as essential a spring green as dandelions. However, in Florida, chickweed (as well as many wild green edibles) only appears in our winter months. Chickweed is very mild tasting (unlike dandelions), being compared to corn and green pea shoots. It should be chopped (excluding stems) and added to salads or dropped into boiling greens during last few minutes of cooking. Young, healthy leaves, shoots, and flower buds are best. The flavor tends to become slightly rank to some in older plants. I don't think so though, and I eat them at any stage of development. The older chickweed and the plants growing under stressful conditions remind some of eating straw. Using scissors for harvesting shoot-tops and leaves is best if you don't want to include the stringy stems. Chickweed is best raw in salads, or as a garnish, but can be added to soups and stews. All aboveground parts are technically edible. However, seeds of grassy plants can be risky and are best avoided.

Chickweed is a cool-climate plant, but comes up here in Central Florida in shady, healthy soil wherever it gets established, but only in our winter starting in December. They are freeze-tolerant, but not heat-tolerant. Central Florida and all of Texas is about as far south as they can handle. In the north, it can nearly reach the Arctic Circle from east to west.

Introduced centuries ago from Europe, it was a prized herb by gardeners until the latter half of the last century, and it now resides as a noxious weed to a shallow, shortsighted, and spoiled society.

Chickweed contains certain amounts of beta-carotene, vitamin C, high amounts of iron and zinc, with modest amounts of other minerals like copper and manganese.

This is one edible wild plant that is a staple of foraging field-guides and one of my many favorites.

Chickweed followed early settlers and pioneers around the world wherever rich, moist soil is found in temperate zones. Chickweed might be higher in zinc and iron than any domesticated green—which is a lot—and high in potassium. I think the flavor is great for a wild salad, as it has such a fresh, clean, and very green flavor it is also high in antioxidants. The flavor has been described as similar to corn-silk.

The stem has as its core an elastic thread. Carefully twist and gently cut the exterior of the stem until the center core is revealed. Then pull slowly on the cord. It has an elastic nature to it which gives it the stringy texture that you will want to avoid by harvesting only the tops and leaves.

I just pick the top portions of the thick colonies in bunches and pull leaves off. Delicate when boiled, just simmer for a few minutes and add butter, salt, and pepper to taste or chop and add to salads.

CLEAVERS, GOOSEGRASS, *Galium aparinel, G. verum*

In my area of West-Central Florida these plants make their appearance in December and stick around until about April. Some experts report that they are found in dry sites but I've only found them in rich, well-drained spots in fields that I would not consider dry. These plants are from a field near a lake in Dade City, Florida, and I've picked the tops off a few and ate them both raw and boiled. Bland-tasting but good, the leaves and young tops have shown promise as a choice salad or stew ingredient. The thin leaves circle around the stem in whorls. One expert reports that these are good when young, stems and all, and the leaves can be brewed as a tea. The stems, however, are covered with tiny Velcro-like stickers that cause whole plants to stick to just about anything, including other cleavers. These mature stems— even boiled vigorously—are unpalatable, fibrous and chewy, and reported to irritate the throat. I tried to boil these older stems but when I noticed the chewy, coarse, Velcro-like texture right away, I spat them out. I haven't tried them since; they just look too fibrous and chewy to me. If you get them young enough and boil them really vigorously, I suppose they should soften enough. I would prefer just the tops and leaves like chickweed if I had to eat them again. The mature seeds are reported to make a non-caffeinated coffee substitute and they are in fact related to coffee. They are so tiny here, however, as to be tedious to harvest. That could be because many plant species that grow here in the Deep South are much smaller versions of the same or related species that grow northward.

Another name for this plant, bedstraw, refers to them being used as mattress stuffing because they don't pack down completely flat, but always retain a great deal of loft. This would also make them good insulating material for shelter or clothing. As bedding material in the wild, I would definitely look for cleavers. Some experts report that some cleavers can also be found at the seashore. Some reports include recipes for stew, soup, salad, and for making coffee.

AMERICAN CANCER-ROOT, *Conopholis americana*

American cancer-root (or squawroot or bear corn) is a perennial parasite that grows on the roots of oak and beech trees. It looks like a pine cone or corn cob when it blooms. It is native to North America and can be found in most states east of the Mississippi River.

COCO PLUM, *Chrysobaloamus icaco* var. *pellocarpus*

Otherwise known as icaco plum, this shrub or smallish tree with roundish, alternating, evergreen, somewhat shiny, leathery leaves are notched on the end for most species. This species here is *Chrysobaloamus icaco var. pellocarpu's* with fruit that starts out greenish-yellow before ripening to dark blue with translucent spots on them (this ripe one had a spot on its underside). These species grow from central Florida southward in oak

Photo by Nancy Fike.

hammocks, cypress swamps, and along edges of canals and beaches but is often used in landscaping. It is reported that it can grow as high as thirty feet in the wild. The color of the fruit ranges from white (creamy white), red, yellow, and this ripe dark blue which is often described as just "blue."

The thin pulp of this species here is creamy white between the skin and the large seed.

If you crack open the seed like a nut you will find an edible kernel inside. The pulp tasted bland to me but edible, and it sticks to the seed almost like glue. The pulp can be canned and used in jams and jellies but is so thin as to not seem doable. The edible kernel may be the more important part, being reported to taste like almonds. The seed kernel can produce an oil which can be used for candles, soaps, and probably as a cooking oil. I don't know what the nutritional content of the seeds are but I'm guessing it is rich in fat and protein.

The plants in my sister's yard (she provided the photo) do not produce much fruit, only these two fruits this year from about six plants over three years old. That could be because we are in the northern section of central Florida (being too far north), or the plants she purchased and put there are hybrids that were bred to be a hedge rather than a fruit-producer, or because they are just still too young. It is reported that the kernel tastes better raw when a hole is punched through the pulp and shell into the kernel, which then allows juice from the pulp to drain into the shell to the kernel.

CORAL BEAN, *Erythrina hercebaa*

(For emergency famine food *only*. Only the flower petals are edible.)

Coral bean flowers. The only part that is safe to eat.

This is a native species of the *Erythrina* genus that has edible mature flowers and grows throughout the Southeast region of the US (except South Florida) but is becoming rare in Texas and the Carolinas. It is also a poisonous plant for most of it. I found this particular species in only one of the edible-plant guide-books I have; Julia F. Morton's book, *Edible Plants for Survival in Florida*. I also found it in the book, *Edible Wild Plants: A North American Field Guide,* by Elias and Dykeman, but they only mention the poisonous aspects of the plant without mentioning the edibility of the flower petals.

Highly toxic coral bean leaves; light green in sets of three.

The book, *Florida Wild Flowers* (Bell/ Taylor) has this plant also but calls it just coral bean and does not mention any aspect of the edibility of the plant. That book rarely mentions the edibility of the plants presented in it but presents lots of info on lots of edible plants that grow in Florida. There is a very similar Southwestern coral bean *Erythrina flabelliformis*. The guide book by Elias and Dykeman (from *Edible Wild Plants: A North American Field Guide*, 1990 Sterling Publishing Co.) describes the seeds as highly poisonous and can cause death, even when consumed in small amounts. The seeds and bean pods of this plant are very poisonous.

Coral bean pods; eating enough of these could easily kill you or a small animal.

When more than one expert reports eating a particular plant, and calling it good or at least entirely acceptable I don't require further testimony than that—I'll try it.

At first, I only found one plant in Dade City, and with no leaves or bean pods on it. I couldn't be 100 percent sure of identification with just the flowers. Then on my next trip to Dade City I found other plants with that exact flower, and these had both the distinct leaves, thorny leaf stems, and bean-like seedpods—giving me 100 percent certainty of its identity.

It grows from a low shrub to the size of a small tree with a woody, beige, main stalk and the light green leaves, divided into sets of three, growing on thin, light green leaf-stems with small hooked thorns. The poisonous bean pods, or seed pods, start off green and change to black-brown when mature. When the seeds emerge from the pods mature they are red. Both the seeds and bean pods are very poisonous at all stages of development—*DO NOT EAT THEM!*

The flowers bloom between February and June here. The flowers are roughly up to three inches long in clusters on a spike (see previous page). The tube-like red flowers are the only edible part for this plant. Just clip the mature flower-tubes off of the spike and boil in plenty of water for fifteen minutes, changing the first water in between. That bright red color turns to green as it cooks. After boiling, drain and squeeze all liquid from it. Then it can be cooked some more, either by adding it to a stew or soup or frying with eggs. These precautions are always important when dealing with any toxic plant.

The poisonous constituents in the seeds and beans is high concentrations of a toxic alkaloid. Even in very small amounts, it can cause nausea, dehydration, and possible diarrhea. When harvesting the flowers, be sure to pick only the mature flower-tubes to ensure that you don't include any toxicity.

Once cooked, it resembles the French-style green beans that are strips of green beans cut into pieces lengthwise. I don't want to suggest that this is a good choice edible because of the very poisonous nature of the plant. So, even though it is used frequently in Mexican cooking, I suggest this being a famine food source to be carefully harvested and prepared.

I brought a pot of water to a boil and dropped the flower-tubes in. They started to turn green almost immediately. I let them boil for ten minutes and then drained and squeezed the water out. To be on the safe side, I suggest boiling them for five more minutes in a change of water and discard that water as well. Some foraging experts might think I'm being overly cautious in these instructions. I'd rather be cautious than nauseous and many guides report this plant as toxic without mentioning the edibility, even from guides about edible wild plants.

They may not be a native plant, most likely tropical to subtropical, and can be found growing in disturbed ground in the open or among thickets throughout this region. As I mentioned in "Warning Signs" and "Doug's Bugs Slugs, and Grubs," nature sometimes provides its own warning signs to creatures in search of a meal in the form of bright colors, particularly the color red. Many of my favorite wild edibles produce blue and violet flowers. Not many have red flowers. This one has red flowers and must be prepared properly to be safe to eat or left alone. I wonder if it is a coincidence that I found these and other plants in a section of Dade City where many Mexican Americans and immigrants live.

CORAL VINE, *Antigonon leptopus*

A member of the buckwheat family and native of Mexico, this creeping vine with the distinct pink flowers and triangular, arrowhead-shaped, heavily veined leaves is considered an invasive exotic, and yet, it could provide much food for many in case of a famine. It can climb high,

shooting out tendrils opposite the leaves and tolerates poor lighting or poor soil conditions. This is another plant with red (well, pink) flowers that are edible.

A favorite of insects and woodland creatures, it has a variety of edible and medicinal uses. The roots have football-shaped tubers, from the size of a penny to a quarter and possibly beyond. The tubers are fairly hard but nutty in taste and texture and best dried, roasted, and ground into flour while the young leaves can be boiled for famine-food greens. The leaves are antioxidant, anti-inflammatory, and a tea can reportedly be made to treat diabetes and high blood pressure (check with experts first). Tea from the flowers can be used for colds and flu.

The pink flowers are known to have been dipped in flour, fried, and served with pasta. I once mixed the flowers in with my omelets with chopped tomatoes and onions. After learning about this plant from two sources, Julia F. Morton and Green Deane, I began foraging on it for experimentation. The seeds can also be used roasted, winnowed, then ground and used as flour. As invasive as it is, and I've seen it climb two stories high on trees, it will be an excellent survival food if needed . . . or when needed.

There is a similar *Antigonon* variety in South Florida with larger leaves, hairy stems, and questionable edibility. My coral vine grows all over here and can be found in all regions tropical, subtropical, and beyond around the world. It has many, many other common names too numerous to mention when referring to this particular species. I know it as coral vine, because of the rich pink color of the flowers. It is also one of the flowers presented in the book *Florida Wild Flowers* by Taylor and Bell (1982, '92, '98 by Laurel Hill Press). Be sure of identification before consuming any wild plant.

CORN SALAD, *Valerianella olitoria*

Sometimes referred to as lamb's lettuce, corn salad grows in great abundance, at least in central Kentucky. Apparently it is less common in other parts of the country, and even rare in many places. It is a mild, tender edible plant from late fall till to mid spring, and is excellent raw in this young stage as a low lying basal rosette. Once it begins to grow taller, and around the time it divides and blooms it isn't as good, but is still edible either raw or cooked. As it matures, it branches off into a pair of stems in a "Y" shape with small clusters of white or light colored flowers. Be careful not to confuse corn salad with cudweed (*Gnaphalium uliginosum*), which isn't edible but does have medicinal qualities. Cudweed has many more leaves than corn salad and the underside of the leaves are gray. Other than cudweed, this plant seems to have no other toxic look-alikes.

Young corn salad is light green with smooth spatulate leaves rounded at the ends with a fine course fringe around its edge. They usually clasp the stem and are small, around three inches long and .5 to .75 inches wide with the leaves growing in a rosette connected directly to the top of a thin taproot. These light green succulent leaves are extremely delicate and tender, and taste much like mild lettuce. This is one of those plants that can be eaten in quantity with no ill effects providing it agrees with you, and, as I mentioned before is best raw, but can be cooked. Take your time harvesting this and all plants, taking care not to accidentally mix other plants that could be harmful in with them. I always carry a tobacco stick or walking stick with me to poke around a little so I don't get snake bit, stung, or cut on something hiding nearby. As with all new foods, follow the edibility test, and eat small amounts at first until you know it will agree with you.

As corn salad matures it takes on a unique "Y" shape, as described above. The central stem is four-sided and stout, sometimes with fine hairs along the ridges. The stem leaves are often clasping the stem which grows to around eighteen or more inches tall. The plant flowers around April or May with four to twelve flowers surrounded by triangular green bracts, and grows from a single thin white taproot. The tiny petals are pale lilac, but so small that the flower clusters do not seem to have any color at all, seeming white. As it further matures, each flower is replaced by a ridged three-chambered fruit that is oval-shaped and longer than it is wide.

Corn salad is a European native cultivated there at one time and can now be found in disturbed areas, edges of fields, often corn fields, roadsides, and other mostly rural areas. It prefers full sun, although I often see it in wooded areas, and soil that is well drained. It is self seeding, and resistant to insects and disease. In North America it has become established on both the east and west coasts.

Like most wild plants, corn salad is dense with nutrients, including three times as much vitamin C as lettuce, beta-carotene, B6, iron, and potassium. These nutrients are in their prime before the plant bolts and flowers.

When I am foraging or just wandering in the country, I seem to always end up snacking on this mild plant no matter what time of year. I won't hesitate to eat it in quantity because I have come to know it well. It is one of those genuine comforts that bring me closer to the source of living in the natural world.

Crabapple, *Malus sylvestris*

This member of the rose family *Rosaceae* includes any of several small trees of this genus. Crabapples grow in both urban and wild settings. If you ever want to find crabapples, just learn to speak Russian, and take a walk when they are in season in the fall, and even into winter sometimes. You just might come upon an old Russian lady collecting the fruit of this often misunderstood tree. For some strange reason, that has often been the case around here. Anyway, no matter how you go about gathering this mostly neglected fruit, it is available in abundance.

When I think of crabapples, urban survival comes to mind first because of their use as an ornamental city tree. They can be found in many varieties, mostly ornamental in town, but with some exploration, you will come across wilder varieties. The ornamentals tend to be smaller than a golf ball, and are generally more tart, or acrid. The larger natural wild ones tend to be larger, sweeter, and therefore more easily eaten raw, in greater quantities. Regardless of which varieties you find, they are all edible. As with most foods, moderation is key, and you want to avoid eating the seeds as they contain cyanide. A few won't hurt you, but eat too many and you will be in trouble All apple seeds, even those found in the grocery store, contain cyanide.

Larger, wilder varieties can be eaten either raw or cooked. The smaller ornamental varieties are best cooked baked by a fire, or boiled, which will often make them palatable, and even sweetened if you just can't stand them otherwise; not an easy task in the wild, but resourcefulness is a vital part of survival, so there are ways. You may be able to harvest honey if it can be found and done without getting stung. There is also tapping a number of trees with relatively high sugar content in their sap, such as maples, sycamores, and a few others. Doing this is very labor intensive, time consuming, and you must be sure to tap trees that aren't toxic in any way. Here is when you must decide whether or not it is worth the expenditure of energy to process the food. Sometimes, just cooking and straining out the seeds is good enough to acquire a little sustenance without too much effort. As I am writing this, I am thinking of the survival adage of not expending as many or more calories than you are taking in. I have eaten enough crabapples to know my limit, and I never prepared them in any way. They seem like they might be good added to other wild mixes of plants to make up a good meal. By the way, the fruit of any variety of apple is the only edible part of the tree.

In actuality, there is really no species known as crabapple. The title I use here is just for familiarity sake There are just wild apples and cultivated apples of many varieties; the proper Latin name for wild apples is *Malus sieversii*. Experimentation is the only way to figure out which variety you prefer to eat. On a health note, wild apples have more cholesterol-reducing pectin than cultivated ones.

Another thought comes to mind when you are foraging and come across an apple tree is that a lot of wildlife enjoy eating apples, so it makes for good hunting grounds. This is great if you are hunting as well, but because such animals as bears, among others, like them, make sure you don't end up ending up being hunted as well as hunter.

Apple trees are usually small and often gnarled in some way with short somewhat horn-like twigs. The leaves are alternating saw-toothed, with veins on either side of the leaf. Five pinkish or white scented petals appear in the spring, and the fruit can be harvested into late fall and sometimes early winter depending on climate and harshness of the season. Trees like south hillsides and soil that is neither too wet or too dry. If you are fortunate, you can often find the delectable morel mushroom in and around old apple orchards appearing for a short window in the spring, at least here in Kentucky and elsewhere I am sure, but that is another topic.

CRABGRASS, *Digitaria sanguinalis*

Americans have done something I consider strange, even if they don't see it. They went from a farming based culture of growing edible plants around them while pushing out poisonous plants, to growing poisonous plants around them while pushing out edible ones. When food is readily available to them through commerce they surround themselves with colorful, chemically infused poisonous plants at the same time that they ignore, vilify, and eradicate useful wild herbs. Dandelions are the best example of this. It is a virtual storehouse of vitamins and minerals that everyone should get into their diets. Yet, dandelions have been labeled a "weed" and a "noxious weed" by a society that values appearance over substance exclusively and absolutely.

According to Merriam-Webster, the definition of "herb" is "a seed-producing annual, biennial, or perennial that does not develop persistent woody tissue but dies down at the end of a growing season."

As a grain, crabgrass can produce literally tons per acre. Crabgrass can be used as flour, a grain, or fermented. Methods for husking and preparing the grain ranges from old mortar methods of pounding it to separate the seed from the husk/chaff, to using a crabgrass husking machine. Ten percent of people are reported to be allergic to crabgrass. It has been used all over the world as a grain for as long as people have been eating grains (a little over ten thousand years). As with any wild grain, avoid any crabgrass seed that has purple, pink or black spurs, which are ergot, a mold/fungal infection, and use only in famine scenarios anyway.

CREEPING CUCUMBER, *Melothria pendula*

The crushed leaf smells like a cucumber. These tiny cucumbers are only edible while light green. As they turn dark green and then black they become toxic and a very strong laxative. The edible green ones are somewhat tart but definitely a cucumber flavor, which brings out the justification for its common name. The vine itself creeps and crawls along ground or shrubbery and up tree branches that hang close to the ground, justifying the name creeping. If you cut one (the light to medium green) open, you'll find it full of seeds that appear exactly like small cucumber seeds. The fruit is reported to have substantial protein — which is a lot for a tiny fruit/vegetable—with significant fiber and carbohydrates. The unripe seeds are edible while the gourd is still light to medium green. I'll stretch that to a medium dark green but no darker. They really taste great raw as a trail snack or mixed into a salad. It's always fun to watch the reactions of people trying it for the first time.

"Green means go." These young, immature cucumbers are safe to eat

The vine is a slender climbing stem with curling tendrils. The green leaves are three-to five-lobed and shaped somewhat like a misshapen star. It can be found pretty much anywhere that one can grow cucumbers and prefers moist, rich soil. As with other edibles, the closer they are to a highway, busy road, or railroad the more contamination of heavy metals and chemicals may be present. It would help to clean or rinse them off first. Having a spray bottle of water when foraging works well for that purpose. I know foragers

"Dark means STOP." Many species of plants/fruits are only edible while young.

who pickle them. I've noticed that the vines that crawl along the ground are usually void of fruit because of critters eating them. When the vines grow up other plants out of the reach of rodent-size critters, you'll find plenty. Just stay clear of the very dark green to black ones. I can't stress that enough. Become familiar with the shape of the leaves and fruit; there are look-alikes that might not be edible.

CROWFOOT GRASS, *Dactyloctenium aegyptium*

The seeds that hang off of these little helicopter-like blades can be eaten after hulling and discarding the chaff as is, or added to flour and baking soda (and a pinch of salt if appropriate), milled or whole, and cooked into campfire biscuits. It's a good survival food because it is plentiful when in season and ripe, which is in the late fall and winter here when the blades turn tan/beige/gold and can be pulled easily from the stem. When they are green they are not edible. They turn a golden-tan when ripening and if you gently clasp the blades and slowly pull them away from the stem they will come off fairly easily when ripe and ready. If the stem does not easily give them up, you can wait till another time for that one and pull at other blades that have turned color.

To winnow the seeds, I suggest rubbing them between your hands as you hold them above a container, newspaper or large leaf or using a mortar and pestle. You can improvise other ways to separate the seeds from the chaff. I also rub them into a screen. The chaff stays on the screen while the seeds fall through to a container. The grain itself is of a tiny salt-like shape and grinds up to a texture like sand. The grass itself is not edible, only the ripe seeds. Don't harvest unripe seeds, be sure they are a golden-beige ripe with no pink, black or brown spurs (inspect them with a magnifying glass if you can). Raw, boiled, baked, and roasted they are reported to be packed with nutrition. This grassy weed is plentiful all around the US and particularly here in the Sunshine State. Look for them in dry, sandy, soil that is well drained.

CURLY DOCK, *Rumex species*

The leaves should only be used when very young, before the stalk is more than a couple feet high, and boiled. The mature reddish-brown seeds can be winnowed and used for a grain or meal.

Dock, *Rumex crispus.*

Like many of our edible weeds, curly dock came here from Europe as people immigrated here centuries ago. This is one kind that they probably brought here purposely, because of its edible and medicinal uses.

Technically, they were introduced from Europe. That's the terminology for a wild plant that is not a native to this part of the world. They've spread throughout the United States and grow in disturbed ground (usually wet or low spots), gardens, and in many cases, roadsides. In northern latitudes from here, they'll grow almost anywhere. In Florida, the species called swamp dock, *Rumex verticillatus*, is

Swamp dock, *Rumex verticillatus.*

prevalent while the curly, yellow, or wavy dock, or just plain dock, is fairly rare. Swamp dock may not be the most edible of the species, even in its very young stage, even in wholesome water. It might at least be too fibrous. I've eaten small amounts of boiled young leaves without a problem. The *Rumex crispus* variety of dock is the best tasting and most edible dock.

Dock, *Rumex crispus.*

In Florida, both of those kinds grow here and mostly in low wet spots like a ditch along a road or along a creek, stream, lake, or river. Roadsides are good spots to get familiar with edible plants—just don't eat the ones too close to the road or downhill from it, depending on how used the road is.

This is one of those well-known foraging plants and is commonly referred to as dock from the genus *Rumex*. There are a few variations of this dock. The variety I've found in northern states is this one (top and bottom photo above), *Rumex crispus*. I've even seen plenty of the very fibrous looking *Rumex* of swamp dock, with all the characteristics of *Rumex*, but with wider, darker, shorter, and tougher leaves rather than the long, wavy, lance-like leaves of *R. Crispus*. I'm hesitant to eat the darkest, toughest-leaved variety unless I become 100 percent sure that they are one of the edible *Rumex* or I'm extremely hungry and decide to take the calculated risk. Youngest leaves are best. If they seem bitter they can be boiled more, changing the water, to tame the bitterness. If they just don't seem right, spit them out and forget it. They should taste like the usual garden-variety greens and I've enjoyed eating the wavy lance-leaved type whenever I've been able—always boiled first. They provide a tasty boiled-greens flavor.

I've eaten the younger leaves that grow along the upper part of the stalks after two quick boils and topped with vinegar. The lower basal leaves are reported be the most bitter of the leaves on the plant in its late adult stage, when the plant is producing seeds. However, I found those to taste rather bland, not bitter at all, after two quick boils of changing the water.

The lower basal leaves start out as a basal rosette (see photo above). This is when the leaves sprout up from the ground at the root and lay around it in a circular pattern. This very early stage does not require multiple boiling. However, identifying them at that early a stage requires a definite familiarity with the plant. It would help to have firsthand knowledge that the plant was at that particular spot the previous year. They usually grow in colonies of patches from one year to the next up north, but around here I only find the occasion lone ones during the winter, like the one in the photo above.

Once you know what they look like during all of the growth stages and the variations in the species, you can identify them fairly easily wherever you happen to see them. They slowly turn color from shades of green to light brown with the occasional pinkish hue with reddish stems and their darker husks of reddish-brown seeds along the top of the stalks (a little like a large, mature sheep sorrel). The docks (over a dozen species reported in the US) are usually covered in most edible-plant guide books. It was one of those staple foods for much of our foraging ancestors.

This plant has been one of my favorite spring greens over the years. Whenever I can find them in reasonably healthy soil I harvest a few of them whole, or just pick a few leaves, always intending to leave something to produce the next generation.

DANDELIONS, *Tarazacum species*

In his 1962 landmark book *Stalking the Wild Asparagus* (David McKay Company, Inc.), Euell Gibbons called dandelions, "The Official Remedy for Disorders," because of the vitamin and mineral content of the plant used to treat disorders caused mostly by deficiencies. Ancient herb doctors dug up the perennial roots of the dandelion, which could be obtained even in mid-winter in the north. A tonic was made by the juice and given to patients. Patients were then advised to eat lots of young dandelions in the spring. Euell Gibbons describes digging up sprouting roots in the spring to peel with a simple potato-peeler then slicing thinly crosswise and boil in two waters with a pinch of soda (baking soda) added to the first boil only. Studies are revealing that baking soda may not be very good for us.

Or, peel the young roots, slice them thin, and then boil them in two changes of water for about twenty minutes. Then cook it in butter until brown with paprika. You can dip the flower blossoms after removing the bitter, green sepals in fritter batter and fry them in oil and then serve with a sweet syrup. It's always best to remove the bitter green bracts/sepals on the blossoms before using them.

Many experts describe a decaffeinated coffee additive/substitute made from slow-roasted and crushed roots. Others might disagree. They also describe a dandelion salad with young leaves and small chunks of tomatoes, bacon, cheddar cheese, and any oil/vinegar dressing. Some guides report the roots are a diuretic. However, the general consensus among guides is that the leaves, eaten in a heaping helping or eaten exclusively for days, are also diuretic. Another consensus seems to imply that the bitterness in maturing leaves is almost unavoidable. It's only the level of slightly less bitterness that can be obtained by picking leaves when the plant is young or boiled two or three times changing the water, or even blanching—by placing tree-bark or a box, bag, or other paper product over the plants in the ground that you will harvest later and leave covered for three days, then harvest. Even so, the bitterness may still be unpleasant to many and some field guides don't provide that info.

For example, I once discovered long ago that the unopened flower buds themselves were mild and offered some of the best wild green-vegetable flavor when simmered with butter and salt. However, I once added a few flower blossoms (opened) to the pot with them, they tasted very bitter and the texture of the flower petals joined together was unfamiliar and strange—causing me to reject any claim that the blossoms were even palatable.

Then I discovered that the bitterness was caused by the green bracts of the flowers. The yellow flower petals themselves are not bitter. Separating the petals from the bitter green bracts before cooking eliminates any bitterness. Squeeze the bract/sepal with force while twisting the whole thing. Some petals will separate from the green part while twisting but I usually end up peeling back the green parts and pulling them away from the flower petals.

I don't have a whole lot of experience with dandelions, as they are rare in my home state. When I have found them here it is either very close to the interstate or growing from sod that came from a cooler climate. My experience with them comes from the occasions over the years of hiking along America's trails and traveling around in my youth. From working at a dude ranch in Wyoming, or a car wash in Colorado Springs to wandering (bumming, as my Aunt Cookie called it) around New England—in all those situations I ate dandelions boiled in a pot or canteen-cup over a campfire or motel stove or hot plate. Some health-food stores import dandelions to Florida, but they're out of my price range. As always, be aware of how far from a busy highway, factory-farm, mill, or railroad to forage from, at what elevation from those places, the purity of the water sources that feed them, and how polluted the soil might be.

The most relevant research on dandelions reveals that they have substantial preventative and therapeutic effects. Their constituents include vitamins and minerals such as (in the leaves) rich in potassium, vitamin A, vitamin C, vitamin B complex, zinc, manganese, and copper. It is well known among foragers that dandelion greens possess diuretic properties when consumed excessively. A similar looking plant is called false dandelion and is used in similar ways.

EAR TREE, *Enterolobium species*

I was ready to experiment on and document the edible seeds of a familiar tree until I learned that there are actually two species of it almost exactly alike except that one has the edible potential and the other, as far as present knowledge goes, does not. The only discernible difference I know of is the shape and size of the seeds. As it turns out, the more common of the two species in my area is the non-edible one. I've identified four of the non-edible trees, still looking for the edible kind.

The less common one here but edible is called *E. cyclocarpum* and has seeds that are rounder, fatter, and not pointed on the ends like the non-edible *E. Contortisiliquum*. The edible species is more localized and common in South Florida, not in central Florida. If the seeds are fatter, rounder, and not pointed on the ends they will have edible uses—and not just with the seeds. The ear-shaped seedpods of both trees are basically the same along with the rest of the trees so the identifier between the species appears to be the seeds.

Non-edible *E. Contortisiliquum* seeds.

Edible *E. cyclocarpum* seeds.

On the edible ones (mainly south Florida), the very young, immature, unripe seeds and pods are reported to be edible when boiled in plenty of water. The cooked white pith of the blue/black mature pods are reportedly sweet and sticky.

The info I have reports roasting and then peeling the ripe seeds before grinding into a coffee substitute (non-caffeine) or flour with significant protein. One large tree can produce a large basket full of pods that contain eight to sixteen seeds each—a substantial harvest in a famine scenario. You can tell the seeds are ripe when the pods turn black and when you shake the pods you can hear the seeds rattle around inside. The outside portion of the ripe black pods are not edible but contain the constituent saponin which when crushed can be used like a soap. Natives used the trunks of large trees to make canoes because the wood is water resistant, light, and easy to work with.

EASTERN REDBUD, *Cercis canadensis*

The Eastern redbud, *Cercis Canadensis,* is a deciduous tree that grows to twenty to thirty feet high, multi-branched, in full sun to light shade of moist, well drained acid to alkaline soil. The flowers are two-lipped clusters of tiny, one-inch-long purplish-pink, bright pink, and white flowers that appear in the spring before the leaves appear. The heart-shaped leaves emerge reddish-purple which changes to green and then to yellow in Zones 5b to 9a of eastern and central America.

The leaves grow down along the branches which grows in a zigzag pattern, bending slightly downward at each of the nodes on at least one species. There are six species of this small tree or shrub which produces the signature pea-like seedpods which places it in the pea family. These seedpods are edible when young, boiled or fried, and appear connected directly to the branches. The flower blossoms and young flower buds are edible raw or cooked. The young leaves are edible raw or cooked. I have not had the opportunity to try any.

However, you can never assume that just because a tree produces bean-like seedpods that they are edible somehow. The Kentucky coffee tree produces seedpods and are not exactly edible in that the seeds can only be roasted to make a coffee substitute. The mimosa tree (silk tree) produces dark-brown, six-inch long seedpods that are not edible at all. The coral bean has edible flower petals but has very poisonous seedpods.

This Eastern redbud tree would be a great find to the survivor looking for a meal.

ELDERBERRY, *Sambucus canadensis*

When it comes to black elderberries, I don't know where to begin. I guess I could start by saying that this is the shrubby little tree with upright to spreading branches that produces crowns of white blossoms followed by bunches of small berries that turn completely black when edible. This is the one that is so common in Florida and more edible than the western cousin called blue elder, *Sambucus cerulea.* Our elder is also called common elder, American elder, and just plain elder. The photo above shows crowns of berries among crowns of flower blossoms.

I've read many books on edible plants going back to the 1970s from authors like Bradford Angier, Nelson Coon, and Euell Gibbons (among others). I'd like to think that I'm pretty book-smart in this field. I've read many authors' take on the edibility of elderberries. I was particularly impressed with Green Deane's work on this plant. Over the years I have frequently eaten a few of the ripe black berries as a trail-snack but never more than a handful at a time. You must be careful not to include the little green stems attached to the berry when you pop them into your mouth, as all of the green parts of the plant are highly toxic.

Elderberry bush.

Some foraging books (but not many of them) include a claim that the young shoots are edible when boiled like asparagus. However, most books do not mention that and with the level of toxicity in the plant, I would like to hear about someone actually doing so and thereby directly and absolutely confirming that it is safe before I would even consider it. Better yet, I would use the Dick Deurling Method of positive edibility. I would have to watch someone harvest it, prepare it, and eat it. If they get through the night without any adverse effects, I'll consider it safe to eat.

Ripe berries.

The berry's tiny seeds also contain small amounts of cyanide-producing glycosides, which occurs during the digestion process and releases the poison. The cooking or drying that is necessary for using elderberry in recipes eliminates that toxicity to some degree. Otherwise, eat only a handful of them at a time when ripe, raw, and no stems. The white flower blossoms (no green parts) are safe when mixed with batter for pancakes, waffles, muffins, etc. or dipped in batter and fried. I don't personally know whether they are good or not; the only waffles I've had went from a store to a toaster. I made pancakes for myself only once (not a fan). I've shied away from fried foods for quite a while now to help keep my heart functioning properly. But I can assure you, every book on edible plants that includes elderberry (many of them) include a batter-the-blossoms instruction—it must at least be safe and taste acceptable.

Don't confuse a water hemlock or Hercules'-club, *Aralis spinosa* for elderberry. The Hercules'-club is also known as devil's walking stick, with many sharp thorns that cover the stalks. The berries and leaf-structure might look similar to elderberry, but elders don't have thorns at all and the berries of Hercules'-club are very toxic. Water hemlock is very deadly poisonous and also has similar leaf-structure and blossoms but does not produce these berries. Water hemlock grows almost exclusively in water itself while elder grows in low, wet or damp spots. You can see that elderberry is one edible that you would need to be familiar with or be sure of identification.

Just look for the clusters of small black berries (they start off green) that form as the blossoms fall off; you can't miss it. Make sure that all the berries you pick are completely black and don't include any green stems. Here's a good tip for harvesting them in bunches. Cut off a whole crown of completely ripe berries (all black) and place it as is in a freezer. Once frozen, the berries come off of the crown quite easily without the green stems. For making jellies and jams it is reportedly suggested to add a little lemon juice. They are loaded with nutrition and loaded with antioxidants with more vitamin C than oranges or tomatoes.

Elders have numerous medicinal applications of which you can research the details if you want. Elderberries contain flavonoid compounds that are antioxidants in addition to having antiviral quality and anti-inflammatory constituents that benefit the immune system. A syrup on the market for fighting the flu called Sambucol is made with elderberries as well as certain lozenges with zinc and other herbs for fighting colds and flu including elderberry syrup. If you try transplanting elder they need moist, well-drained soil with a slightly acidic pH between 5.5 and 6.5. Their root systems are delicate during their first year and will require frequent watering during dry spells to establish them. Consuming any green parts of elder can result in nausea, vomiting, diarrhea, dizziness, or confusion.

FALSE DANDELION/CAT'S EAR, *Hypochaeris radicata*

There is more than one kind of false dandelion, all similar, with one being identified in the book *Florida Wild Flowers: and Roadside Plants* by C. Ritchie Bell and Bryan J. Taylor (1982, Laurel Hill Press) as *Hypochaeris radicata*. Some books describe that one as well. However, the recent book by Peggy Sias Lantz, *Florida's Edible Wild Plants: A Guide to Collecting and Cooking* has a similar looking plant that grows in the northern half of Florida with a completely different botanical designation, *Pyrrhopappus carolinianus*. They appear to be similar in that they resemble the real dandelions (*Taraxacum species*) but there are several different kinds.

These dandelion look-alikes have edible similarities. Experts report that the *Hypochaeis* species have edible young leaves with a mildly bitter flavor that can be added to salads or cooked as greens, edible flowers (I take off the green bracts first), and the early stalks while still tender can be cooked like asparagus before the flower buds begin to form. I personally haven't tried eating the stalks yet.

However, Peggy Lantz reports only that her false dandelion (*Pyrrhopappus spp.*) is used by eating the young leaves raw or cooked. The flowers of real dandelions are more dome-shaped than these look-alikes and the flower stems are the biggest difference. The dandelion flower stem is hollow, clear, no leaves, and grows one flower bud per plant. Our look-alikes (a.k.a. cat's ear and false dandelion) have thin, solid, green, branching flower stalks with leaves and multiple flower buds (one on each branch or the stalk). In other words, the real dandelion grows a singular, translucent, hollow flower stem up the center of the basal-rosette while the look-a-likes grow an actual green stalk. The leaves of each species seem to be slightly different as well. Compare the leaves in these photos to the leaves in the photos of the dandelion.

FALSE HAWKSBEARD, *Crepis japonica/youngia*

This is a genus that can be found across North America, Europe, and Asia. The usual common name includes the word hawksbeard. However, other plants commonly known to include the word hawksbeard are not the same kind of plant as this *Crepis* species. For that reason, I prefer to call the local one *Crepis* after the genus. Also, the variety designation of the species has changed recently from *japonica* to *youngia*, so it would be called *crepis youngia* now or even *youngia japonica* with the names reversed. Botany can get complicated that way.

This particular species, *Crepis japonica/youngia*, is found from about Pennsylvania south to Texas and the gulf coast states, also in parts of Asia. All *Crepis* species have the same basic edibility as far as I know, the youngest leaves are fine in salads but better cooked as a potherb and mixed with other greens. The taste of the older leaves gets a bit rank to me while the youngest leaves are mild enough to mix with other greens. Because of possible anti-cancer and anti-viral activities in crepis it should be investigated and researched by doomsday preppers and survivalists. The leaves frequently, but not as a rule, have dark colors giving the appearance of a ring around the leaf. If it has dark colors in the center of the leaves it probably is the wrong plant. If it has the dark center and is velvety to the touch it is not crepis and might turn out to be a toxic plant called lyre leaf sage, *Salvia lyrata*. Crepis leaves are thin and delicate, but not velvety. The firm little flower stalks produce multiple little yellow dandelion-like flowers (see photo above) which turn into puff-balls of pollen when turning to seed—similar to dandelions.

FIREWEED, *Erechtites hieraciifolia*

This is not the plant called fireweed found in some books on edible plants with the botanical designation *Epilobium angustifium*. That plant is also edible but is not found growing in the Southeast except for high areas in the southern section of the Appalachian Mountains. That fireweed is found in Alaska and all of the southern half of Canada down through most of the US, except for my native area here in the Southeast.

Both my local plant called fireweed and the northern one have the distinction of being an edible for famine food resources but not known for being a tasty treat to most authors on the subject. I haven't been able to get past the smell of it to try it (I will, eventually) but would make an effort to make it palatable as emergency famine food if I had to. They can be blanched to improve the flavor and used raw or cooked to blend in with other foods. There are people out there who regularly blend the tops, leaves, and flower buds into culinary works of art that they enjoy in a variety of ways. I find this plant in disturbed ground in low lying areas and deep woods at varying times of the year.

FOOTFRUIT, *Podocarpus macrophyllus*

This yew pine (though not a pine) is in a grassy parking area of a church in downtown Zephyrhills, Florida near the local park. Technically a *Podocarpus macrophyllus*, this specimen stands at least thirty feet tall and is just starting this summer's production of edible grape-like tasting fruit with its hard, inedible, green seed attached. The fruit is ripe enough to eat as it turns shades of yellows, blues, and reds. The fruit begins to form some time in summer and ripen either in late summer or early fall.

It's known as footfruit because the genus name *Podocarpus* comes from the Latin for foot-fruit. This evergreen is used in landscaping frequently as a hedge for its ability to be shaped by trimming. A native of Japan and China, it does not care for alkaline soil or low wet places. The lance-shaped, leathery, needle-like leaves are arranged spirally (practically like whorls) around the branches and measures about three to six inches long (usually four) and as much as a half-inch wide (usually a quarter inch).

The fleshy fruit is attached to the single, large, green seed which must be removed. Any toxicity that might remain in the fruit from the seed can be eliminated with cooking, as one would do to make jellies, jams, pies, syrups, etc. Just pull the seed off of the fruit and discard the seed (or save it to plant with).

I've eaten handfuls of the raw fruit with no problems; however, some sources report that young children have experienced nausea from eating the raw fruit. As a famine food, it is plentiful in suburbia, rural communities, and big cities alike. The genus *Podocarpus* has about a hundred species in areas of warm temperate to tropical zones, from Zones 8a to 9b specifically. It has both the taste and texture similar to grapes but with a very sweet flavor. The fruit begins to form around here in late summer or early fall. Don't eat the seeds!

GOLDENROD, *Solidago species*

I don't feel there are enough reports on the edibility of goldenrod to justify eating boiled leaves or using the seeds as a mush or as a stew thickener even though you might find an old report stating it. In a doomsday/famine/survival situation I would barely even consider it. It will always be better to be safe than sick in any scenario where foraging is a necessity.

The best-flavored goldenrod tea comes from a sweet goldenrod, *S. odora* and is reported to have an aroma similar to anise. Some reports include the leaves for a tea as well as the flowers but most reports only include the flowers for making the tea. There are reports of not finding the exact sweet species in Florida. However, I've drank tea made from our local wild species that tasted okay, but nothing special. Yes, I'm quoting myself.

The "book" on Goldenrod is that the tea can be a diuretic; the flowers used as a yellow/green dye, the leaves have antiseptic properties, and infusions

and oils from this plant are used medicinally for a number of things. Pick the flowers off when the plant is in full bloom and place in a paper bag for seven to ten days. For tea, simmer the dried flowers gently for ten minutes (more or less) depending on how many cups of material and water. The tea is a traditional remedy for urinary disorders and kidney or bladder stones. Our local goldenrods don't produce a sweet tea but I just add a little honey to make it turn out more than acceptable and I'm really not a tea drinker.

GROUNDNUT, INDIAN POTATO, *Apios americana*

Without specifically looking for it, I had always wanted to find a staple of Native American and pioneer food called groundnut, a tuberous root-chain of a vine that can be found in low, wet spots around the country.

Then one day I spent five hours hiking the trails around here, which was my custom to do when I had the opportunity. I saw cattails, water lilies (*Nymphaea odorata*), *Nuphar* lilies, pickerel weed (*Pontederia cordata*), greenbrier (*Smilax spp.*), assorted palms, poke, bullrushes (*Scirpus spp.*), and a few other interesting plants. I'm not necessarily looking to forage on wild edibles there, just identify them wherever they may be. I focus on learning about what I could eat out there if I had to, by careful experimentation.

I spooked a small deer, a large black snake, and some other large animal which I heard running away through the brush but didn't see. I was about to cross the railroad tracks to enter the southwestern portion of my hike and spotted a strange looking flower on a thin vine growing up about

Leaves alternate along the vine with pinnately compound leaves that have three, five, seven, or occasionally nine ovate leaflets.

Apios americana courtesy of James St. John, CC BY 2.0.

twelve feet high on tall bushes. I thought it looked like something I'd been looking for and it was.

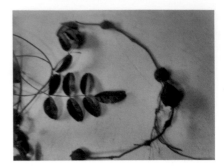

The groundnut, also called Indian potato, has the direct distinction for being a pivotal plant pointed out by the continent's natives to the freshly landed Pilgrims near Plymouth, Massachusetts a few centuries ago. That act of kindness greatly assisted the early settlers in getting through that first winter in the New World. Unfortunately, those pious Puritans treated their helpful neighbors badly. Not even twenty years later, this same tuber of the groundnut vine, which the natives called hopniss, became illegal for Indians to forage for on English land—punishable by jailing for a first offense and a whipping for a second. It makes our laws against foraging (where they do exist) look rather tame comparably.

Members of the pea family, the seed pods resemble a bean or pea pod. They can be harvested the same as the cultivated pea, but I don't know the details. Since those are seasonal, the more significant food source is the starchy tubers that run along a root-chain just under the soil, even becoming exposed in particularly low spots during wet spells.

The groundnut is reported to be a native of China. Some say that they taste like rutabagas, others say turnips. They are reportedly not good raw, but edible. Peel, slice, and then boil them slowly in salted (optional) water until they are tender enough to pierce easily with a fork or knife. From there they can be prepared as you would with any starchy vegetable.

It is a thin vine, leaves alternate along the vine with pinnately compound leaves that have three, five, seven, and occasionally nine ovate leaflets (photo above). From the vines grow small purplish-brown to maroon flower spikes. The flower blossom in the top photo on previous page is several inches large. The plant is a perennial legume. Many writers report that the tubers should be eaten hot, as they become "tough and tasteless" (Euell Gibbons, *Stalking the Wild Asparagus*, 1962) as they get cold.

From southeastern Canada south to Florida and west to Minnesota, Colorado, and Texas, the *Apios americana* is a plant that I had known about for some forty years before I finally positively identified it in the field here deep in the woods of Zephyrhills, Florida.

I share this experience with the father of modern foraging, Euell Gibbons. In his famous book, *Stalking the Wild Asparagus*, he mentions learning about groundnuts when he was young, but not actually finding them himself until his middle-age years.

Hawthorn, *Crataegus* species

This is a medium-sized deciduous tree, fifteen to thirty feet tall, branches often hanging in a somewhat chaotic manner. There are over a hundred species of native and cultivated hawthorns in North America, which are quite variable and can be difficult to distinguish from one another. Some hawthorns are native to Britain and Europe but have become naturalized in the United States and Canada. They can be found north and east of Tennessee, up the west coast from California to Alaska, as well as in Utah, Montana, and Arkansas. This isn't important. They are all equally edible and useful. One of the telltale signs you have found a hawthorn are the thorns protecting the precious food and medicine of this gnarled strong tree. Leaves vary greatly from the many varieties of this tree. The leaf shape tends to be shallow to deeply lobed as well as serrated and pyramidal. The berries grow in clusters in the fall lasting into winter, and are small and red with a dark circular "crown" at the end of the berry. I have even encountered a couple that have no thorns at all. Even with all the different varieties available, this tree is pretty easy to spot. Tracking a hawthorn through its seasons, one can easily spot its red berries in the fall near harvest time even from a great distance. They resemble both tiny apples and rose hips, and rightfully so, as they are all in the Rosaceae family of plants as their patterns reveal. They have oval-shaped leaves (albeit in hawthorn's case often deeply-lobed), with serrated margins. The flowers produce five green sepals behind the five white petals, surrounding the numerous stamens at the center. You will likely find a pink tinge to ripe stamens, and some specimens show pink petals. The flowers are usually in full bloom during May, or earlier. Do not be deterred if you detect a slight fishy odor of the fresh flowers. Your nose is picking up a compound called trimethylamine. This is hawthorn's ingenious way of attracting flies and other pollinators. The smell disappears when the flowers are dried.

As toxicity of the seeds goes, they are similar to apple seeds I know people who make tinctures, and I have asked them if they remove the seeds first, and some do, and some don't with no ill effect. I always remove the seeds, because why take a chance, especially in a survival situation where medical help may be nonexistent.

Most important and the first thing you need to know about the hawthorn berries is do not eat the seeds. They contain cyanide bonded with sugar, called amygdalin that changes in your gut to hydrogen cyanide, and can be deadly It is fine if you eat the raw berries. They are really the best part; just spit the seeds out. If an adult mistakenly eats one or two seeds they aren't deadly, but they could be to a child. Long ago someone discovered that very young hawthorn leaves and blossoms in April and May could be eaten together right off the tree, thus the "bread and cheese tree" was born because very young spring leaves traditionally used on sandwiches are called bread and cheese. The leaves, flowers, and berries are all edible, and one may even get a second harvest of new growth leaves and blossoms around the end of July during what is known as the lammas flush however, this will yield far less of a harvest I'll say it again—don't eat hawthorne seeds. Also avoid mature flowers, or any part that smells like almonds when crushed as this smell is a good indicator of the presence of cyanide.

Once the seeds ripen in the fall, squeeze the seeds out of the berries by mashing the berries with your hands, then quickly filter the thick slurry into a second container through your hands one handful at a time. In about five minutes the liquid will jell. Flip it over onto a flat rock, or improvised plate and enjoy. It can be eaten as is or sliced thin and sun dried like a fruit leather. It will be sweet and can last for many years. Remember, just ripe berries have more pectin than overripe berries. If you've had a dry year, add some water to get a workable consistency. You have to do this all very quickly.

Hawthorn itself often has little apparent taste. However, some hawthorns are tasty enough.

Hawthorns are hard to pick in quantity so improvising a method to save time and energy is a good idea. Try making a basket from a shirt or other cloth connected to a frame of some sort on the end of a stick long enough to reach the berries, then holding the container under the berries. Whack the branches and berries with another stick, knocking them into your improvised container. Once you have enough berries, process them as described above. This process is to remove the seeds, and other particulate matter from the berries get as many seeds out as possible one or two won't hurt, but too many is trouble.

Hawthorns are a very nutritious addition to your wild foods and contain many nutrients particularly good for the heart and regulation of blood pressure. If you have a heart condition, this could well prove a very good thing, but make sure if you are taking any sort of heart medication that hawthorn works with rather than against you. Do your homework before you are in an actual situation with this and all new and wild foods.

HEDGE NETTLE, a.k.a. Florida Betony, *Stachys floridana*

One of my favorite edibles is the *Stachys floridana*, a.k.a. hedge nettle. A member of the mint family, this prolific-growing violet-lavender colored beauty is also commonly known as Florida betony. Another common name for this plant is wild radish because the white, grub-like tuber having the taste and texture of a mild radish.

Described by the book, *Florida Wild Flowers* as "somewhat of a weed," the flowers resemble a group of very small lilies circling near the top of a non-branching, square stalk. The musty leaves can be dried and steeped for tea. The opposite leaves can also be boiled as a green, but the musty flavor makes that use of this plant a famine food.

The best edible part is the fleshy, white, and segmented underground tuber. The tubers can resemble grubs, but not always. They have the texture of a radish (but usually a little softer) and can be eaten out of hand (rinse off dirt first), or chopped and added to salads, or boiled. Sometimes the segments of the tuber are close enough together and numerous enough to resemble the rattler of a rattlesnake. The larger ones in particular do, however, the largest ones usually have issues like stale, discolored, or mushy spots. During the heat of the Florida summer, you most likely will not find this plant above ground. However, if you know where they grow the rest of the year you can still dig up the tubers when the aboveground parts are not in season. When you find some, you may end up finding hundreds if you keep digging. You won't always find the tubers under the plants. They range in size from tiny, to large, to non-existent. I've seen fields the size of a football field loaded with them.

The tubers can resemble grubs, but not always. Sometimes the segments of the tuber are close enough together and numerous enough to resemble the rattler of a rattlesnake.

They can be found throughout the Southeastern US except for the Everglades. I haven't looked into whether their range extends further away than that. However, there are species of this plant that grows in several regions around the world and are considered a delicacy in some places. The *Stachys affinis* is a

commercialized variety that reportedly has practically no differences from the hedge nettle, but is considered an expensive delicacy. Our "weed" variety blooms around here in winter and our early spring in low, moist, sunny spots. Before it blooms, it would appear to be just another minty looking weed to most people. After the flowers appear, it is remarkable how colorful it can transform a landscape until idiots on lawnmowers cause their usual inept destruction.

The common name hedge nettle shares its second name with one of my favorite starchy-tuberous wild plants commonly known as spurge nettle, as well as a stinging edible green (after boiling) called stinging nettle. Touching any of the aboveground parts of stinging nettle or spurge nettle is like getting stung by a bee. However, that is not true for the hedge nettle. Our hedge nettle is just a harmless colorful flower with a tasty treat underneath.

HENBIT, *Lamium amplexicaule*

Henbit is a pretty little herb that was introduced to our con-tinent from places around the world where it has existed for thousands of years, much like many of our wild edibles. Very low growing, it mixes itself in with other weeds and wild herbs in our Florida winter and in the spring up north. I can usually start seeing it here in December about the same time as false dandelions, chickweed, pellitory, and stinging nettles and not long after I start seeing our fall crop of *Crepis japonica*, wild mustards and radishes, field/wild garlic (looks more like an onion), sow thistles and Florida's other cooler-season edible plants.

The upper leaves have no stems (no petioles, the leaves are attached to the stalk/main stem), are opposite (in pairs along the stalk/main stem), rounded, and scalloped. The lower leaves have stems (petioles) attached to the stalk/main stem.

The young leaves on or near the tops are fuzzy (as is the whole plant) and slightly sweetish and succulent. They can mix well into a salad, stew, or as a potherb. The fuzzy texture can be a little off-putting to some, but when adding just a few to your salad, stew, or stir fry you shouldn't get any complaints.

It is reported to being found in all parts of the US except the north central region. It is reported to go well in salad recipes. It likes to grow in colonies in full sun in our winter but dies out quickly as the spring here approaches.

Shagbark Hickory, *Carya ovata*

This tree litters the ground with such a prolific number of nuts that at its peak you could easily pick up five pounds or more in a matter of less than half an hour. Granted these nuts still have to be shelled, but they are among the easiest of this type of nut to harvest. The fruit of the shagbark hickory tree falls covered with a green-to-brown fleshy husk, between two to three inches across with a seam that breaks open easily and won't stain your hand like its cousin, the black walnut. Inside is a hard light colored shell containing a pecan or walnut looking nutmeat which is the edible part. When sorting through nuts, after peeling away the outer husk, check the hardshell nut inside for any small hole and throw away any that do as they have been invaded by a grub, or weevil that feeds on the nutmeat inside. Also throw away any with mold growing on them. Next, place remaining nuts in a container of water and toss aside any floaters you may have. All the good nuts will sink to the bottom. Crack the floaters immediately though as there may still be a few that are good and can be eaten right away. Although not as hard as walnuts, hickory nuts still have a hard shell surrounding the delicious nut inside. Incidentally, varieties of Hickory nuts range from delicious sweet ones to bitter and inedible. With a little foraging experience, you will figure which are good, and which are not.

To get at the nut inside, crack the nut by hitting it on its side with a rock, hammer, set of vise grips, or something that will break the outer shell leaving the meat inside intact. Be careful not to crush it so hard that you can't salvage the good parts. Eventually you will know the right pressure and the sweet spot to hit the shell to break it just right. You may have to use a pick to extract the nut after cracking. A lot of work maybe, but worth it as the nuts are highly nutritious and tasty. You can eat a few nuts right out of the shell, but they are best roasted by the fire to neutralize enzymes that make larger quantities harder to digest. Be sure to save the outer hulls and shells to burn in your fire as they burn hot and slow, and smell good burning. The best time to harvest hickory nuts is in late summer to mid-fall when they are ripe and falling from the trees. Try to beat the squirrels to them as they are a favorite. Be sure to harvest only what you need, as they have to eat too. Hickory nuts contain large amounts of very good fat that is valuable in any survival situation.

As for edibility, like oaks and pines there are no poisonous hickorys, and no poisonous look a likes. Some just need more processing than others, so don't overdo consuming those. They are edible, but they may be astringent or bitter. Often those qualities can be leeched out. Two hickories that are common in this regard are the pignut hickory, *Carya glabra*, and the water nut hickory, *Carya aquatica*. It has been said the first is not palatable and the latter is not edible. Actually, both were used as food by Native Americans.

These seemingly inedible nuts can be eaten, though, and the bitterness leached out like you would with acorns. The water nut hickory's major claim to fame is it is the hickory wood used to flavor foods by smoking and in barbecues.

As for shelling by hand, remove husks if they are not off already. Wash and dry the shells. Lay the hickory nut down on its narrowest side and hit the closer seam with a hammer one third the way back from the stem end. It takes some practice. Second method: If you soak the nuts for an hour or more and work with them wet they will open without shattering. Either method is a personal preference. Some say you get a greater yield by soaking them. The nuts can be ground into a meal and used to thicken soups, etc. A nut milk or butter can also be from the nuts and this is used as a butter on bread, mixed with other edibles and so on. The shell is normally thick and hard. The nut can be stored for up to two years in a cool location away from animal and insect invaders. You do not want the nuts to freeze but you do want to keep them cool. Refrigeration isn't likely going to be an option so you are basically at the mercy of the weather, but be sure to keep them out of the heat/sunlight as much as possible. They can last a couple of weeks at room temperature but a number of months if you can keep them cool. Very cool but not frozen if possible. Just eat at least a few every now and then to make sure they haven't gone bad or become infested with critters If you have, or can make a suitable container, storing them underground is an option, and they don't have to be buried very deeply so you can get at them as desired. The tree can also be tapped in spring and cooked down into a syrup.

Hickory trees range from thirty to 150 feet tall, have furrowed bark that is sometimes shaggy. Leaves are usually leaflets of five or seven, two to four on the main stem, three leaflets splayed at the end, terminal leaflet often the largest. Hickory trees are often confused with ash except their leaves alternate, whereas the ash leaf is opposite. Hickory nuts can be eaten raw or roasted as a nut, a flour, or a meal in water. They have no toxic look-alikes. They flower in June. The flowers are individual male or female and both sexes can be found on the same plant. They are pollinated by wind, and the plant is self fertile hickory trees *Carya spp.* are found mostly into the Midwest US, as well as North and Southeast and tend to grow individually rather than stands of trees. They are often found among trees such as maples, oaks, and evergreens, as well as others While they are tolerant of most soils they seem to prefer rich moist well-drained, but not soggy areas in sunny areas that receive some shade.

Other trees belonging to the hickory family include the bitternut hickory *Carya cordiformis*, pignut, or black, hickory *Carya glabra*, sand hickory *Carya palida*, red hickory *Carya ovalis,* and the mockernut hickory *Carya tomentosa*. The pecan *Carya illinoinensis* is also a type of hickory, grown for its valuable nuts. Lesser-known hickories include the nutmeg hickory *Carya myristiciformis*, whose nuts are edible and whose bark is smooth throughout the tree's life spans and curls as the trees age. Others, such as the scrub hickory *Carya floridana*, are more localized and found exclusively in parts of central Florida.

Hickory is a very hard, durable wood used to make all sorts of tool handles, and the smoke produced by burning the wood is used to cook and cure meats. Hickory nuts are loved by people, squirrels, ducks, turkeys, and all sorts of creatures, and the shagbark and shellbark's peeling bark provide shelter for bats, moths, and squirrels.

HORSEMINT, *Monarda punctata*

USE WITH CAUTION: Also known as spotted bee balm and bergamot's bud, you might find this interesting plant in most of the US along dry, sandy, and well drained areas. I've seen it in places where opuntia cactus and passionflower grows and along railroad tracks. The high plains in the center of America is just about the only place you will not find it, along with a few states in New England. When I find one I usually find others close by in colonies in our late summer and early fall.

However, I do not find the colonies that often. A patch of horsemint is a great find for a survivor/forager. One leaf simmered for tea makes a relaxing, weak, minty tea, as the name implies. A few leaves in a cup of tea can produce a strong relaxant for medicinal purposes or as a cold remedy to induce sweating. But beware—consuming large amounts of horsemint can be fatal because of its toxicity—as many powerful medicinal herbs can be. An even stronger concoction can be used as an antiseptic or antibacterial wash and ingredient in hair shampoo. A chemical in it called carcacrol is particularly good for memory problems. So, using a horsemint extract in an elderly person's shampoo might help to prevent or treat dementia or Alzheimer's disease. Use both leaves and flowers for tea, an antibacterial and antiseptic, a depressant, a cold remedy, a poultice for arthritis, and as an ingredient in hair shampoo. The flowers have a more lavender color to them than the photo above depicts. BUT USE CAUTION!

KUDZU, *Pueraria montana var. lobata*

This is the invasive famine-food spreading throughout the southeastern US called kudzu. The kudzu flowers in bloom are reported to smell like the artificially flavored grape chewing gum. (Or so I've been told; I've always identified some that was past its bloom.) This patch is growing in a thirty-foot area adjacent to a short (one-mile) hike/bike trail in downtown Dade City, Florida, the county seat of Pasco County; a mostly rural section of west-central Florida just north of Tampa and where the American tennis champion Jim Courier grew up.

Introduced to the US around 1876, kudzu was encouraged by the government during the Great Depression and Dustbowl era for soil conservation. They found out that it could grow a foot per day and smother an entire forest. By 1970 it was considered a weed and finally added to the "Federal Noxious Weed List" in 1997.

As an edible plant, it is yet another example of a potential famine-food resource which is hated and ignored by the government, general media, and American culture. The young leaves can be used as a cooked green salad ingredient, juiced, or dried for tea. Older leaves might work for some of that in starvation-desperation, but young is usually best. The shoots can be used like asparagus. Blossoms can make pickles or jelly. The root can be used in a number of ways. As with all potential edibles, research other sources for more details. Beware of Wikipedia, as it is not always accurate.

One key to identifying kudzu is that the thick hairy stems are hairy even on the youngest portion of the vine and new growth. For absolute identification, kudzu is unique in the way the leaves have a line of small, fine hairs along the margin (edge), as if extending beyond the perimeter of the leaf.

Kudzu is a very hardy vine. Its extremely hairy stem is reported to reach as much as four inches thick and one hundred feet long. Only the seeds and seedpods are NOT edible; the rest of the plant is.

Lady's Thumb, *Polygonum persicaria*

This is an annual edible plant that is not particularly tasty, or high in nutrition, and even has potential for mild toxicity if used in very large amounts You may ask why include it in a book about wild edibles? Well, it's because it is one of the most easily recognized and prolific of edible plants, is very mild and good if used in moderation, and has no toxic look-alikes. It is found at least somewhere in every state in the US, and has identifying features that make it easy to distinguish from anything poisonous, and it is good added to other edibles to fill out their portions a bit, or make them less strong tasting. Then it is a safe and serviceable plant to add to your wild foods diet. It is of also fine as a rather mild food in its own right. This makes it a good go-to plant for novice foragers, and those lacking knowledge of what to eat in a dire situation. Most, but not all lady's thumb have a distinctive dark thumbprint like mark on each of its lance-shaped leaves. It looks like an ink stained thumb print.

This plant likes sunny areas and is commonly found in yards, fields, beside streams and lakes, but also thrives in drier areas In other words, you can find it most anywhere from farm fields to city parks, and everywhere in between. Other characteristics are its long stem spikes with pinkish flower clusters at the top that appear in early summer, and papery sheaths that are hairy at the bottom of the nodes surrounding the stem. As the plant progresses through the season, the jointed stems often turn red, giving it the nickname "Red Leg." The lance-shaped leaves, wavy at the edges, grow alternately and staggered below the flower cluster and are up to six inches long, and two inches wide (although usually smaller) and can grow over two feet tall branching out and swollen at the nodes, from a taproot.

Look-alike plants include other members of the *Polygonum* genus that feature jointed stems and pinkish flower clusters, the thumbprint remains the best identifying feature of lady's thumb from its near relations such as green smartweed—*Polygonum Scabrum* a similar plant, but with green flowers and glandular dots on the undersurface of upper leaves. Both are edible. Many other relatives have a spicy quality lacking in the rather mild tasting lady's thumb. As always, do your own research and always test the plant to ensure your own personal tolerance to it. Lady's thumb is a member of a subgroup of the buckwheat family of plants known as smart weeds which, if eaten in large quantities, can cause one to become more sensitive to sunlight and may contain oxalates. This isn't a big concern with lady's thumb because of the quantity you would have to eat to be affected.

Lady's thumb can be found from spring through fall and the leaves can be eaten either cooked or raw. As mentioned earlier, because it is so mild, it makes a good mix with stronger tasting plants. It can also be steamed or boiled for eight or ten minutes or mixed in with other foods such as soups and stews. If this plant is found growing alongside streams, ponds, or any questionable areas it is probably best cooked to destroy any bacteria that may be present. This applies to anything you find in the wild, or the grocery store for that matter. Cleanliness is always of the upmost importance. Cooking the plant also reduces any toxins which although unlikely, may be present. According to the online database "Plants For A Future" (PFAF), lady's thumb contains natural fibers, sugars, fats, and tannins. Although it is not high in these or other nutrients and is rated as of minor nutritional value, it is still a good addition to one's arsenal of survival foods.

LAMB'S-QUARTERS, WILD SPINACH, *Chenopodium album*

Most experts on edible plants specifically call this lamb's-quarters. They usually mention that it is also called pigweed, goosefoot, and fat hen. But the best descriptive name for it is the one that some writers (mostly from the West Coast) call it: wild spinach. I've known this plant as lamb's-quarters because the edible plant guides and related books that I have read these forty years call it that almost exclusively. Its botanical name is *Chenopodium album*. It's related to real spinach,  and a quinoa (*Chenopodium quinoa*) from South America, and possibly even beets. Almost every writer of edible plants includes this one.

I can see why. I've seen it grow to over eight-foot-high with multiple branches and loads of seeds growing in dense spikes at the ends of each branch. While the fibrous, five-sided stems and stalk is better left alone, the long taproot is reported to make a substitute soap, but is not edible. The leaves and seeds are very edible though. As with all wild seeds that are edible, always be careful of a purple mold/fungus spurs called ergot which is quite toxic, interfering with the body's digestive system. While this is more prevalent in grasses, herbaceous plants are not excluded from contracting it.

Two particular characteristics stand out about *Chenopodium album*. The leaves are waterproof until boiled. Water slides off the leaves as if they were layered with silicone. The texture of the leaf does not feel or look like it would be waterproof, but it is. Then there is the white powdery look to the tops of the young plants (photos above). It's not powder; it's natural and quite harmless. Look for lamb's-quarters in rich soil where mostly full or completely full sunshine is available.

Many writers express the general opinion that this plant is a staple in foraging food. Some even prefer it to spinach. Its abundant seeds can be winnowed and ground into a meal, cereal, or flour additive reported to have a buckwheat flavor. The leaves are good boiled or raw, and even fried in an omelet or baked in meatloaf. I look forward to its southern season which emerges toward the end of the year and lasts until summer. However, I've been able to keep a plant or two productive all the way through our summer by planting them in northern exposures of fences and my trailer where no direct sunshine can reach them.

It was one of those species that I learned about years ago but didn't absolutely positively identify until I was in my middle-age years and hiking around New England. After that, I was finding it all over the place. The ones that appear (sparsely) around here usually do so when sod comes from cooler climates. However, I'm able to transplant some that I find and even plant some from seed. Sometimes they pop up along inclines of drainage ditches after fresh sod has been lain. The ones I've grown from seed require rich, well-drained soil and then bolt (go through their life cycles quickly) to seed before reaching over a couple feet high. I've seen it wild around here up to six feet high. The root of lamb's-quarters can be shaved and used as soap. Leaves prepared for tea might reduce fevers and treat intestinal worms.

This is a plant that many people refuse to eat, partly because it is a weed to them, and partly because some people know it under the name pigweed. That name has been used for many other wild plants as well. This is why the botanical name is usually best for positively identifying it. To most modern farmers it is a troublesome weed. Up until this most recent century of our modern civilization, most farmers thought of it as the edible wild vegetable that it actually is. Call it what you like. When I find enough of it for a serving of greens, I call it "Dinner."

LILY PADS, *Nymphaeaceae family*

Lily pads. That is what I learned to call them as a kid while swimming and fishing in the ponds, lakes, and water holes around my west-central Florida home. They come from a family of plants called *Nymphaeaceae* and otherwise called the water lily family.

They are aquatic freshwater plants with a variety of flowers; from the small, red, lily-type blossoms of the *Brasenia* genus commonly called water shield, to small, round, cup-shaped, yellow flowers (*Nuphar* genus) commonly called yellow pond lily and another of that genus called spatterdock, to medium-sized, multi-petaled, blossoms of yellow, white, or blue (*Nymphaea* genus, bottom photo), and to the largest flower of North America—well known as the lotus lily or American lotus (*Nelumbo* genus, top photo) with its solitary, showy, white and yellow flower up to ten inches in diameter and stands on top of a slimy stalk which normally reaches above the surface.

American lotus, *Nelumbo* genus.

Nyphaea odorata will grow medium-sized, multi-petaled (like a smaller lotus flower) white flower with a thick yellow stamen in the middle.

The photo of the lily pads resting gently on the surface of the water is the fragrant water lily of the *Nymphaea* genus. They almost dominate the lakes and ponds of this area (when they are allowed to grow). I suspect that those have no confirmed edible parts, unfortunately

The first indicator of the species within the family will be the flower bloom. They vary from genus to genus.

I'll be looking to get a photo of a *Nuphar* lily (as described above) with oblong to ovate heart-shaped leaves and smallish, cup-shaped, yellow flowers. Some of those leaves appear almost round but always have a slit down the middle. They produce edible seeds after soaking in fresh, clean water for a few hours to leach any possible bitterness, then parched to remove hulls, and then roasted and/or fried like popcorn. The flower petals have been used to make a tea.

Spatterdock *Nymphaea* genus.

There's edible quality to the seeds of *Nuphar* as well as the seeds of the large lotus lily. However, the roots of the *Nuphar* are a different story.

The roots of the lotus lily (*Nelumbo* genus, top photo with a seedpod), has a distinct tuberous root section that is difficult to locate under the mud but very edible. Native Americans got very muddy wallowing around in search of the prized roots of that water lily—it was simply cleaned up, peeled (before or after cooking), chopped, and boiled as a starchy root vegetable.

The *Nuphar* water lily may have roots of some species that might be made edible by boiling but definitely not all or even most. Some guidebooks make the mistake of implying that all *Nuphar* lily roots are edible after boiling in one or more changes of water. However, many credible reports of actually performing that task with some species of them have failed to make them palatable and led many a practicing primitive to an evening of stomach cramps, nausea, and vomiting.

Note: The best sign that a root (or most plant parts) is not edible—whether boiling it once or a dozen times—is rank bitterness. The general rule for most edible wild roots (but not all) is, "If it is bitter, spit it out." The bitterness is often of such an astringent nature that it may have medicinal uses in the hands of a seasoned expert but for edibility it is a bad sign. Not so much for greens as for roots.

As stated here, some guidebooks make the mistake of assuming that all *Nuphar* species have edible roots based on past reports that were not always based on all of the facts, unfortunately. One expert reports that he has tried boiling the roots of some local *Nuphar* lilies over and over without success. Another reports that Tom Elpel and a friend made themselves sick on a camping trip with *Nuphar* roots and the TV survival expert Les Stroud of the Science/Discovery show *Survivorman* (Now *Survivorman & Son*) had the same experience in one of his earliest episodes called "Boreal Forest."

Again, the American lotus lily (*Nelumbo* species) does have edible roots, albeit hard to find. There are also sufficient reports that the water shield lily pad of the *Brasenia* genus (which has a round leaf with the stem attached to the middle like the lotus but floats on the surface rather than standing above it) also has an edible root. So, while we can be sure that the roots of the lily pads with completely round leaves (no slit) that attach the stem to the middle of the leaf are edible with only one (most likely) boil, the roots of the other two genus of the water lily family either has questionable edibility or none at all. If the leaf has a slit, don't eat the root.

So, the key to knowing for sure that the roots of a water lily are edible is in the leaf structure. If the leaf is completely round, no slit or heart shape at all, that root/rhizome is definitely edible.

Now, about the water lily in the bottom photo on the previous page showing the floating roundish, heart-shaped leaves with the obvious slit down the apex where the stem is attached is a *Nyphaea* water lily commonly called fragrant water lily. I had just about concluded that nothing is edible on that one, as the reports on them indicate that the plant (especially the root) has chemical, medicinal properties and very likely not edible. I have since learned that the unopened flower buds and still-curled leaves might be edible. Apparently, the unopened flower buds and young unfurled leaves can be cooked thoroughly and eaten according to at least one source. The flower stem and leaves are curled as they rise up under the surface. Pick them when they are still under the surface and the flower stem is still coiled. Chop and add young buds to a survival stew. Boil young unfurled pads for at least ten minutes before adding to a stew. However, that is just one source saying it is edible. As shown in the photo above, *Nyphaea odorata,* which will grow medium-sized, multi-petaled (like a smaller lotus flower) white flower with a thick yellow stamen in the middle. There is also a *Nyphaea Mexicana* with smaller yellow flowers and even a blue-flowered *Nyphaea elegans*—both native to Mexico. These particular *Nyphaea* species can be found (as far as I know) throughout the Southeastern US. The other species, as far as I know, can be found as far north as central Canada and in cold-temperate to temperate areas around the globe. I can't be sure about them, maybe young, coiled flower buds and unfurled leaves from under the surface, but nothing else from *Nyphaea* should be attempted. If bitter, discard them.

In the 1974 book by Nelson Coon, *The Dictionary of Useful Plants*, the author goes down the list of the four genus of water lilies. Starting with the three with mostly edible qualities he mentions edible reports on *Brasenia* (water shield), *Nuphar* (yellow pond lily, a.k.a. cow lily, spatterdock), and *Nelumbium* (lotus lily, a.k.a. lotus, American lotus). However, as he gets to that last one (bottom photo on page 99, our most plentiful species), *Nyphaea odorata,* fragrant water lily, a.k.a. pond lily, bonnets; he only reports on the folk medicine uses of the plant; not a word about edibility.

Many water lily plants produce large starchy roots. Some are edible, but some species have strong medicinal qualities that might exclude them as being useful for food.

My conclusion here for the purpose of survival/famine/doomsday is to look for the lily pads that are completely round, no slit down the side. Those will have edible roots at least if not also seeds and young unfurled leaves. The lily pads that are heart-shaped but have small, yellow, round flowers buds have edible seeds when mature for roasting or frying. All other lily pads will have questionable edibility whether seeds, leaves, or roots, like the fragrant water lily.

While many reports indicate the edibility of the young, unfurled leaves (often still under the surface and somewhat dark in color) I haven't tried cooking them for greens. I'm fairly sure I could find enough edible greens from the many edible plants I could forage on already without resorting to these. If I had to, the same rule applies. Round leaves, no slit or heart-shape, is the most likely edible type. In an emergency, I could try any of the plentiful young pads and flower buds that pop up in many lakes and ponds in my central Florida woods. As tempting as it might be to try to get some carbohydrates from the roots, I would be very reluctant to try eating the boiled roots of lily pads with heart-shaped leaves.

The *Nelumbo* (lotus) seeds require sun-drying the mature pods, pounding them to remove the seeds, then parch them in a skillet and pound them again to remove the shells. They are then ready to be eaten roasted or ground into flour. For the *Nuphar* seeds, just dig them out and fry, bake or roast. One expert suggested soaking them in fresh, clean water first to remove bitterness.

Water quality is also an issue. All edible parts of aquatic plants should be boiled vigorously for killing possible pathogens and parasites. If there are plenty of water lilies in a body of water, and other aquatic plants as well, the chance of the water being free of toxic waste, heavy metals, or chemicals is fairly good. It is when you see a body of water with no aquatic plants in it at all that you might want to pass up on it for purifying drinking water, unless you have a water-distillation system. Look for a shiny sheen on the surface indicating a petroleum product, a foamy substance in the water, or smells. Best to avoid those as water sources.

I've recently learned something new to me about American lotus, *Nelumbo species.* When you open up the green shower faucet-looking seedpod while still green you can remove the large seeds and eat them raw after simply peeling off the skin of the seed. They taste bland but edible. My Asian friend Vicky showed it to me when I brought her some green lotus seedpods. I think they can also then be boiled and added to soups and stews.

LOQUAT, *Eriobotryae japonica*

Although I was taught to call them Japanese plums, it is a member of the rose family and is more closely related to apples, peaches, and pears. The most common name is loquat. The names, loquat and kumquat (not related), comes from old Chinese names where loquats originated. The fruits contain calcium, vitamins A, B, C, and probably other nutrients. The top photo shows a tree's branches before the fruiting season.

A large green shrub to medium-sized tree; they like full or mostly full sun in warm places around the world—escaping cultivation rather easily. Introduced to Florida around the time of the Civil War, its range can extend north to South Carolina in the US.

The fruit starts off green and toxic (not sure how toxic or which toxins), turning yellow and quite tart (my favorite kind), then turning orange and sweetish before turning discolored, spotty, and drying before dropping. Birds like the fruit, which explains why this plant escapes cultivation so much—the birds drop the seeds to the ground as they eat the fruit.

The fruit doesn't transport well and won't stay fresh for long in the fridge. Each berry contains anywhere from one to five seeds. The seeds are not edible, containing properties of cyanide, but can be made into a cherry flavored liqueur called, grappa. There are reports of using the seeds in various other ways, though I would not recommend them. The fruit can be made into jam, pie, jelly, sauce, etc. My favorite way is from the tree to my mouth, minus the seeds. I prefer to squeeze out the seeds before consuming rather than put it in my mouth and chew the pulp off the seeds and then spit out the seeds. Consuming one or maybe two seeds accidentally might not adversely affect me. I just don't want to find out. The fruits can also be dehydrated—minus the seeds—to produce a preserved dry fruit for the trail or recipe. You end up with a leathery, brown dried but sweet fruit. The tree (or shrub) has some herbal and medicinal uses, which you can look into if you wish to know about that. A loquat marmalade would be good.

Loquats, mulberries, and Surinam cherries are berries that I (Doug) remember eating off the tree or shrub when I was very young and living in Tampa, Florida. My family also lived in New England for a few years in my early youth where I remember how great it was to eat wild blueberries right off the bush—which all began me down a path to self-sufficiency through the study of foraging and survival.

Common Mallow, *Malva neglecta*

Also called cheeses in some places because of the shape of its seed pods resembling a tiny cheese wheel, is a plant I have encountered everywhere from cracks in the sidewalk, all sorts of urban areas, and occasionally but rarely in wild, less inhabited places Because it likes areas inhabited by people, be mindful of where you collect it. In most of these areas it is common to have been subjected to manmade toxins, herbicides, and the like, so use common sense and seek this plant in less occupied areas when possible The common mallow is part of the family of *Malvaceae* that include okra, rose of Sharon, hibiscus, marshmallow, and others found throughout the world. Cotton is the only toxic member of this family. When comparing differences in members of this diverse family of plants, rose of Sharon is one that comes to mind, and while a member of the same family as the small, low lying *Malva neglecta*, rose of Sharon is a common tall bush or shrub covered in medium sized papery flowers I have snacked on these characteristically mucilaginous hibiscus flowers many times on hot summer days. It is synonymous with, and a variety of hibiscus tea is a great thirst quencher and healthy deep red tea that is very cooling on a hot summer day.

All parts of the mallow plant are edible. Flowers, leaves, fruit, seeds, stems, and roots are highly nutritious containing protein, vitamins A and C as well as potassium, calcium, magnesium, iron, and selenium. Plants containing protein are fairly uncommon so that adds street cred as a desirable for your diet. The seeds contain 21 percent protein and 15.2 percent fat according to my research. The leaves can be harvested like spinach and are edible raw or cooked. The cooked leaves mucilaginous quality characteristic of this species is very similar to okra and makes a good thickener to soups and stews. They can be added to salads, and have a mild flavor, that lets them take on the flavor of everything else, along with being highly nutritious. The flowers have the same mild flavor of the leaves, while the fruits are pleasant and a little nutty. Dried leaves make a great tea. Mallow roots release a thick mucus when boiled in water and apparently make a serviceable egg substitute although it is green—I've never done this, but hear it can be done, and the root can be used as a toothbrush, something I will try one of these days. Make sure you wash this plant very well if you plan to eat any part of it raw, especially if harvesting in a populated, or agricultural area.

Common mallow seems to be most everywhere, and has no toxic look a likes. The most obvious identifying characteristic for mallows is their leaves. On some plants the lobes are very distinct, and on others the leaves are almost completely round. The one thing the leaves all have in common is that they all have veins radiating from a central point, with lots of little veins branching off of those veins. Mallow leaves and stems are also always mildly fuzzy. There is only one leaf at the edge of each stem, and all those stems branch out from one main stem. If you pick a leaf, rub it between your fingers, you should feel a slimy quality, which should clue you in that you've got the right family of plants. It is occasionally mistaken for ground ivy which is okay, as that is another edible plant but with a distinctively strong smell mallow can also sometimes be confused with certain varieties of geranium, many of which are also edible and medicinal as well. It is considered an invasive plant, so once you know you can integrate common mallow into your diet, eat up and enjoy, but first maintain the habit of performing the Universal Edibility Test on it just to be safe I find this plant growing year round, depending on just how cold it gets. It is a plant found all over the world in one form or another, so a good one to know.

MILKWEED VINE, *Morrenia odorata*

Also known as latex vine, latex plant, and strangler vine, I was very pleasantly surprised at how much the boiled immature fruit/vegetable (boiled for at least twenty minutes) tasted like a cross between yellow-squash and zucchini. Fact is, in survival foraging, finding this vine with multiple young fruit and plentiful flowers on thick vines would be priceless. It may also go by the name strangler-milkweed vine.

The flowers, young leaves, young fruit/vegetable, and shoot tips can be eaten if boiled. The thick latex sap would be detrimental to most if eaten raw. I don't advise it. You very likely will not find this plant in other edible-plant guides.

The bumpy, discolored, mature fruits are too old to be edible once the seed-ball in the center begins to form. And if the core has turned to a fluffy white pollen-like substance with multiple brown or black, sliver-like seeds bunched up in the center, it is now toxic and the whole fruit is not edible at all. For best results, pick only the smooth young gourds and cut in half to see if the seed-ball is starting to form. Any seed-ball beginning to form is NOT edible and must be removed before boiling. If the inner-flesh of the gourd is receding into the seed-ball the entire fruit is not edible.

Inedible mature fruit: large, discolored, and bumpy.

Multiple parts of the vine are reported to be edible. I wouldn't try boiling a fruit that is large, discolored, and bumpy. I've tried to boil fruit like that only to find the insides turning into a seed-ball and the corm (pulp directly attached to the inside of the skin) thinner and somewhat rank smelling, bad enough to not risk it. Once the fruit gets bumpy in the winter (January here) no matter what size it is it has seeds beginning to form in its center and probably shouldn't be eaten at that stage. I don't know the specifics of how inedible it is or why after the fruit begins to mature. I do know that the very young ones boiled and eaten whole (including skin but minus any beginning stage of seed-ball) tastes exactly like yellow squash (bottom photo above).

Pick only the smooth, young gourds.

Any seed-ball beginning to form is not edible and must be removed before boiling. If the inner-flesh of the gourd is receding into the seed-ball the entire fruit is not edible.

Again, the young edible fruit/pods have a smooth shape and skin, always green, and usually smaller. Those are delicious. You can find the young ones in central Florida from spring to late fall but once December comes around most fruits will be too old, even if small. They all resemble a chayote and are about the size of a Haas avocado. The fruit/pods turn yellow, tan, and eventually brown when growing old and will eventually split open to release the fluffy seeds.

The smooth-skinned, young, immature fruits can be roasted or baked but the preferred way to utilize all of the potential nutrition in a survival scenario is to boil whole. The nutrition is on the same scale as squash.

A little butter and seasoning makes for a perfect side vegetable. Those star-like, greenish-white, five-petaled flowers have an aroma of vanilla, a kind of sweet perfume (a good identifier), and are reported as edible cooked as well as the shoots (growing tips of the vines). The opposite leaves start out heart-shaped and larger than the older leaves that become smaller, elongated and arrowhead shaped like they are in the top photo. That's the opposite of a strangler vine, which starts out heart-shaped and stays that way and without the flowers. You might also find the fruit and flowers growing on what looks like the strangler vine with heart-shaped leaves rather than the typical arrowhead-shaped.

Milkweed vines are reported to produce year-round from sea to shining sea. Around here they produce fruit in the summer. They are considered noxious, non-native, and invasive. There are similar vines that do not produce these flowers and the leaves stay heart-shaped. There will also be ivy-type vines that will look similar. Look for those sharp, pointy leaves, the flower-bursts, and the fruit to positively identify it. I've found lots of vines growing in orange groves on citrus trees.

If a person has an allergy to latex or other plants that produce a white sap they should not eat this one. Many guides will say that a white sap is a sign of something toxic, and usually that is the case. In other cases of edible plants, a white sap is a sign that it just needs to be or should be cooked (like the sow thistles, *Sonchus species*). The sap will be very sticky. When you pick a milkweed fruit, flower, or shoot-tip you will very likely notice the white, sticky sap dripping off of it for a minute or two—particularly the fruit.

This is definitely a choice edible. A good name for this might be a wild green chayote squash, or just wild squash. I found it to be delicious, and I wasn't in a survival scenario. For some edibles, the hungrier you are, the better they will taste. Which also means that the good ones will taste great if you are really hungry.

My system for foraging on them has evolved to taking only young looking fruits and cut them in half before cooking. If there is any formation of the seed ball in the center I remove and discard it before dropping the two halves into the pot. If the cooked product has any rank flavor or smell—not the delicious squash fragrance and flavor—I spit it out and/or just discard it.

MORINGA TREE, *Moringa oleifera*

The moringa tree, *Moringa oleifera*, is a native of India and has spread around the sub-tropic and tropical zones around the globe. Its uses and health benefits are extensive. I've been drinking a tasty iced tea made from the leaves as well as a nutritious green bread.

It is reported that the young, long, slender seedpods/fruits can be cooked many ways. The leaves are eaten raw or cooked and has a spinach-type flavor. The young green seedpods are cooked like green-beans, a cooking oil can be made from the seeds, and the flowers are reported to taste like mushrooms.

Research into this tree's remarkable nutritious and healthful attributes are extensive

Excellent reporting claims that the leaves are high in vitamins A, C, and B, rich in minerals like calcium and potassium, and even high in protein comparable to yogurt while being low in carbs and fat.

It may be so beneficial to so many ailments that the common name of miracle tree is appropriate. If you have one (or more) of the many common health problems, this one will probably help.

There are reports of using this tree to fight starvation and malnutrition in third-world countries. If dandelion is the most nutritious weed in the world, the moringa tree is the most nutritious tree in the world.

MULBERRY, *Morus species*

Mulberries are loaded with nutrition. They are reported to be low in saturated fat, cholesterol and sodium but high in vitamin C, vitamin K, iron, dietary fiber, riboflavin, magnesium and potassium. The young leaves are reportedly edible cooked, boiled, or even stir fried. I haven't tried that. There are so many good edible wild greens available once you know what they are that resorting to tree leaves for greens (unless from the moringa tree) is not necessary.

The nutrition in the mulberry leaves is significant. However, the leaves can be tough and chewy, must be cooked, and only the youngest leaves should be used.

There are three kinds of mulberry trees: the white mulberry, *Morus alba*, a.k.a. Chinese mulberry, the black mulberry, *Morus niger*, and our native red mulberry, *Morus rubra* which is found only on the eastern side of the US. The red and white mulberries grow here in the US and the black mulberry is found in Europe.

Any recipe for pie, jelly, vinegar, sauce, etc. that involves blackberries can be used for mulberries. Only the black mulberries are edible—unripe mulberries are toxic, especially the very early whitish, translucent ones. Use only black ones here.

Mulberry berries are one of my favorite berries and look somewhat similar to blackberry fruit and its closely related dewberry (*Rubus species*). The mulberry is a tree without thorns, the blackberry is a thorny cane, and the dewberry is a thorny crawling vine.

OPUNTIA CACTUS, *Opuntia species*

The two major species that are edible have large spines, very tiny ones, or both. All cacti with these pads are edible unless it has a milky white sap. The pads must be flat like these to be the edible species, not cylindrical. The very tiny, thin spines are called glochids and grow in bunches on the pads and the fruits. These glochids are so small that you need a magnifying glass to see them. However, if you notice little bumps or white spots on the pads, that's where the glochids will be. Once they get into your skin they will stay there for a day or two. Even tweezers don't work very well for getting them out, even with a magnifying glass. The spines and glochids can be burned off of the pads and fruit by roasting over a campfire while holding it with tongs or a skewer. The skin is said to be too fibrous, but lightly roasted, baked, fried or boiled it should be edible in small amounts and combined with other foods.

The author in front of an opuntia cactus.

The youngest pads are the least fibrous and most edible. The glochids on the pads can be cut out at the "eyes" with the scooping end of some potato-peelers. Another way to remove the spines and glochids is reported to be by scraping or brushing them off with leather, canvas, or a scraping tool. That process may be somewhat inefficient though.

After being sufficiently rid of spines and glochids, cut into chunks or slices and cook any way you wish. Another method is to cut through the pad lengthwise to remove some of the skin. However, trying to peel the skin off by any method is difficult being that the pads are usually too thin to begin with to peel the skin. It isn't the kind of skin that separates from the meat of the plant. It's more like two thick skins attached to a thin goocy layer of pulp.

The pads should be boiled, or otherwise cooked, to be edible in sufficient quantity to make a meal. To harvest the pads, cut the youngest pads off at the nodes (joints) with a sharp knife. Use a skewer, leather gloves or tongs to hold the pads. The glochids congregate in bunches on spots that will remind you of potato ears.

Those pads are a commercial product that are sliced and pickled. They can be purchased at just about any grocery store's international aisle as nopalitos, a spicy fleshy pickle that would taste good to me if I cared for hot-spicy pickles.

In the wild, one can chop them, and add them to a survival stew. If you want to skip cutting out the glochids you can roast over the fire holding a pad with tongs fashioned out of sticks (or metal tongs if you have some) or skewer, provided the sticks are not from a poisonous plant or a pine. If you make the mistake of using a branch from a shrub/bush called oleander, or chinaberry, or Brazilian pepper as a skewer or tongs you could poison yourself. It's always best to make a skewer or tongs out of oak or hickory or some other clean burning wood.

You can also chop the young pads into chunks that you can run a skewer through (in Florida, a whittled down palm-frond stem works fine) and then roast over the fire like a shish kebab.

The young pads sliced or chopped are reported to be prepared like you would eggplant, or fried like you would in stir-fry or using with scrambled eggs. It can be cut into strips and boiled like string beans, which can also be deep-fried like onion rings. The thick sap reminds me of the texture of butter and the taste and texture of them boiled reminds me of a combination of cucumber and bell peppers. The inner pulp can be used medicinally to cool dry or burnt skin. Cut a pad through to expose the thin, pulpy, gooey flesh inside and put that on irritated skin for a few minutes.

The fruit has its uses as a dessert or making into a juice or jelly. The seeds of the fruit can be dried and ground into a flour additive. The teeny-tiny seeds should not be eaten raw with fragile teeth, as they are hard enough to break teeth. The fruit can be wrapped in duct tape before being removed from the cactus. Then it can be cut down the middle lengthwise and be ready to scoop out the pulp with a spoon. This pulp can be eaten raw, but carefully.

This cactus has many common names, which is why many foragers call them by their botanical genus, *Opuntia*. Among the names are, prickly pear, Indian fig, Indian pear, paddle cactus, devil's tongue, beavertail cactus, tuna, nopal, or nopales.

While there is detailed information on using the fruits, I wanted to cover the pads for their substantial food source potential. I recently found this (top photo above) large, wide *Opuntia* cactus where a trailer park once was. The whole plant reaches as high as approximately fourteen feet and as big around as it is high. It is very important to check the sap of a cactus when you cut off a pad for any milky sap. *Opuntia* is known for having a thick, mucilaginous, clear sap which can thicken stews, but not a white colored sap. The expression milky sap refers to white sap. Any white sap coming from any cactus is poisonous and signals to you that it is a poisonous species. It is like that for many species of plants, not just cactus. There are exceptions though, like in the case of dandeliions, milkweeds, milkweed vine, sow thistle, and other plants, but the general rule is to stay away from a plant with a white milky sap unless you know exactly what it is and how to prepare it. However, you really shouldn't eat any wild plant at all if you can't positively identify and safely prepare it.

The fruits of all *Opuntia* range from yellow to red to purple. Another way to eat the fruits requires cutting in half lengthwise, scooping out the pulp, and forcing the pulp through a screen/mesh to separate the seeds from the pulp. The pulp can also be mashed, seeds and all, with a pitcher of water, left to sit for an hour or simmered lightly for a few minutes, then strained to produce a fruity beverage.

One guide reports that the fleshy fruits and segments of all flat-stemmed *Opuntia* species are edible. By the term, "flat-stemmed," I suppose they mean the pads. Still, check for white milky sap. No guide book is perfect.

Opuntia is originally from Central America. Cacti as a group is reported to be native to the western hemisphere, but has become naturalized all over the globe wherever they can. They're not just found in the desert anymore. The *Opuntia* species all have the flat-stemmed and slightly oval pads like these. They grow only in well-drained soil, not necessarily dry. They just don't like to get their feet wet. The older pads get stringy and stale.

PAPAYA, *Carica papaya*

This native plant of Central America produces one of my favorite fruits. They are frequently planted here for the nutritious fruit, containing the highest source of natural digestive enzymes. As soon as they start to turn yellow—at least 20 percent of the fruit showing yellow through the immature green—they can be picked and set out in the sun for anywhere between a day to four days to completely ripen with the inner corm (flesh) soft enough to eat with a spoon (not the soft black seeds). The corm will not be soft enough yet until the outside is completely yellow. There is a lot more than just the corm of the ripe fruit that is edible or useful.

But first let me state some of the nutritional value as revealed in a report: 88 percent water, 43 calories (per 100 grams) 0.6 percent protein, 0.1 percent fat, vitamins B1, & C, thiamine, niacin, riboflavin, calcium, iron, and potassium.

The edible parts include unripe green fruit that can be peeled, chopped into chunks, and boiled or baked. Young leaves and flowers are edible cooked. The inner core of the trunk is reported as edible raw (no mention of cooking). The ripe, dry, black, seeds can be used like pepper and keep for as long as three years or so. And the roots are reportedly edible if boiled for an extensive amount of time. There is also the report that the mature leaves have the soapy constituent called saponin and can be used like a washcloth.

With all of the digestive problems that could occur in a survival/famine/doomsday event, a delicious fruit that assists in digestion would be a great fruit to have hanging around. However, my first exposure to papaya fruit left a bad first impression on me and has afflicted others as well, including my sister. After the fruit has completely ripened and begins to become overripe the inner flesh begins to smell with a similar aroma to methane and sulfur (not that it has those substances, that I know off). I wondered how a fruit that could smell so bad actually taste good. A visit to any health-food store will show you that papaya is used in supplement form to treat digestive disorders by assisting the breakdown and absorption of food into the body. Papaya is the best natural source for helping your body with digestive enzymes. I knew this was so and my mother ate the fruit so I forced myself to get past the smell and taste it, chilled first before cutting open. It doesn't taste anything like the smell. That was many years ago now and I eagerly await every opportunity to partake of the ripe, yellow, smelly fruit. As a matter of fact, I only notice the smell now when the fruit is way overripe and even then, I just barely notice it.

The trunk is reportedly weak and will break easily under the weight of a grown person. The young leaves and flowers might require a second boil. These trees can be found in oak hammocks, shell mounds, and scrub-lands. They are prolific growers in central and south Florida but will be few and far between north of there. The milky sap from green parts of the plant is dangerous to the eyes but will tenderize tough meat. The young leaves and flowers might require a second boil to make edible.

PASSIONFLOWER, *Passiflora incarnata*

Passionflower is native to North and South America and its range extends through all of the Southeastern US—a sub-tropical invasive vine that grows along fences and bushes wherever people go (or have gone), including along hiking trails, highways, and even around campsites throughout Florida. They spring up and crawl around for most of the year, dying down in the winter.

There are different kinds of passionflower and most are known for making a relaxing tea. The species that grow wild and plentiful in the southeastern portion of the US is probably the one (or one of the ones) that can be used as a tea for relaxing the mind. Some of the passionflower species has as its protection from herbivores a chemical which might turn into cyanide when consumed by the animals and people who might attempt to forage on the flowers, shoots, and leaves. The kind of species that doesn't have cyanide-causing constituents has a kind of neurotransmitter, a chemical which harmlessly relaxes and soothes the brain. That is the species that is used in herbal teas. There is a report out there that our local wild species was tested and no cyanide triggering chemical was in it. It supposedly had the neurotransmitter. I also have a report from an herbalist friend that she uses a cultivated species for medicinal purposes. However, the cultivated species is not the same as our native wild one. They are different. The fruits have the most obvious differences.

I (Doug) was camping along the Florida Trail a few years ago when I decided to dry some wild passionflower leaves and make a tea with it. I crumbled up a leaf and put it in the sun, but only for an hour or two, not long enough to dry sufficiently. I noticed that I started feeling slightly nauseous for a minute or two not long after sipping the tea. When I learned that there was this debate over whether it had cyanide-causing constituents in that species I assumed it was why I felt nauseous that evening. I never tried to make the tea after that. If I did now, I would dry out a flower for a couple days the best I could, maybe use an improvised clay oven or put the flower in a pan and put in on the hot ashes/coals of the fire until the material shrivels up.

You can make a jelly, Jell-O, and beverage from the ripe seeds and gel that covers the seeds. Simmer the Jell-O and seeds of several fruits for a refreshing drink after straining or add pectin for jelly or Jell-O. The ripe seeds and gelatinous substance surrounding the ripe seeds are edible raw. When the fruit starts to turn yellow and shriveled it is ready to use, but as long as the seeds are still whitish and covered in a gel without too much discoloration they can still be used for a beverage. The largest green fruits are almost always ripe enough. Also, when the fruit is yellowing, scrape out the fleshy inner-corm (the inner rind, inside of the skin) and sun-dry to add to soups and stews or eat as is. In a survival situation, filtering and purifying water is an everyday occurrence. The taste of the water after going from pond to filter to pot will not likely be pleasant. Making a fruity beverage with it might help the hydrating medicine go down. I make a beverage by cutting about five mature fruits in half and scooping out the gel-covered seeds to simmer in a pot for five minutes with a quarter cup of sugar in three cups of water. If I have a lemon you should add some drops of lemon-juice to the mix after it cools and serve it as cold (with ice if you can) as you can (after cooling in a fridge if possible). The flavor might be somewhat strange to conventional palates.

The leaves are tri-lobed, large and palmate that grows along the vine with the distinct and large lavender flower blossoms. This is one of those flavors that might be an acquired taste for most people. The cool beverage has a unique tropical-fruit flavor that should be sweetened a little with sugar but not really necessary and it would probably mix well with lemonade. Your best bet of the fruits are the ones on the vine that are turning yellowish from its green color and slightly wrinkled skin.

The thick gel covering the maturing seeds and the seeds themselves are edible and are sweet and tangy. I cut them in half and start off with a big swipe of my tongue over the gel-covered seeds. The tangy sweet burst of flavor is quite a treat and quite unique. While they are edible raw as is I have been told that they produce a laxative effect when eaten raw.

Papaw, *Asimina triloba*

This is native to the eastern woodlands of the US. It was spread by the native Americans ranging as far west as eastern Kansas and Texas, and north to the Great Lakes, and almost as far south as the Gulf of Mexico. You can't live long in rural Appalachia, or any of the twenty-six states it is found in and not know something about papaws There's even a song about it often taught in grade school: "Way Down Yonder in the Pawpaw Patch." If you are fortunate, you may have even run up on one while out walking in the woods with an old timer, and sampled this delicious fruit. Although the fruit of the papaw tree is edible, you have to get it at just the right stage of ripeness, and then be sure to beat all the other wildlife waiting for the same thing. It is loved by squirrels, opossums, raccoons, foxes, and many others I am sure. When ripe, it tastes kind of like a cross between a banana and a mango. It is quite sweet, and has a custard-like texture. It usually has ten to fourteen large bean like seeds in two rows, and a thin skin, neither of which is edible. The soft fruit inside is the only edible part of this native tree. The fruit itself is about the size of a medium-size baking potato and is oblong with a green to yellowish brown color. It is best picked when it is soft and just about ready to fall off the tree. It doesn't store well, and should be eaten soon after collection. As with any new or wild food. Perform the edibility test on it, no matter how hard it may seem to resist this delicious wild delicacy. Even though papaw is considered safe to eat in moderation some people can be sensitive to it. There have been a couple of reports of this fruit being toxic, but you would have to eat hundreds of these things to reach the toxicity found in these studies.

Papaw, also known as Hoosier banana, poor man's banana, and I'm sure numerous other names is a small deciduous tree native to the eastern United States, producing a large, yellowish-green to brown fruit and is a member of the *Annonaceae* family of plants as are the custard-apple, cherimoya, sweetsop, soursop and others. It is not to be confused with the papaya which is sometimes called Papaw in Australia, and possibly elsewhere.

Young trees are sensitive to full sun and require filtered sun for the first couple of years after which they prefer full sun. The trunk of the papaw is around eight inches in diameter and does not grow very tall, usually between twelve to twenty feet with some reaching as tall as thirty feet with dark green, oblong, drooping leaves up to a foot long, giving it a tropical appearance. The only other regional tree that comes to mind that has a similar appearance is the big leaf magnolia (*Magnolia macrophylla*), which incidentally has both edible and medicinal properties, but papaw is generally much smaller. The leaves turn yellow and begin to fall in mid-autumn and return in late spring after the tree has bloomed with its foul smelling upside-down maroon blossoms up to two inches across, and lasting from early to late spring depending on location and climate conditions. To get an idea of its habitat, consider that it needs a minimum of four hundred hours of winter chill and at least 160 frost-free days, and can withstand temperatures below -25º F, and it is seldom found near coastal regions. One indicator that you have found a papaw tree is the zebra swallowtail butterfly's larvae feed exclusively on young, pawpaw leaves but only in small numbers.

The fruit ripens during a four-week period between mid-August and into October, depending on environmental conditions and is quite delicate and thin skinned. When ripe it is soft and lightens in color sometimes developing dark patches on the skin which doesn't affect the quality of the fruit at all. It should be eaten right away, within a couple of days at most, unless you have the luxury of a freezer where the pulp can be frozen for up to six months. It is high in protein, antioxidants, vitamins A and C and several essential minerals.

As a final thought, Thomas Jefferson grew papaw trees at Monticello in Virginia near our nation's capitol, so that should speak something of the value of this unique, delicious, and nutritious fruit.

PELLITORY, *Parietaria floridana*

Pellitory smells like cucumbers while raw, although you may have to crush some leaves a little to get the full aroma, and it is the reason that another name for it is cucumber weed. The flavor of the whole plant from the ground up is a good salad ingredient (hard to describe, other than just good) but becomes somewhat bland when cooked—making it also a good addition to any greens. It has a variety of herbal uses. It is used in a poultice for burns, scratches and minor cuts. Pellitory tea might be good for bladder stones and as a laxative.

While it is kind of high in sodium, it also has nitrates—one raises blood pressure in some people, the other lowers it by lowering the retention of water. It is also reported that it may cause rare allergic reactions in some people (an itching sensation) when eaten. Its pollen is known to affect people with hay fever and asthma. However, I have both problems and can sniff the plants excessively without adverse reactions.

It comes up in our (Florida) winter in very shady spots and dies off in May. While you're looking for it, be reminded that our local stinging nettle looks similar but has toothed leaves instead of entire. If you grab the tops of the pellitory and pull you'll get the best parts, raw or cooked. If you grab a stinging nettle by mistake, it will sting you with a pain that can last for anywhere between a few hours to a few days. The physical difference between pellitory and our local dwarf stinging nettle is that the nettle leaves are toothed along the margins (edges) and not as pointed on the tips.

PENNYWORT/DOLLARWEED, *Hydrocotyle specics*

A member of the carrot family, pennyworts are members of the *Hydrocotyle* genus. Also called dollarweed, the stem grows to the middle of the round scalloped leaf. The flavor is strong (semi bitter) for salads and should probably be boiled anyway because it grows in very wet spots and is considered an aquatic plant.

To best kill possible pathogens and parasites from any groundwater boil rapidly for a few minutes, or less rapidly for at least ten minutes, and add a minute to every 1,000 feet of elevation (above sea-level) you're at. There may also be traces of chemicals and heavy metals from soil and water close to a well-traveled roadway or landscaped property where herbicides and pesticides may have been spread. However, fields and streams far enough away from these hazards (including railroads) is where you'll find safe places to forage from. Always boil aquatic edibles that contact questionable water.

Cattail cores are an exception to this because the core is not in contact with the water. There is a very large (up to a foot high) pennywort

Hydrocotyle, H. umbelatta, which can be used the same way. On previous page, the middle photo shows the leaf of one of those at about the size of a half-dollar or a little more. The species in the bottom photo is the smaller one to about the size of a quarter or a little more. A commercial beverage can be found of pennywort and these plants might be worth looking into for its medicinal properties.

There is another similar plant called pennywort with heart-shaped leaves called *Centrella erecta/asiatica*, a.k.a. gotu kola, which is reported to have inedible look-alikes but very healthy benefits if you positively identify it. The other two pennyworts that are completely round are the easiest to identify. Strong flavored and best cooked for greens, they are rich in nutrients. I always wondered if they had edible quality, and now I know: Pennywort is related to carrots and has similar nutrition.

PEPPERGRASS, *Lepidium spp.*

Species of edible peppergrass include; *Lepidium fremontii, Lepidium virginicum,* and *Lepidium campestre.* Common names for the above species include, peppergrass, pepperwort, field cress, poor man's pepper, dittander, and New Zealand cress.

In medieval times, when spices were rarely seen and very expensive, peppergrass seeds and leaves were commonly served as a pepper substitute. The root was crushed, ground, and mixed with vinegar to substitute horseradish. I use the green seeds and leaves in salads, soups, stews, and even sandwiches. The flavor of the raw leaves reminds me of radishes.

I never cared much for pepper, but I make use of peppergrass whenever I find it in safe soil of disturbed ground anywhere in Florida most of the year (it doesn't like our hot summers). Related edible species grow up and down the Eastern US. I've seen the dead stalks still standing in July around here. It usually waits until our cool weather has arrived in earnest before sprouting up in mass quantities. It seems to be most abundant in the winter here but hangs around until the summer heat chases them away.

This member of the mustard family is a weed that I depend on for a salad ingredient and potherb. The leaves are small, so their strong flavor makes a perfect addition to a bland salad or stew. The flavor is not spicy or hot, not exactly like pepper. It is somewhat hot or spicy in the same sense that radishes are but milder.

With most edible plants, we can describe a flavor by comparing it to our conventional foods. Sometimes it can taste like a blend of conventional and familiar foods. In a few cases, like this one, it just has a flavor unique and is somewhat different from anything else. Some people do not find it pleasing to their conventional palates, but when you realize that it is a plentiful food source that was introduced and grows widespread throughout the US, and in fact, around the globe, you should use your power of suggestion on yourself to become accustomed to it and grow to like it. As I did when I was very young, in order to develop a taste for onions. I was convinced that onions were good for my health, even though I didn't like them, and forced myself to eat them anyway. Now I can't imagine a salad or stew, or hardly any meal without them. The leaves of Peppergrass are reported to have high levels of vitamins A and C. The seeds will be green and used both raw or cooked. The nutrition is on par with other mustards.

Few plants are truly deadly poisonous and many are just inedible for a variety of reasons. However, it is not necessarily the fear of poisoning that prevents many people from eating a wild plant; it's a general fear of wild food and wild places. There's even a phobia name for a fear of eating plants, *Phytophobia*.

When you are raised in our modern world, the woods can be an intimidating, alien, and foreboding place. However, the main definition of the word forage is "a search for provisions." In the event that one must forage for his/her survival, looking to the wild plants for nutrition beats searching for a store that is open and stocked with food that you must pay for . . . if you can pay for it. You might be surprised at how many Americans become faced with no food, no money, and nowhere to turn. If they knew what was around us all the time in our environments, they would be more secure and self-sufficient.

Incredibly, it is older than the human race itself. It's how we evolved. We had to learn what we could eat and what we couldn't. Many people before us had to learn to forage in order to survive. Before my grandparents lived, pretty much everyone had to know how to forage for food.

We can learn from what they found out. Sooner or later, the way things are going, future generations will need to know as well.

PERENNIAL PEANUT, *Arachais glabrata*

Although they don't grow wild here, if at all, the ordinary peanut plant we all know and could be deathly allergic to is *Arachis hypogaea* and has reportedly edible stems and leaves raw or cooked. A close relative of the peanut plant is this little, bright-yellow flowered, almost tropical, carpeting plant which is commonly called rabbit bells, golden glory, ornamental peanut grass, and perennial peanut.

In downtown Dade City in the summer, these little flowers carpet the landscaping around one of the main intersections near the post office and spreads around that block in places. As soon as I read that the flowers themselves are edible—nothing else on the plant—I picked one at the next opportunity and ate it. I rolled it around in my mouth for a few seconds as I chewed to seek the flavor I was expecting to find, the flavor of peanuts. It does taste like peanuts. Be warned that many places where these have been planted, from here and southward throughout Florida, have probably been sprayed with poisons to kill weeds or mosquitoes. I don't know how weed-killer sprays would affect them, so I can't rule out that they wouldn't be sprayed with that. I am fairly sure, especially once the rainy season starts, that there has been spraying for mosquitoes in the downtown districts of even the smallest of towns here. Also, be warned that eating too many of them could have a laxative affect. If you are allergic to peanuts, I don't know if you should steer clear of these as well. They are reported to being so closely related that you should probably skip nibbling on them altogether.

Remember, only the flowers themselves are edible (maybe the flower-stems as well) but the rest of the plant is not and where I have seen them grow has probably been sprayed with something we should not consume.

PERSIMMON, *Diospyros virginiana*

The fruit of the persimmon tree should stay on the tree as long as possible until dropping off naturally. The sweetest ones are the ripe ones that fall naturally to the ground when ready. Even the ones on the ground are still ripening somewhat, not unlike the wild plum.

Euell Gibbons called it "The Sugar-Plum Tree" and devoted five pages of his landmark book, *Stalking the Wild Asparagus* (1962) to it. He reports using the fruit for many things including vinegar, molasses, and beer. He reports that they range from Connecticut to the Gulf of Mexico and west to the Great Plains but most plentiful in the mid-Southeast.

There are many recipes out there for bread, pies, and desserts using persimmons (the fruit) in combination with or in place of bananas, nuts, or pumpkins among others. A persimmon butter can be made like apple butter. Persimmons are native to the Southeast and were a staple of natives and pioneers around the Mississippi River Valley along the edges of fields, meadows, fences, highways, rivers, and railroad tracks. While native to the Southeast, they can also be found introduced in Utah, California, and range into Mexico.

The leaves fall off well before the fruit ripens in late fall and can be found still hanging on to the tree even in the snow of its northern range. The fruit starts off green when they form in the mid to late summer then turn from yellowish-orange to a fleshy purplish-orange with sooty black spots on them. The black spots that appear on the leaves and fruit are natural and harmless. The fruit should probably be washed off to some extent before use, but not required.

When we get to late fall or even the early Florida winter months you'll have all the leaves fallen off of the trees before the fruit really starts to drop. If you shake some fruit off they can sit in a window sill or in the sun somewhere for a few days before eating or processing but they won't be as sweet as when dropping off naturally. The pulp does not taste particularly good when not sweet. The unripe ones will make you pucker your mouth. They contain one to six seeds that should be discarded or dried for sewing back to the soil or sewing for use as buttons as was done by Confederate soldiers during the Civil War. Some reports include the seeds being ground for a coffee extender but not recommended as a coffee substitute.

However, it will not have caffeine, and nothing tastes like coffee except coffee, and if you want a caffeinated drink in a survival/famine/doomsday scenario you should have yaupon holly, *Ilex vomitoria* and it's *variations* of trees or shrubs. The leaves of persimmon trees can be used for tea but not recommended. However, using hot water, not boiling water, to steep dried leaves can produce a vitamin C–rich beverage. Boiling-hot water kills vitamin C. The fruit-skins have been used to make a fruit-leather but the strained pulp, minus seeds and skin, is used in many kinds of recipes and/or frozen for later use.

Before the fruit completely ripens and turns sweet they are extremely tart to the point of prime pucker power, not a pleasant kind of tartness at all. The ripe sweet ones can actually appear overripe to the uneducated forager—soft, gooey, spotted, and somewhat wrinkled. The old wives' tale of the fruits being better after a frost is not true for persimmon. I repeat, while you can put ripening fruits on trays out in the sun or on a window sill to ripen they will not become as sweet and perfect as the ones that stay on the tree until they look soft, gooey, spotted, and somewhat wrinkled before dropping off naturally.

The seeds can be pressed for oil. A person with gastric digestive issues may not want to overdo it by consuming large quantities of the fruit as they can inflict intestinal blockage issues.

PICKERELWEED, *Pontederia cordata/lanceolata*

There are two different kinds of pickerelweed around here, the *Pontederia cordata* has arrowhead shaped leaves and the *P. lanceolata* has lanced (longer) arrowhead shaped leaves. Both species are used the same ways. Experts say that the two are very much the same. Although I haven't tried it yet, there are plenty of sources that report eating the youngest leafstalks in early summer before the leaves unfurl after washing, chopping, and adding some to salads or boiling as a potherb for about 15 minutes. The greens are then drained and seasoned to taste. Not all experts report that; most just report the use that I've partaken of on the rare occasions when I can, the edible ripe seeds raw.

Pickerelweed grows along wet margins of streams, ponds, and retention areas. One expert reported that the whole plant can be cooked and eaten. The most commonly known edible part is when that flower turns into small furry fruits that mature into seeds. You simply pull gently, cupping your hand around the seeded flower bud, letting the loose, mature seeds fall into your hand. They can either be eaten as is (a trail-snack) or dried and ground into meal or flour. The trick is to cup your hand around the end of the stalk and squeeze just hard enough to release the seeds that are ready to drop.

Where these plants grow tend to colonize by spreading along the pond, stream, ditch, wet gully, or whatever water source they might populate. I've seen them in town and in the deep woods. Seeds are generally much higher in fat and protein than any other parts of a plant, which in a survival scenario could provide a much-needed boost.

PINDO PALM, a.k.a. JELLY PALM, *Butia capitata*

This is called pindo palm, also known as jelly palm and wine palm. I recently learned of this delicious fruit and looked for the tree for quite some time before I found this one.

Similar looking to the queen palm, the most notable difference is its height and the color of the fruit. While reported to get up to twelve feet high, pindo palm rarely reaches over eight feet tall while the queen palm gets much higher. The fruit of the pindo ranges from bright yellow to caution-yellow while the queen palm's fruit are always shades of orange. Both trees have spines along the edges of the fronds, the pindo palm spines appear to be sharper and longer, but I could be mistaken about that.

While the orange fruit of the queen is very fibrous to eat raw, the fruit of the Pindo is quite edible raw—just spit out the large seed—and the taste is surprisingly sweet with a blend or hint of tartness, quite unique. The fruit starts out green before ripening to yellow and falls to the ground where you can harvest it for days after. Just look for spoilage and smell each one before deciding it is fresh enough. The seeds are not edible but are reported to have 45 percent oil which can be used for products that contain any palm oil. The fruit itself has a natural pectin so that jelly can be made without adding any commercial pectin (just add sugar). The taste is described as either a cross between banana and tangerine or apple and citrus but I can't decide how to describe it because it seems to have a unique flavor to me (as many wild edibles do).

Because of its fibrous contents, some people could experience upset stomachs from eating more than a few handfuls raw or on an empty stomach. To avoid this, and the way I forage off of the queen palm fruit, one can chew the flavorful juices from the fruit and then spit out the fiber, skin, and seed together. Most Americans aren't use to eating fibrous fruit as part of a regular diet. This is why they should be cautious to just chew out the juice and maybe eat just a few with the fiber when trying these for the first time. The same can be said for almost any wild food. When forced to, or choosing to, eat wild food of any kind for the first or second time one should try small portions, especially with the naturally fibrous foods.

Pindo palms range on this continent from tropical to sub-temperate climates up to the North Carolina and southern Virginia area across to the Pacific seaboard states and up to British Colombia and over to Hawaii.

Frequently used in cemetery landscaping, I found this one (my first) here in front of the hospital in Zephyrhills. As with all landscaped edibles, beware of pesticide spraying and soil contaminates. Both the queen and pindo are so closely related that they can hybridize. This is a choice and unique edible fruit worth looking out for.

PINES, *Pinus species*

The western side of the United States has species of pine trees that produce substantial edible nuts called pine nuts, piñon nuts, or pinyon nuts. On Florida's side of the continent we don't have those kinds of pine trees. What we do have are pines that produce nuts about as large as mustard seeds—if you're lucky.

In a survival scenario, don't bother with the cones that are already on the ground or any green cones. The cones on the ground have already lost their nuts—actually better described as seeds—which are usually so small that you'll have a hard time finding any even if the woodland creatures haven't already eaten them all. The green unopened cones are immature, having no seeds, so those needed to stay on the tree until turning brown. If you can easily get your hands on brown unopened ones, the seeds can be coached out of the cones by putting the cones in paper bags and set aside for a few days. The seeds will be released into the bag. The seeds of some will be so small that it will look like coffee grounds. Another and quicker way is to put the cones into a cooking pan and set it near the campfire, preferably set right on the hot ashes mixed with hot coals. The heat will entice the cones to release the seeds. The cones open up naturally when in contact with high heat—as forest fires are essential in a pine forest to propagate new growth. The seeds contain just shy of 15 percent protein. Our local species of pine are recognizable by their needles. A cluster of needles is called a fascicle or bundle and the length of the needles and shape of the cones determine the exact species.

The needles of Florida's pines range from three to five per fascicle (bundle) and up to 18 inches long. The needles contain vitamin C and I have frequently chopped the young green needles and steeped in hot water (not boiling) for a vitamin C rich tea. The resin that the tree produces from dried sap might be used in fire-starting, as wax, as a topical antibiotic for dressing wounds, and as a glue. The most significant and year-round resource from pines may be the starchy, white, soft, and sticky layer that appears to separate the bark from the wood and is called cambium or cambia. Edible cambium can be obtained from elm, possibly birch, and all pines of the *Pinus* genus (as far as I know). However, even though many guide books that include info on tree cambium call it an inner bark I wouldn't call it that, being that it is much softer and more pliable, starchy and gooey, than any kind of bark I know of. This white, smooth and moist cambium is carb-rich and can be stripped off and eaten raw, or boiled like noodles and eaten as is or mixed into a survival stew; or boiled, then dried and ground into flour.

(Keep in mind that removing cambium can kill the tree, or leave it open to disease and pest infestation. Please be a good steward of our woods.)

There is also the possibility that pine pollen is edible cooked. Pine trees can be found in just about any environment in the Florida wild except the actual cypress swamp and very swampy conditions. If you are in swampy conditions and see pine trees in the distance you can be fairly sure that there is high ground there.

PLANTAIN, *Plantago species*

Foragers learn about this one early on. It's usually included in guidebooks on edible and/or medicinal wild plants. Even some survival guides include this one in chapters on edible/useful plants. It's called Plantain most everywhere—not to be confused with the fruit.

The species on top is, *Plantago major,* the most common one in the US and was introduced here by European Immigrants centuries ago. Well over a dozen species exist in the US, they are easily distinguishable by the shape, structure, and texture of the leaf and the kind of flowering seed spike/stem.

The one on the bottom photo above is our most common species in Florida. That one is native to here and has elliptic, slightly fuzzy leaves. That species is probably designated *Plantago lanceolata.* All species have elastic, fibrous veins running down the leaves. There are some slight variations in the other species that grow in Florida and elsewhere. The seeding spike growing up the middle looks roughly the same for all species with some forming seeds only near the top while others produce them through most of the spike.

The small green and thin flower spike grows up from the center of the basal rosette. This is where the valuable seeds are produced in the fall (our spring here). The seed-husks (chaff) of a similar species are used commercially as psyllium, the main ingredient in Metamucil and other commercial laxatives. For a field laxative, soak a small handful of seeds (with husks) in hot water for 10 to 15 minutes and drink it as a tea. The seeds will soften up during the soaking process and you should swallow a few along with the tea. Be sure to drink plenty of water when taking any kind of laxative. These husks are also used as a hunger suppressant.

The seeds have also been used as a grain; the whole, shelled seeds make a kind of wheat-germ. They also help to absorb excess stomach acid, making it useful for treating heartburn.

The seeds are easily removed from the stem when mature by pinching the stem with the thumb and forefinger, then running them down the stem as you pinch off the seeds. This method can be used for harvesting the seeds and leaves of many plants.

The leaves of *Plantago species* are best eaten raw when very, very young but should be boiled with other greens. Older leaves get too fibrous and stringy—some people cook them and then remove the stringy fibers. The fibrous veins run lengthwise down the leaves and can stretch like elastic when pulled apart similar to chickweed stems. It's one of the identifying factors of the plant.

Their medicinal uses are well known among herbalists. A poultice of mashed leaves is beneficial for a variety of skin problems, boils, insect bites, and for simply preventing infection in a field dressing. As a tea, the leaves might benefit a cough and even ease ulcers.

Plantain leaves are reported to be rich in vitamins A, C, and K. There is a report that consuming a few seeds before a meal will decrease the absorption of bad cholesterol and that the plant provides certain quantities of protein, fiber, fat, and potassium.

There is also a sea plantain which can be found on every saltwater, brackish, or saline shoreline from Newfoundland—around the continent—to Alaska. It is reported that fishermen of New England have been using sea plantain as a cooked vegetable for generations. Those species include, *Plantago oliganthos* and *Plantago juncoides.* There might be another plant species also called sea plantain that is not the same nor of the same *Plantago* genus and might not be edible. Always make sure you have the right plant if you are going to consume it.

While living in New England periodically over the years, I remember using young *Plantago major* as a cooked green along with other wild edible plants. They were so prolific, you could see them growing along the cracks of sidewalks and pretty much everywhere that human development ventured. They were not nearly as plentiful there on my most recent trip. I blame Roundup for decreasing numbers of wild plants. Plantains are considered by most to be a noxious, ugly weed; not a resource to protect. The use of chemical poisons as weed killers is more popular now than ever. Which is not just a mistake because it destroys and contaminates wild food and medicine, but also leaves behind trace-amounts of toxic chemicals in the soil and leeches into surface water systems, and eventually, the aquifers/oceans. When future generations are forced to search for water sources and wild food that is not contaminated by toxic levels of heavy metals and poisonous chemicals they can look toward their preceding generations to blame.

POKE, *Phytolacca Americana*

There are foragers out there who say that the shoots do not require more than one boil to be safe to eat. That may be true, but I've seen and heard enough evidence to take the safest course of action concerning this plant. Better safe than sick. Better cautious than nauseous.

Warning: All parts of this plant contain a natural toxic chemical called phytolaccin, which is so toxic it is both cathartic (a purging of the bowels) and emetic (induces vomiting). So, why even mention this plant in a survival book about edible plants?

The youngest shoots—up to six or seven inches high— with no red or purple on it (maybe a slightly pinkish color on the stem is alright, in which case, just pick the leaves), can be made edible and delicious through the proper boiling process. That requires boiling the young shoots at least twice in a certain way.

First, take an empty pot that will hold all of your uncooked greens easily and put the greens into it in order to estimate how much water will be needed to put in the pot to cover the greens. Keep in mind that the greens will reduce in size as they cook.

Second, do not put the greens in yet. Put water in to where you estimated will cover the greens and bring the pot with water to a boil (without the greens).

Third, once the water comes to a boil, dump all the greens in and stir just a few seconds. Allow the greens to come to a boil and cook for roughly a minute or two depending on how much greens you are cooking. A small amount, boil a little; a bunch of greens, boil for at least two minutes with a few stirs.

Fourth, now take the pot off the fire and pour the contents into a colander (yes, I have a small metal one with my survival supplies, stainless steel is best) thus discarding the water and then setting the greens aside. (Or improvise by draining the water from the pot and then pouring the greens into something to keep safely aside.)

Fifth, rinse out the pot a little and refill the pot with fresh water. Now put the pot back on the stove or campfire to bring the new water to a boil.

Sixth, when the new water comes to a boil you put the greens back into the pot. The first boil is called "the first-

Mature poke plant. HIGHLY TOXIC!!!

boil" and this second boil is called, "the second boil." This time you can boil for five to ten minutes longer and then strain out the liquid again—this time making sure you press as much liquid out of the greens as you reasonably can with a spoon, fork, or stick.

Seventh, now you can eat these nutritious and tasty greens as is or cook it with spices and herbs for a few more minutes, cook it into a stew for the same amount of time, or let it cool and then put it into a Ziploc bag to freeze for later. You can also put the greens in a freezer bag after the first-boil and mark the bag as such before freezing.

Practically every foraging guidebook will report a variation of this method to some degree—few people agree on the exact method and most other variations should be safe enough as long as the basic rule is kept. . .

RULE: NO SHOOTS OVER 6 OR 7 INCHES HIGH IS SAFE AND THE WATER FROM THE FIRST BOIL IS NOT CONSUMED. A shoot may also be unsafe to cook if it has just stopped growing after reaching a few inches high and you can clearly see the blood-red or purple color on the stalks and leave-stems.

Toxic chemicals in plants are nothing to take lightly, especially in a famine or survival situation. When one is badly in need of nutrition and growing weak, anything that is even a little toxic could actually kill. If prepared properly, this plant is both safe and delicious.

A real-life victim of over-confidence in one's ability to survive in a survival situation is Christopher McCandless. His tragic story led to a book and then a movie called *Into the Wild*, directed by Sean Penn. It was reported in the press that Christopher poisoned himself by mistaking a toxic plant for an edible one and the movie portrayed that. However, many experts did not agree with that assessment, as also reported in the book by Jon Krakauer, *Into the Wild*. There is probably info out there that reports of the actual cause of his death or just more speculation. I have one possible theory.

A fungus can grow on some grass seeds, giving them a purple, pink, and/or brownish tiny spur-like growth. It is called ergot. It can cause the digestion system to shut down temporarily for days. Other types of grain fungal infections and diseases can produce the same effect in humans. This might be what happened to Christopher in an already weakened state that led to his death. Any healthy individual in our modern society could spend a couple days or more in a hospital depending on the severity, but a person who is going through slow starvation already, tens or hundreds of miles from civilization, could easily die from advanced starvation as a result.

When you go into the field or garden to harvest poke, always cut the shoots off (preferably with a cutting tool or your fingernails) well above the root. The roots are the most poisonous part of the plant and even a trace of it accidentally included in your harvest could result in an extreme emetic and cathartic internal reaction. Losing it from both ends!

The process of boiling a plant a second time with new water is also a trick/method to use on otherwise edible plants that turn bitter with age (sow thistles, dandelions, etc.). Any very bitter substance consumed on an empty stomach could result in the purging of the contents of that stomach. In any famine or outright survival scenario, getting sick from something you ate is very dangerous. This is why I hesitated to include poke in my book. But I realized that it would assist me in making an important point about foraging (know what you're doing or else), and that I like poke greens after the proper procedure.

Note: The southern expression, poke salad, is a mistake and has probably killed people. It is a mutation of the Cajun word sallet (not sure of exact spelling), which is loosely translated to "a mess of cooked greens."

You will probably read or hear of conflicting information on poke and claims of medicinal uses for it. All I say to that is to be very cautious with poke, as well as other plants that require a preparation procedure of some kind to make edible or to use as a medicinal. The reason some medicinal concoctions need precise preparation is because they often contain poisonous or toxic substances, nothing to take lightly. Take my word on this, you'll thank me later. Or else, you could end up letting someone lead you to your doom by uttering those famous last words to you, "Trust me, I know what I'm doing!"

Purple Deadnettle, *Lamium purpureum*

This is an annual plant, and possibly the most prolific wild edible and medicinal plant I have encountered. Its name has the Greek translation "the devouring purple monster." When you see entire fields of these reddish purple flowering plants as far as you can see in early to mid-spring it is easy to imagine how this translation came into being. One would think it a cultivated crop if they didn't know better. It is a perfect example of too much of a good thing. An annual winter plant in warm areas, it will turn a plowed field  into a purple sea the leaves, flowers, and tender parts of the stem are edible when young, and as a cooked potherb as it matures. I find this plant year round in Kentucky and many other areas, and have foraged it along with a few other low lying green plants throughout winter as well as the rest of the year. Purple deadnettle leaves are considered dead, because there are no stinging hairs. It is in the mint family which is distinguished by its four sided square stem, and is often confused with henbit, a relative of deadnettle, and equally edible. The green henbit leaves are kidney shaped and are attached directly to the stem, whereas the purple deadnettle has a triangular shape, and the stalk is attached to the stem's leaf blade. At that point it produces four nutlet seeds, which can be used to replant for additional growth. The flowers are tubular in shape, and the upper and lower lip ends will incline toward each other. Bees are also known to enjoy the pollen and nectar of the flowers. The upper leaves often have a reddish or purple coloration to them and appear similar to stinging nettle. It grows up to a foot or so in height if given a chance. Another similar plant associated with the other two is ground ivy, edible, but known more as a medicinal than an edible. Still, it can be eaten sparingly. It tends to have a slightly stronger flavor. All three of these plants are edible in moderation. All have medicinal properties, and spread like wildfire given a chance. I have used both deadnettle, and henbit interchangeably with no noticeable differences, but have used ground ivy sparingly as a food, and more as a medicine. By all means pull this plant up, till it under, harvest it, etc, but please refrain from using any sort of herbicide or toxic means of eradication. These chemicals create a danger to foragers, wildlife, and the very ecosystem itself.

All three of these plants share a similar appearance such as tiny purplish flowers, the leaves are similar in shape and structure, and the plants are similar in size and growing conditions, with at least purple deadnettle blooming in April and lasting about six weeks. All of them share a strong taste and smell, and are in the mint family, and yet each have very distinct differences. To someone integrating any, or all three of these plants into their survival diet, I would say purple deadnettle and henbit are the closest associates, with ground ivy being ever so slightly different.

Purple deadnettle tends to grow on roadsides, waste places, farm fields, pretty much anywhere. It seem to love lawns, and disturbed areas as well. For these reasons, take extra care when harvesting to consider what sort of chemical or fertilizer treatments have been introduced to the land. In an extreme survival scenario you may have to loosen up on these rules, but in everyday foraging, stick with the most pure locations possible.

These plants are common throughout are common throughout Europe, especially Britain, Israel, Norway, northern Africa, western Asia, and the Mediterranean. It was introduced to the US and Canada and now grows in many areas throughout both countries.

In the spring, the young leaf shoots are harvestable and can commonly used in salads The leaves are also useful as a good tea, which helps treat chills and promote kidney function and perspiration The plant is very nutritious, high in iron, vitamins and fiber Sometimes mint stems can be so hairy the best way to tell the stem is square is to feel it with your fingers through feel you will notice the characteristic square stem.

The entire plant is edible. The flavor can be somewhat strong and earthy you can eat it stem and all, or pick off the tops The hairs on the leaves give it a unique texture, and contribute to its strong flavor, but you get used to it as you do any new foods introduced into your diet.

If it smells like a mint and looks like a mint it is edible, but they must do both. A lot of mints do not smell minty, some of them are edible and some not. Follow this rule strictly Anything short of obsession when it comes to edible or medicinal plant identification could make the difference between life and death. Some of the mints can make you quite ill.

Purple deadnettle is often confused with henbit and neither smell minty, but both happen to be edible mints, and have no poisonous look a likes The differences can be seen in the leaves purple deadnettle, in this case dead means not stinging, has more triangular shaped leaves that grow in large areas henbit has heart-shaped leaves with scalloped edges with a stem that seems to grow right through the middle of its neatly stacked leaves.

Nutritionally, both are high in iron, vitamins, and fiber. The seeds of the purple deadnettle, *Lamium purpureum*, are loaded with antioxidants and presumably the henbit, *L. amplexicaule* does too.

Although all these plants can be consumed within reason, we should still make sure they agree with us individually, hence the good old Universal Edibility Test.

PURSLANE, *Portulaca oleracea*

While walking past a flower shop years ago now, I spotted something laying on the sidewalk in front of me that stopped me dead in my tracks. It was a plant I didn't see very often and it was laying right there on the middle of the sidewalk, roots exposed, dying, completely out of place—one of my favorite edible wild plants. It's a simple little plant called purslane. Someone had been pulling "weeds" up and leaving them there to die. This one had been thrown over to the sidewalk a few feet away from the area around the flower shop's fence.

To your average American gardener in this pre apocalyptic world of the two-thousand-teens, purslane is a noxious invasive weed that digs into the soil right next to those poisonous-but-colorful, ornamental, landscape favorites.

Most people I know must think it somewhat crazy of me to study the edibility of the common weed, at least in our time they would. Way back when my mother was young nearly a century ago, it was a common and important knowledge to many people to know which "weeds" were edible and nutritious and which were not. Before that time, it was a matter of survival to know. It was life-or-death serious way back when! Now it's just crazy? It will become a matter of survival for everyone again someday. I guarantee that!

"Feed a child a fish, you feed him for a day. Teach a child to fish and you'll feed him for a lifetime." Teaching self-sufficiency means more than just fishing. Besides, there won't be a lot of fish left when the human population of the planet exceeds eight billion. Marine biologists know that the amount and variety of fish that existed fifty years ago will never be seen again. If that amount of fish was ever restored to what it once was just fifty years ago, it could only happen if there were no human eyes around to see it—or hardly any. Even then, the diversity of life in the seas may never be the same again after we're done with it.

In a world of billions of hungry mouths to feed and contaminated soil, dwindling fresh-water supplies, and mass-extinctions of species by chain-reactions of a diminishing food-chain, caused in part by profit hungry capitalists, everyone will need to know more than just fishing, even more than just fishing and hunting. I'm talking about a fate that people seem to be avoiding discussion about. A coming mass-extinction event!

There will not be much wild fish or animals left by the time young children today get old. Eight billion people and counting is a lot of mouths to feed.

Knowing this plant, the purslane, as well as hundreds of edible wild plants, will be an advantage to all those who know exactly what to look for and how to use them. One of the strengths of purslane is its ability to survive. Unless one pulls them completely out of the ground, including all of its roots, it will fight to live. It will even try to put its roots back into the soil when pulled up and left there. I knew this was so, so I picked up that discarded plant, put it into one of my large cargo-pants pockets, and took it home—walking a mile away. Once home, I put some potting soil (they love that stuff) into a planter-container and carefully placed the purslane in, roots first of course. I gave it some water, TLC, and placed it in a neutral spot, half-sun and half-shade. The next day, its stalk was standing up, still somewhat droopy, but definitely alive. Within a week, it was flowering all over and happy as can be. It helped that I watered it once every day for a while. It became twice as large two weeks later and sprouting new growth the next year.

It is also very nutritious. It contains carbohydrates, calcium, protein, phosphorus, iron, vitamin A, thiamine, vitamin C, vitamin E, antioxidants, and even small amounts of vegetable fat and fatty-acids (Omega 3). Every part of the plant is edible from the surface up. The leaves have an oily, nutty flavor.

I can clip leaves off of its stems here and there without hurting it. It can continue to produce and reproduce for quite some time, as long as conditions don't get extreme. Not too much heat, cold, water, drought or shade. They love moderation.

You can find purslane all over the world. The edible parts are succulent stems and leaves, as well as the seeds. The whole plant can be eaten raw from the ground up but don't eat the seeds raw (possible toxic fungi and infections). There are other edible *Portulacas*, even a coastal salty one, and they are generally easy to identify once you become familiar. Discard any seeds that are purple, spurred, or oddly discolored.

Learn it, find it, and know it! Just be careful of where people have sprayed their poisons around and stay away from factories/mills that release water into a water source, the drainage areas of railroad tracks, major roadways, and nuclear power plants.

The leaves, stems, and flowers of the purslane are delicious raw, eaten in salads, cooked like spinach, or added to baked dishes. The stems can be pickled with vinegar and sugar. The tiny black seeds can be threshed from their husks while dry, lightly roasted and ground into flour.

Purslane was one of the first edible plants that I positively identified well over forty years ago. Foraging became a major interest of mine after being abandoned in a big city a thousand miles from home. It was an eye-opening experience, and one that led me down a path to the self-reliance that survival skills and foraging enables. I knew I had to learn it. Sea purslane looks exactly the same, grows near salt-water, and is salty.

The purslane plant is one of those plants that are easy to identify once you know what it looks like in three dimensions coming up out of the ground. A pink flowered cousin of purslane is reported to be edible but the taste was so different along with the design of the stem, leaf, and flower structure that I don't consider it the same as purslane and question its edibility.

RUSHES, BULRUSH, *Scripus species*

In general, the edible roots of perennial plants (herbaceous plants that live for several years) are high in starch (carbohydrates) and sugar (energy), particularly during their dormant period—winter for most climates—when there is none or little aboveground activity. They basically store the plant's energy in their roots until spring—or whenever the growing season might begin for a particular climate and/or plant.

Rushes are native to the Western Hemisphere and many kinds can be found around the world. A member of the sedge family, the nearly round reeds fooled me into thinking it was a form of grass plant. The reed (stalk) itself is actually triangular in shape, but roundish. The significance of that is because all members of the sedge family have edges, (sedges have edges) apparently some more than others. The best identifier for this plant is the flower/pollen growth at the tip of the stalk in the fall.

The roots are a rhizome, the root expands lengthwise along the ground as it grows and puts up new shoots along the ground as it produces new growth. These roots have edibility in various forms. The whole thing can be processed like cattail rhizomes—drying, pounding, and sifting out the fibers to produce flour. You could also pound the root into a mash, boil it to make it a mush, and then pull out the fibrous strands and pieces before drying and grinding into flour. The flour or preceding mush can be used in a poultice when soaked in a tannin solution and placed on a venomous insect bite or sting to draw out some of the poison. There are reports that the pith of the stalk can be used like a wick for candles (it has the texture of a soft Styrofoam), lanterns, or used as is when soaked in an oil or fat and ignited. If you take a stalk and pull off just enough outer layers to allow air to flow to the core but leaving enough of the outer layer to ensure its structural integrity, you can use it like a Tiki torch after soaking it in oil or fat.

Because of the thick habitat of rushes in wetlands, many animals frequent them for feeding, shelter and camouflage. Native Americans (First Peoples) used rushes for weaving mats and for thatching their shelters. They even wove together floating structures in which to fish and gather edibles from aquatic edible plants. A beetle grub that is very edible and makes a very effective fish-bait lives inside of the upper part of some stalks. To find them look closely at the largest mature stalks for a brown streak accompanied by a small hole. A grub might be living inside. These same grubs can also live inside of the hollow parts of cattail stalks.

There is also a species of *Scripus* that lives in brackish water. The photos above show the flower/pollen tops. When these seedpods form at the tip of each stalk they are easy to identify as a species of *Scripus*. These are probably the species *Scripus californica*. Larger species north of here include *Scripus acutus,* or hard-stem bulrush, and *Scripus validus,* or great bulrush, a.k.a. tule.

The rhizome can be baked as is in a campfire. The core is hard when raw but wrapped in a banana leaf or aluminum foil you can dig out a little hole in the hot coals of a well-established campfire and stuff (or just place) the wrapped rhizome into the hole. Then cover it with hot coals and feed the fire on top of it. It could take hours to fully bake, so if you do this in the evening as you would normally sit by the fire in the wild, you could wait until the next morning to dig out your breakfast from the now warm ashes. It just requires chewing the soft white substance off of the stringy fibers.

The seeds themselves may also have edible quality other than winnowing for flour. More research needs to be done on this plant for survival fare. Like cattails, the young shoots can be peeled and eaten raw or cooked. The tips of the root-rhizome is reportedly edible after roasting and the seeds can be parched and then eaten as is or used for flour. The potential nutrition in the roots is reported to provide sugar, starch, and 1 percent protein.

A few other foraging books will also provide information on this plant. Not all field-guides are the same, not all are completely accurate, so I advise having several of the most comprehensive and in-depth ones available for comparing. I have no direct experience using this plant, the info presented is based on research.

SANDSPURS, *Cenchrus species*

These are familiar mostly to Floridians and called sandspurs. They are protecting an edible seed. The seed pods dig into your clothes and flesh with tiny spikes, thorns, burs, spurs, whatever you want to call it. The three local species contain a prize to anyone willing to make the effort to release the seed from its spiny casing or just burn off the spines over an open flame. It's like roasting a marshmallow over a campfire. The goal is to just burn/singe off the spines, leaving the seed inside lightly roasted without burning the whole thing up and the sharp spurs reduced to nubs or charred off completely. The seeds have oil that can ignite it into flames if held too close to the flame of a campfire for too long. Just singe the spines off completely and eat, or place the charred spurs into a mortar and crush them until the seeds separate from the scorched hulls, then winnow (remove and discard the hulls).

They can be used in a number of ways associated with edible grass seeds. The other methods of freeing the seeds from the spiny spurs require much more effort than the calories are worth. One can try rubbing them vigorously between pieces of leather. Another method requires pounding them with a rock against a hard surface, or in a mortar to free the seeds from their casings. Utilizing calories wisely in a survival situation or even just while camping-out is important. Taking the time to closely inspect your seeds is worth avoiding any possible hazard. Since the seeds of the sandspur are surrounded by their casings the threat of ergot is much less than with other grass seeds.

Use only the sandspur stalks that turn yellowish from their original green, those are the ripe ones and ready to prepare and eat. They first come up in the early summer and continue putting up spur-topped grass-shoots throughout the summer and well into the winter.

Nature has a way of protecting its seed, even in the plant kingdom. The seeds of the sandspur plant evolved the spines to protect it from herbivores. Many plants use spikes, spines and thorns, while some other plants use bright colors to warn predators of toxic substances. You might be surprised at how many thorny vines have edible potential.

In a pinch, you can cook the spurs over the campfire to sufficiently burn off the spurs and char the casing, then chew it down. Don't use the green ones—they turn yellowish when they mature.

SAWGRASS, *Cladium jamaicense*

For finding water and obtaining quick and easy calories in the Florida wetlands the sawgrass species called *Cladium jamaicense* is near the top of the list. You usually find sawgrass in standing water and low, wet spots bordering cypress swamps, rivers, and lakes but I have seen them in somewhat dry scrubs of pine forest and oak hammock where either a gully drains rain to some low, wet spots or a spring hides beneath them or nearby.

Sawgrass appears similar to cattails and the starchy, white, inner core along the base of the stalks tastes similar too. The differences in appearance is the much thinner, darker green and sharply yet finely toothed, V-shaped leaves of sawgrass. The sharp teeth point upward, making them able to cut through clothing and flesh if you rub them the wrong way—literally.

The white core is edible raw or cooked.

One way to harvest the bottom white core is to grab the innermost bundle of leaves near the ground and pull up sharply. With luck, you will pull out the core without its outer leaves attached or roots. Or, just pull the whole thing out of the ground and peel off the outer layers. I've done both. I try to pull up just the core but the whole thing comes out of the mud sometimes. That white core is edible raw or cooked. It usually includes the bottom six to eight inches before turning green and tough above it. It has similar flavor to the cattail stalk and heart-of-palm and a little like cucumbers. They typically grow to between 4–6 feet tall but some reports put them as high as nine to ten feet. The inedible flowers form at the top of the center spike that extends above the grassy leaves in the form of rusty brown colored plumes of inedible seeds.

The seeding stalk of a sawgrass. Notice how different it is compared to the rushes of the *Scripus* genus.

There are other species of *Cladium* with unknown edibility and while there are some around the world with roots reported to be edible our local species' roots are reported to be too tough to eat even after extensive boiling—too woody. All sawgrass species are members of the sedge family and sedges have edges, this one with sharply toothed edges like a saw—hence the name. This species covers many parts of the Florida Everglades in marshy, fresh or brackish swamps often called a sea of grass and range from there north to Virginia and west to Texas.

SAW PALMETTO, *Serenoa repens*

The photos here show saw palmetto sections being harvested for the heart as well as pulling up the core of a new frond for the starchy white bottom. The most abundant edible palms here, the cabbage palm, sabal palmetto and this saw palmetto, *Serenoa repens*, have fan-shaped fronds (leaves). The saw palmetto is the low growing, sprawling, multiple sectioned palm with a blue or yellowish tint sometimes and rises from the ground like a multi-headed monster. The end of any one section can be cut off and peeled to produce an edible core—raw or cooked—called the heart of palm.

Saw palmetto.

As long as there are multiple "heads" coming off of the base of the plant, one can harvest from one head without killing the entire plant. Just imagine this multi-headed edible monster coming out of the ground with its heads crawling parallel to the ground before aiming upwards. Eeeeeeeeeek! It's scary out there at night if you let your imagination run away with you.

These palms have barely palatable, large, black and very dark blue when ripe, berries rich in oil and sugar and can be found throughout Florida's sandy prairies, dunes, pinelands, oak hammocks, and along the edges of cypress swamps west from here to coastal Louisiana and up to the North Carolina coast. There is much info on uses of the berries, but it is the hearts of these palm heads, terminal buds or trunks, that I'm focusing on here. The other palm, the cabbage palm (*Sabal palmetto*), is somewhat protected by law (debatable, especially if one is in a perceived survival situation), very difficult to harvest (which kills that plant), and suffering now from a disease (called, cabbage palm disease) that is killing them in some counties (not in Pasco or Hernando yet at the present time, as far as I know) but the saw palmettos here are plentiful, healthy, not protected (as far as I know), and much easier to harvest than cabbage palm.

Palm hearts.

The saw palmetto is a noxious, native grass-plant that does not need protecting. In dry conditions, they are very slow growers but in swampy conditions they grow faster. As a survival food, the heart of the palm is practically all carbohydrates with a variety of other nutrients—as you might typically find with any starchy vegetable. When identifying them, there are clear differences between the saw palmetto and the cabbage palm. One way is that the cabbage palm frond's stem connects to the fan-like leaf

The cores of new fronds have starchy white bottoms.

in a pointed, spear-shaped fashion. The saw palmetto frond's stem attaches to the fan-like leaf bluntly—no spear-point shape. Also, the frond stems of the saw palmetto have hacksaw-like teeth along it, hence the name, saw. The cabbage palm frond stems are usually smooth with the exception of a few large, sharp thorns close to the trunk in some species.

Be aware that snakes—particularly rattlesnakes—like to curl up into palmettos to either get off of the hot ground or cold ground. While bees collect honey from the blossoms, wasps like to nest on the undersides of the fronds. I once disturbed a wasp nest underneath a live cabbage palm frond that sent me running. Many animals use saw palmettos in many ways—sometimes the berries are all that they have available to eat. The berries in many places are protected by law because of their value for prostate-health medicine. If you actually eat the flesh off the berries any test for prostate health can be obscured.

As a nibble, I pull up the center, growing, emerging frond of young emerging plants and chew off the tender white bottom. In any survival situation where nutrition is needed some estimates report that our diets benefit most from high-starch, high-carbohydrate foods. While we need protein and fat in certain amounts to keep us going, we need even more in carbs to give us energy. The saw palmetto could become a staple diet of the survivor here.

On the medicinal side, the ripe berries contain the main ingredient in today's supplemental/herbal preparations for enlarged prostates. Medical experts have concluded that significant improvement in frequent urination can be obtained by decoctions (boiling the berries and consuming) and tinctures in specific dosages made with the ripe berries. The berries start off green, turn to yellow, and ripen to black.

SHEEP SORREL, *Rumex acetosella*

A very tasty leaf! The top photo is a mature adult plant in February. The bottom photo is part of Florida's winter crop of young edibles beginning to come up in October. Sheep sorrel is strictly a winter crop here with the plants going to seed and dying in April or May. You can find it in disturbed ground of open fields, acidic soil, from dry to well drained and (in these parts) sandy soil. It covers a range that includes all of the US and southern half of Canada Including the southern portions of Alaska. It grows frequently in colonies, but not exclusively.

A Florida sheep sorrel in February.

Other than sheep sorrel, its common names include, sour grass, sourweed, and surette. A stalk will come up the middle of this rosette. The stalk will form red to rusty brown seeds when mature, similar to buckwheat and curly dock *(Rumex crispus/persicaroides/obtrusifolius)* which are all members of the buckwheat family *(Polygonaceae)*. Very similar to wood sorrel, *Oxalis species,* sheep sorrel has a very pleasant tart flavor that I like to snack on as a kind-of trail-nibble whenever I find them and I add some to salads.

However, if eaten in large enough quantities in one sitting they can cause diarrhea and other gastric problems such as nausea. But you would have to eat a lot for that reaction. That may or may not be attributed to the oxalic acid content (experts vary on this) and has been established to cause problems with people who get kidney stones (if they consumed significant amounts on a regular basis). Along with kidney problems, it may also

Florida sheep sorrel by October.

adversely affect arthritis and gout sufferers, also if eaten in large quantities. That being said, it is tasty and reportedly harmless in small to moderate amounts. The juice from sheep sorrel and wood sorrel is good for cleaning silver and effective on mildew and rust stains because of the oxalic acid content. There are recipes of both plants available out there including sheep sorrel soup.

You'll find these plants in many edible plant guides and even some survival guides that include a chapter on edible wild plants. Sheep sorrel is an easy one to identify—it looks just like those photos. Even when the stalk comes up, the leaves attached to the stalk will have that same exact unique shape and tart flavor.

I've known about, and been snacking on, sheep sorrel and wood sorrel for most of my life now. This was one of the first edible plants I discovered through the edible plant guides that I started reading way back in the 1970s as I emerged into adulthood.

SKUNKVINE, *Paederia foetida*

The word *foetida* means stinking, which you may have noticed if you've ever encountered this vine up-close and personal. I never thought that the smell was that offensive. My sister seems to think its odor is as offensive as a skunk. When I told her that it is edible she probably wondered if I had lost my mind, while knowing that I had already lost that old thing many years before.

Note the tiny dull spikes ("stipules") at the apex where the leaf stems meet the main stem.

The smell can also remind one of a strong sulfur aroma because that's what it is—the *Paederia foetida* contains sulfur compounds that cause (at least in part if not completely) the stinky smell. The leaves are "opposite" (two leaves at each node—on opposite sides of the stem) lance-shaped to oval and tapering to a point. If you look closely at each node where the leaves grow on the stem and on the underside of the leaves (at the apex of the leaf and stem) are tiny, dull spikes (one per leaf) protruding from the apex and called a stipule. That is a classic example of a characteristic that aids in identifying this plant. I also identify it with the odor. You might not notice the odor unless you crush some of the leaves. When I'm pulling mature vines out of my garden I've noticed the toughness of the vine itself and wondered if it would make good cordage if braided together. As it turns out, that was its main function when it was cultivated. Skunkvine is not native to this continent. It came here from Southeast Asia and China in 1897 exactly for its fibrous cordage potential—ground-zero being just north of me in Hernando County—and escaped into all southeastern states.

There are many other species of this genus around the globe. This one has a slightly bitter flavor that mellows when cooked. When I cooked dark-green leaves the flavor gave me an extremely distasteful reaction that I haven't experienced from the light-green leaves. However, this is one of those greens that

As attractive as many poisonous ornamentals, Skunkvine looks prettier than it smells.

I think is best added to other greens. While you can eat them raw, in spite of their stinky aroma, I would suggest mixing just a few leaves in with a salad (if at all) and just use the youngest light-green leaves only if possible. The same with boiled greens, mix them in with other greens sparingly. It is reported to be used in soups and minced in steamed food.

SMILAX, *Smilax species*

This is a thorny vine that you can find in every heavily wooded area in Florida. There are so many varieties and common names for them that any experienced forager calls all of them by their genus name, *Smilax* (like smile with an axe). I've known about this one for a very long time as greenbrier.

One of probably several hundred assorted "Smilax" species.

Also, experienced foragers know that the smilax with the best/most food potential is the thick green shoots of the *Smilax bona-nox*, even though other plant parts of that species are reported to be edible in some guides as well as other species of smilax.

Some report that the *Smilax rotundifolia*, with its nearly round leaves, has edible young leaves, tendrils, and shoots (boiled or steamed). They also report the same info on *Smilax herbacea*, which is commonly called carrion flower. However, the growing tips of the vines (shoots) of those *Smilax* species looks nothing like the *Smilax bona-nox* in comparison and some do not have the tender edible shoots at all unless they are very small and only appear in the spring. I am not certain of this. I am

fairly certain that I would only use the youngest leaves boiled of the most delicate of species. Some *Smilax* species have leaves that appear much too thick and tough to be useful as a boiled greens ingredient.

However, it is the thick growing tips, or shoots, of the *bona-nox* vine variety that is a substantial choice food available nearly year-round (raw or cooked, but sparingly raw), looking somewhat like the large insect called a walking stick, and is a great boiled green vegetable with a unique flavor of its own. This is one vegetable that Monsanto won't get their hands on, I hope.

It has common names like greenbrier, catbrier, and bullbriar, the crux of which focuses on the word brier because of the thorns that has grabbed and/or cut many a hiker and forager. Along with the blackberries and dewberries that grow on thorny vines, the smilax is a delicacy that can trip you up, rip your pants, and cut your flesh. It is a prime, plentiful, and choice famine-food source. However, because of the fibrous nature of it, it's best cooked like asparagus or eaten raw only in small quantities as a trail-snack.

When harvesting them, find the growing tip of the vine. Try bending it about seven inches from the end. If it doesn't break off easily, move your fingers closer to the end and bend it over there. The tenderest portion will break rather easily, making sure that you get all of the potential food that is there. To be sure that you have the right vine, a single leaf grows with two tendrils all along the vine, even to the tips. The best way to remember how to identify smilax is to recite a mantra over and over, "One leaf two tendrils, one leaf two tendrils, one leaf two tendrils . . ." all the way down the vine.

The berries are not particularly edible in most species. I would just skip foraging on the berries. The roots of some species are reported to be ground into a flour and/or used to make a reddish tea, beverage (sarsaparilla), or jam. However, even young roots are too hard to grind down to the flour. Large, old roots would seem impossible to grind. The effort will probably not be worth the results. Though, I won't discourage you to try. Again, the young leaves on some species might be edible boiled, just use the most delicate-leafed of species. Some have tough, indigestible fibers from the earliest stages of development.

This is one to remember should you ever need to, or whenever you might just want a totally wild, green vegetable right from the woods. And remember, many foraging books will claim that the root can be used for a number of things, but I can't confirm that they would be useful to a survivor.

SOW THISTLES, *Sonchus species*

This is a variety of our Florida sow thistles of the *Sonchus* genus, which, rather than being a thistle, is more closely related to the northern wild lettuce of the *Lactuca* genus. These plants are not true thistles. True thistles (bull thistles) are the somewhat similar looking plants that produce prickly, sharp thorns all along the plant which can cut bare hands easily. *Sonchus* leaves should not draw blood like the true thistles can. Two kinds of *Sonchus* are featured here in Florida with possible interbreeding, *Sonchus oleraceus* (common sow thistle) and *Sonchus asper* (spiny sow thistle). The spiny sow thistle has sharp pointy edges on its leaves that appear thorny but is actually just sharp but soft, pointy-edged but fairly delicate, grassy leaves. Those edges cause that particular species to be better as a cooked green than a salad ingredient. The edges and points of *Sonchus* soften up completely when boiled. True thistles do not soften with cooking.

All *Sonchus* species provide delicious cooked greens, but as a salad ingredient, even the young soft *oleraceus* are usually a little too bitter raw. As the plant matures the leaves become rank and are much too bitter, even boiled. However, the unopened flower buds can be added to stews and the stalks can be boiled twice to remove bitterness. You can usually find this plant featured in edible-plant guides. Many foragers look forward to them as a tasty cooked green. If the leaves get too old, they can still be eaten if boiled twice to mellow some of the rank tasting bitterness. *Sonchus* is plentiful and quick growing through our winter season from about December to May and is one of my favorites. Keep clear of plants growing too close to a road or where poisons may have been

sprayed in recent years. There are toxic look-alikes, some with round, velvety stalks that produce pinkish to purplish colored tassel flowers. I've seen the look-alikes around in the summer here when real *Sonchus* is nowhere to be seen. *Sonchus* will have yellow flowers only.

SPANISH BAYONET, *Yucca aloifolia*

This is another of the yucca species with very much the same edibles if not exactly the same as the *Yucca filamentosa*. However, I decided to examine this one separately from the *Yucca filamentosa*. First, I've had more experience with the flower blossoms of this one and the taste seems cleaner and the texture crisper. I once used them to mix in with scrambled eggs and battered and fried them until excluding most fried foods from my diet.

One of my plant guidebooks says that this one is a native to Florida, yet, another guide says that it is a native of Mexico. I suppose that it could be both. This one grows wild in coastal regions and sandy scrubs or escaped cultivation and range from here to New England and down to Texas. The examples in the photo above are in a vacant lot a few blocks from me where a house burned down a number of years ago. The lot has been unkempt and grown-over ever since. I love to see unkempt lots close to home where I find many varied edibles growing freely without decapitation or poisons. Let that be a tip to where you will be able to forage the most abundantly and safely. The lots and lawns that are well manicured and landscaped are the most dangerous and least productive (and the residents might be hostile toward someone picking at their weeds and flowers).

So, look for the most unkempt, grown-over and abandoned of areas to find the best variety and safest of environments—usually. As you can see, the biggest difference between this Spanish bayonet and the *Yucca filamentosa* is the way the green leaves are thicker here and grow in layers up the stalk until shooting up its flower stalk. The *Yucca filamentosa* has the thinner basal leaves at the base only without expanding upwards.

One thing that I forgot to mention on *Yucca filamentosa* is the way the points of the leaves on both species can be cut off and filed down to a thin, sharp needle—hence the common name also used for this plant, Adam's needle—and the leaves can be stripped into fibers for a strong cordage. I have sources that repeat the same report on the fruits, that they are edible raw or cooked but are bitter and rubbery. Yet another source only mentions the edibility of the flower petals. I can only report to you at this time that the flower stalks, while still young, tender, and green (before the flowers appears) are perfectly edible when peeled, cut into sections and boiled. You may want to boil them twice to take out any unpleasant rank flavor. After one boil, they had an icky flavor to them. I'd rather have slightly-bland than slightly icky taste any day.

The ripe seeds will require a regimen of roasting and boiling to produce a boiled vegetable or roasting and drying to pound into flour. You may have to do some more research on the seeds and fruits. I don't have enough info on them to be specific about the edibility of the fruits and seeds.

From examining both species up-close and personal I get the impression that the stalk of the *filamentosa* is not just taller than the Spanish bayonet but stays green and tender longer, yet, they both flower at about the same time of year (May/June) here. Some people might have a nauseous reaction to the flowers eaten raw. Try just a couple or so at first and wait for thirty minutes. The roots of this species are not edible, but can be used as a soap.

SPANISH MOSS, *Tillandsia usneoides*

Spanish moss might provide a "gotcha" moment the way Bear Grylls does when he eats a bug raw on camera. You can pull off a tiny, green, growing tip of Spanish moss in front of an audience and eat it knowing that it is edible just to get a response from anyone watching you. However, this one will not provide any measurable nutrition at all (that I can surmise). Spanish moss does not have a parasitic relationship with the trees in that it does not feed off of the trees in any way. It is an ediphyte, which according to Merriam-Webster's is "a plant that derives its moisture and nutrients from the air and rain and grows usually on another plant."

I believed for all these years that the annoying bugs, chiggers, lived in the moss that hangs in the trees. Chiggers are microscopic bugs that work their way to your skin around your clothing to eat your skin cells and causes intense itching for days at a time if you don't find a way to get rid of them as soon as they appear. Try covering the spots where they've established to feast on you with nail-polish. I've walked through Florida's woods for many years and only got chigger infestations around my feet and ankles and to a lesser extent above the knees. I've never found one above my waist, which stands to reason if the bugs were in the moss that hangs, and I've had contact above my waist with hanging moss on many, many occasions, I should have found one on me above my waist by now if they were there. I have it from good authority that the moss that is on the trees does not have chiggers and would only have them after being pulled off the tree and thrown to the ground or fallen off on its own and landed on the ground.

The name Spanish moss might come from the look of the beards of early explorers and founders of Florida from Spain. It has had other names but the one that finally stuck is the one that the vast majority of my fellow Floridians have called it, Spanish moss. Soaking the moss in water for weeks (as much as six) is reportedly sufficient to strip off the bark or outer layer to leave just the fibrous material that can be used to make cordage. You can build a makeshift wall of tied tree branches around your camp to lay Spanish moss on and create a kind of privacy fence or drape large amounts of moss around the trees that encircle your camp. The only damage that they do to the trees is cut off some of the sunlight from them and weigh down the branches somewhat. It absorbs water like a sponge and I've used it for insulation from the ground along with fallen leaves under my tent to cushion it from the ground and provide the illusion that I've set my tent on a mattress. I lay a tarp over the debris-pile before laying my tent over the debris-pile to help ensure that bugs will be impeded from crawling around on the exterior of the tent from the pile. I've also used a relative and very similar looking moss called ball moss, *Tillandsia recurvata*, for insulation that appears to attach itself to trees more so than the Spanish moss species. I usually find these mosses on oak species. The edible part is the teeny-tiny, green tips of growing moss-strands which has, reportedly, less calories than it would take to pull the tips off and no nutritive elements or constituents that I know of. That being said, they are reportedly edible raw and I know of direct knowledge of that being so from multiple sources.

SPANISH NEEDLES, *Bidens alba/pilosa*

This is food, tea, and medicine to those who know how to use it. Those who don't know how to use it are, of course, ignorant of its real value. So, they call it a weed that must be poisoned away from their homes as they poison their own environment around them. In my experience, there are no "weeds," it's either potential food or not potential food. Imagine being chronically homeless and under-employed or unemployed most of the time. You might want to look at everything that grows around you as potential food. People once lived that way all the time throughout their lives. I wish the people around me weren't so purposely ignorant of that, but they are.

Spanish needles have edible flowers (raw or cooked) with a tangy pleasant taste. I like to add them to my salads. I don't use the leaves in my salad though, they have an off-putting taste to me. You can try adding a few young leaves to your salad and judge for yourself.

The tops of the plants before they flower are the best for salads or boiled greens. I prefer to mix them with other wild greens, like: amaranth, lamb's-quarters, spiderwort, young crepis, young dock, young sonchus, peppergrass, young mustards, young dandelions, and others.

The Bidens *alba* is the larger of the two, I've seen them over eight feet high, with five or more petals. The Bidens *pilosa* is the smaller plant with less petals on average.

Both are perfectly edible except in areas where opals are mined. It is an invasive species and around here you can find it virtually everywhere almost year-round. There are many medicinal uses you can research this plant on. The thin .25–3/8 inch seeds have two tiny "teeth," or prongs, on one end to attach themselves to creatures (like us) that spread them around. These seeds are crushed, powdered, combined with moisture or a mucilaginous sap as a topical anesthetic and aids in clotting. The dried leaves make a pleasant non-caffeinated tea, if you are into tea, but you should drink it sparingly because of the high nitrite content of the plant. However, nitrites might help reduce high blood pressure. Spanish needles range from here to Louisiana and up to about the Carolinas.

I prefer to study the edibility of invasive plants more than others. Because, if all hell breaks loose and the more you know the less you need, the edible invasive plants will be the best ones to know because of their great abundance.

SPIDERWORT, *Tradescantia ohiensis*

When I once told an elderly woman that a certain edible plant becomes bitter as it gets older she replied, "I can relate to that."

Spiderwort is a plant that does not taste rank or bitter with age. The clasping leaves running off the stems that shoots up from the base looks like thick grass blades that were folded up the middle. While the young stems that grow from the base are always best, they are almost equally good in the latter stages of the plant's life. I like to use the thickest stems chopped and added to my salads, stews, or omelets. You can use them in stir-fries as well. Anything that you can do with a typical green garden vegetable you can do with this plant. Talk about a wild vegetable that has been labeled a weed by ignorant, spoiled, and arrogant Americans, this is definitely one of those.

However, the sap of the plant has a somewhat thick, mucilaginous, gelatinous, viscous nature to it not unlike okra. After chopping it up, I rinse them off thoroughly before using them, not that there's anything wrong with a slimy, green vegetable.

They like to grow around us along roads, paths, trails, meadows, thickets, disturbed ground or not. They grow at least this far south and from Maine to the Mississippi River. They are virtually year-round in Florida but don't like the hottest part of the summer or coldest part of the winter. In early November, they pop up around here en mass. In all points northward they are the usual spring to fall plants, producing an abundance of flowers and seeds at the top of each stem/stalk. I resist calling it a stalk, since so many can grow up from a single inedible root. Each stem has the traits of a stalk, which may or may not produce a forking branch or two and then flowering on the ends.

Even the outstanding blue, three-petaled flowers, as reflected in the photos provided above, are edible and best picked after opening in the morning as a garnish or made into a candy substance. I haven't tried to make the candy myself, but, suffice it to say that it's just sugar and flower. That's right, flower, not flour. All parts of this plant from the ground up are edible. I would exclude the seeds for fear of ergot and other hazards.

Here is an important fact for the future of foraging. In case of radiation contamination after a nuclear event the stamen hairs of the flowers of spiderwort will turn from its bright blue to pink. This plant could become a very important foraging food here should they ever be needed. Or, should I say, "When they will be needed!" Be aware that the species *Tradescantia zebrina* is NOT edible. I'm pretty sure that that particular species does not grow around here.

I pick the flower stalks of spiderwort, *Tradescantia ohiensis*, and chop them up to add to my salads, soups, and stew. They are fairly bland, so they mix in well with the other ingredients. To me they have the clean flavor of a typical green vegetable. The name come from the medicinal use of the sap to treat spider bites.

SPURGE NETTLE, *Cnidoscolus stimulosus*

These perennials have starchy edible tubers averaging up to the size of a large carrot, or bigger when healthy and usually about a foot down underneath the plant itself, which is covered above ground with tiny stinging hairs laced with formic acid. They can be found in dry, sandy dunes, cattle fields, open pinelands, and roadsides from every section of Florida, north to Virginia, and all along the Gulf coastal region to Texas. Texas has a similar species but without the edible tuber. One report on those is that the aboveground portion is edible after boiling but I can't suggest that without two or more reputable sources confirming it.

A Gulf fritillary butterfly harvesting nectar. He had no use for a tuber, and we can't survive on nectar.

The lobed leaves attach to a main stem that becomes a woody thin root leading down into the ground to the edible tuber anywhere from a few inches to a foot-and-a-half down. If you touch any of the aboveground parts, you'll think you were stung by a bee (bee venom is very similar to formic acid). The pain and irritation will last a few minutes or a few hours

Dig along one side of the plant until you find the root leading down to the tuber. You're trying to dig down along the main inedible root without cutting it so that you can follow it down to the cigar-shaped tuber. The inedible root is woody and tough but thin, so when you get down to the tuber you'll know it. I've heard that some people expect the tuber to always be a foot down. They don't follow the root down as they dig, and then can't find the tuber because they cut it and tossed it with a shovel full of dirt. Sometimes the tuber can be quite small.

Boil the tuber as you would a potato-like vegetable. There is usually a woody string at the core of the tuber which is easily removed or otherwise discarded after boiling by eating around it. I've tasted one tuber, reminding me of a potato and another that reminded me of a parsnip-like carrot flavor, so

Notice that we've started digging alongside the plant, so as not to sever the string leading down to the tuber.

the taste can vary. They grow in colonies which can spread for miles along open fields of large pasture and pinelands. The butterfly, a Gulf fritillary, just happened to be checking out the bright white five-petaled flowers (top photo). The local natives reported eating the

Enough carbs to keep you alive.

This is spurge nettle and bull nettle (not to be confused with bull thistle), *Cnidoscolus stimulosus*.

tuber at the end of the root but nothing else. If you don't find the tuber after you've dug two feet down, you should look to see if you didn't already shovel it out of the hole. Sometimes the tuber can be very small but you can't tell what size it will be from the size or shape of the aboveground plant. Some might question whether the caloric-cost of digging up the tubers is worth it. However, it is very high in much needed carbohydrates that your family might need and some roots can be quite large and they only seem to like sandy soil, which makes the digging easier. Cook until soft enough as is or add to stew. It is not edible raw, as far as I know.

STINGING NETTLE, *Urtica chamaedryoides*

Could a weed that stings you when you touch it with your bare hands, brush against it with exposed legs while wearing shorts, or step on it barefoot, even with socks on—and then sting for a few days even to (sometimes) leave a red rash, serve any useful purpose?

It can sting sometimes for a few hours or a few days but usually for 24 hours. The pain turns to an irritation that feels like tiny needles pricking you just under your skin, being amplified when it gets wet. My southern wild local species has a very potent punch to its sting. The plant looks a little like a hairy species of mint, which is closely related to our nettles, as these are often called.

Two plants of the dwarf species that ranges throughout the Deep South and Florida. While the northern species are much taller, with longer leaves, the dwarf species gets up to barely a foot tall.

The stinging hairs (or, nearly microscopic spines) containing formic acid can be rendered harmless by boiling, drying, or high heat. The stems of the taller species are reported to be made into cordage for things that include fishing line and snare wire. Only the young leaves are reported to be good for food, as they form hard crystals with age that can't be completely unarmed and don't digest well. However, nettles have been used for quite a while—European monks and nuns used its broth, made tea, and as a boiled green and they were quite healthy for it. They used the fiber for their apparel, used leaves to curdle milk for cheese, made a liquid fertilizer and organic pesticide from it, and maybe even made a soup with the roots (questionable).

It's somewhat sharply toothed leaves are what distinguishes our local dwarf variety from a similar looking little edible wild plant called, pellitory or cucumber weed—which does not sting, smells and tastes like cucumbers, and grows at the same time around here as our nettles in shady spots but with no teeth on the leaves. Use the leaves of stinging nettles boiled or lay the whole plant on the hot ashes of a campfire until thoroughly heated and wilted and eat the leaves.

America's many species of *Urtica*, both native and introduced, prefers rich disturbed ground. Using tongs or gloves to harvest and then scissors to cut the leaves off of the stems is the preferred way. Other than hanging the whole plant out to dry and making a powder from the leaves for soup thickener or flour additive, the leaves themselves can be placed in a pot with a little water and boiled or placed in a steamer and steamed before consuming.

It has medicinal uses as well. It is reported that an arthritic-based pain and inflammation can be eliminated by purposely stinging the joint or part of the body where the inflammation occurs daily for anywhere from a few days to a week. If stung by one, the best reported way to relieve the pain is reported by making a paste of baking soda and placing it on the sting. Reports say that these plants are high in basic nutrition. Many report also that they are high in protein. Also on the medicinal side, stinging nettle has been a traditional remedy for rheumatism, gout, hay fever, and lately it has found usefulness in the treatment of enlarged prostates.

A stand of nettles.

Toothed leaf edges.

Stingers along the underside of the leaves.

SURINAM CHERRY, *Eugenia axillaris*

This plant is native to South America but was introduced to India by Portuguese explorers centuries ago. From there they carried seeds all the way to southern Europe and finally to Florida. It is cultivated and naturalized in tropical and subtropical regions around the globe where temperatures only rarely get below 32°F. Between the 1930s and the 1960s they were widely planted in central and southern Florida—even to escape into many wildlife areas as a somewhat invasive species. I'm trying to let some invade the property around the trailer where I'm living at the moment.

When they are completely ripe and blood-red they are harvested for their tart sweetness. I'll admit that the berries are sweet and juicy when blood-red ripe but the resinous tartness of the slightly underripe berries will not harm you and I enjoy their strong flavor. I've been eating them on rare occasions as far back as I can remember. Some of us here in parts of Florida are lucky to have two crops of fruit per year—a spring crop ripening in May or June and then a completely different crop around October/November provided the season is not too dry. It is a sub-tropical plant but can grow through most of the Southeast. You may have to save some seeds for after the possible occasion when a hard-freeze kills them. It is also reported that some areas could see more than two crops per year. Even though they are called cherries, they are not related to cherries. The name Surinam comes from a small country in South America. They don't exactly come from there, generally from Brazil, they just happen to grow in Surinam, South America also and the name stuck.

They are reported to be used in pies, preserves, jellies, jams, syrups, relish, vinegar, wine, and liquor. I've seen a syrup made from them but whenever I've found them I just pop them into my mouth and delicately chew off the pulp from the large, single (sometimes double), roundish seed. The seeds are not used for anything, as far as I know, and are not edible (swallowing one probably won't hurt you, but they are usually too big to swallow mistakenly). There is a cousin of these which produce the berries as well but turn almost black when ripe and grows in Europe. That kind is reported to be less sweet than the red-ripe species shown here.

My sister Nancy bought me a young plant from somewhere and brought it to me to plant in my garden. They might require more than one to produce fruit, I don't know. I wouldn't mind another Surinam cherry bush around my trailer—or a few more.

SWEET GUM, *Liquidambar styraciflua*

The saplings of this tree look like bushy shrubs with hanging branches but they can turn into some of the tallest trees in Florida, potentially up to seventy feet high with canopies that can spread out to fifty feet wide.

Abundant in my central Florida woods, sweet gum ranges from central Florida north to about Maine and across the lower portion of the mid-west to the continental divide. The leaves remind me of the star-symbol with five to seven very pointed lobes and slightly toothed margins. The leaves turn from their original bright green to orange and finally to red in the fall and hang on to the tree longer than most other deciduous trees. The trees produce spiny, tan/brown and round, inedible seed-balls that fall off after turning brown in the spring. No part of this tree is edible, at least as far as actually consuming it for a meal. However, the sap/juice dries into a thick, gummy resin that is a sweet tasting sap and is not officially edible but can be extracted and consumed in very small amounts by chewing the resin like gum—just don't swallow the gum.

This juicy sap and dry gum has been used by natives and pioneers as a perfume, an incense, and the sweet chewing gum that gave this tree its name. Sweet gum trees are reported to attract wildlife, tolerate drought and has very colorful foliage. If it wasn't growing wild here it would be an introduced species because of its many positive attributes. It is also reported to be good for cleaning teeth by using the skinned twigs like a toothbrush.

SWORD FERN, *Nephrolepis cordifolia*

Edible, brown tubers (also called "stolens") that grow on the root-mass of this particular fern. The tuber itself contains about 96 percent water with small amounts of protein, carbohydrates, and other nutrients. Considered a pest plant by the state, it grows profusely around here year-round in well-shaded lots and woods and makes a good garden perimeter (if controlled). To harvest the tubers, you just grab the plant near the ground and pull up. There will frequently be no tubers, or a few, or many.

Mature tubers are light brown and slightly fuzzy.

There are reportedly five kinds of sword fern in Florida, yet, only one produces the brown, marble-sized, fuzzy, edible tubers. The ferns without tubers is the native varieties while the one specie with tubers is non-native and very invasive. The best way to tell if you have sword ferns with edible tubers is to just pull up a plant at the base. If it has those tubers along the roots close to the root-ball, they are edible. I don't know how prolific they grow in other parts of the state but around here there are thousands in many wooded areas, used lots, and vacant lots. Unfortunately, there are also many areas where similar species without the tubers grow in abundance.

The tubers have a dirty, earthy flavor even when rinsed off well and are a crunchy delight to anyone in need of water or in desperate need of a meal. The dirty/earthy flavor is a little off-putting but when hungry enough it won't matter. They have so much water in them that you get a burst of it when you bite into one.

I pulled these up in a patch of woods on the outskirts of a tent city where homeless people live in tents hidden away from public view. I teach some of them about the plants around them. They need not go hungry just because society has cast them out. The round tubers are edible raw or cooked. Boiled, they turn out mushy. Raw, they are crunchy. The young tubers are white and taste nutty. The mature ones are light brown and slightly fuzzy. The young white ones can be baked at 350°F for about thirty minutes and then crushed to powder for a non-caffeinated coffee substitute. Bake mature ones for a while to make a slightly chewy and sweetish treat. However, the water inside gets very hot when cooked, so let them cool first.

This is a prime, invasive, prolific, foraging food to know. There's one similar looking fern here that does not grow the tubers, in particular a fern designated as *Nephrolepis exalta*. There are other kinds of ferns that produce young sprouts that are edible up north and in other parts of the world in their young unfurled state known as fiddleheads. There are three species in particular that are edible in that very early stage after being washed and rubbing off a brown fuzz or scales from them and then boiling them. Those species include ostrich fern, *Matteuccia struthiopteris*; bracken fern, *Pteridium aquilinum*; and cinnamon fern, *Osumunda cinnamomea*. None of these fiddleheads are supposedly found in the Deep South as they are in northern areas and the ones that do are reportedly not edible here for some reason. However, even those edible fiddlehead ferns have warnings attached. Edible fiddleheads can be found worldwide, even in the Amazon. The edible ones in upper New England and New Brunswick, Canada will be the spring fiddleheads without any fuzz on the heads. The ones with fuzz might be toxic. You will have to look to other sources for detailed information on fiddleheads.

I've been planting these tuberous *Nephrolepus* sword fern around the perimeter of my garden by harvesting the tubers in vacant empty lots where there are thousands of them and planting the tubers like seeds. They take only a few years to mature and continuously produce new tubers around them. I've pulled up many sword ferns and picked a dozen of those tubers or less from each plant. You can even pull up a plant, take the tubers off, and replant the plant. The tubers are attached to the roots by very thin root-fibers.

Be aware that the toxic vine *Dioscoria bulbifera*, the air potato, the toxic cousin of the edible winged yam, frequently attaches itself to sword fern roots to grow their vines from. The young seeds from the toxic potato, *D. Bulbifera*, will sometimes look similar to the sword fern tubers when young and small. The young white sword fern tubers are not fuzzy or brown like the mature tubers. Their white appearance is very similar to the very young air potatoes but the toxic air potatoes will almost always have a thin, round, green vine attached to them and a slightly bumpy surface. Do not mistake the young air potato roots for the young sword fern tubers; the offending air potato root will taste very bitter—whether boiled, baked, roasted or raw—and must be spat out. They are not edible. A general rule in foraging comes into play that if a root is very bitter tasting—particularly if it is not supposed to taste bitter—just spit it out immediately. The sword fern tubers have no bitterness at all. If you bite into what you think is one and it's bitter, spit it out.

TANSY MUSTARD, *Descurainia pinnata*

This member of the Brassica family (the mustards) has distinct characteristics similar to the *Lepidium* species genera like our local peppergrass and even similar to our *Brassica* genera of wild mustard. Another similar looking edible cousin, but of a more northern species, is called shepherd's purse. Their main similarity is the seedpod structure near the top of each stalk. The leaves and peppery little fruits that turn into seedpods are edible raw or cooked at any stage of development. The seeds make a good seasoning and soup thickener. A poultice was used for toothache pain. An infusion of the leaves was used as a wash on sores. The leaves, flowers and seeds are edible raw or cooked.

D. pinnata (tansy mustard) ranges from Quebec to British Columbia, then down to Florida and across to California and Mexico. Our species is also called Western tansy mustard because of a species that also exists on the other side of the globe. Being in the western hemisphere makes some things "Western" to Europeans, Asians, and elsewhere other than the western hemisphere.

Many Native American tribes around the continent used this plant in many ways. The seeds were even traded among them for other goods. A mush made from the teeny-tiny seeds helped quiet a queasy stomach—no doubt because of the mucilaginous nature of the plant's seeds. Note that this plant is toxic to grazing livestock in large quantities.

As a survival strategy, I would dry some seeds now to save for an event that requires foraging to survive and use them for planting.

TAR VINE, *Boerhavia diffusa*

I see this plant around in disturbed ground near sidewalks, stores, houses, and such so much that it only seems to grow where people go the most and nearly year-round, locally. That is a problem with many edible wild plants if survival among a wilderness environment becomes a necessity. Most of our most common edible plants tend to stay close to human activity. When I venture out on the local hiking trials I notice many an edible plant species near the roads and trail-heads. As soon as I hike into the woods, however, most of those usual plants dwindle down to nothing until I see fewer kinds of edibles.

The young leaves of tar vine when boiled have an interesting flavor, somewhat bland, that mixes well with other greens or sparingly in soups and stews. If they have a rank flavor, put fresh water into the pot and boil them a little more.

It is a tropical, subtropical, and southern temperate zone plant around the world which can be found here and as far north as South Carolina.

The scientific, botanical genus is *Boerhavia* but the exact species/variety name is somewhat disputed by botanists. You won't find this plant in any of the usual published edible wild plant guidebooks. Not many experts know about this one.

The root can be woody, and it certainly appears to be, but when lightly roasted and peeled (remove outer skin) before consuming as is or adding to soups and stews it is reported to have a flavor similar to parsnips. I haven't tried eating the root yet. If eaten raw, it can raise blood pressure. People with high blood pressure should never eat it raw and maybe sparingly, if at all, thoroughly cooked.

I've tried the young leaves boiled. In a survival situation, the roots could be wrapped in aluminum foil and placed within the hot ashes of a campfire or laid on top of burning hot coals. Because of the woody nature of the roots I examined I suggest baking in the hot ashes of the campfire for several hours as a famine-food resource. However, it might still turn out too woody to eat.

There may also be the potential to bake and grind the seeds into a powder and then add that to baked goods like ashcakes.

This is a plant that I've seen around for many years while wondering whether it was edible. I would classify the boiled young leaves as a good, but not great, added ingredient to a survival stew. I wouldn't advise including it in everyday home-cooked meals until trying it first. A little salt and pepper might make an interesting side dish for the hungry survivalist. Finding it growing in clean soil will also be a challenge considering it likes disturbed ground.

TINDORA, IVY GOURD, *Coccinia grandis*

I have a neighbor from India down the road that has many tropical plants and vines surrounding his property. The vine plants all died out for the winter but are now (March/April) producing prolific new growth of vine, blossom, and fruit.

Larger than the creeping cucumber but similar, this is called ivy gourd by some and Tindora by my Indian friend. The skin is tougher than the creeping cucumber and the garden-variety cucumber but this one has an interesting feature. The creeping cucumber turns black, becoming quite toxic and inedible. However, this ivy gourd turns red from the inside out, becoming soft, delicate, sweet, juicy, and pleasant—very edible. The young leaves and tops of the shoots can be used as a potherb in soups and steamed with rice. However, allowing the plant to proliferate to produce just the fruit is your best course until a famine situation. The best fruits for a salad are the youngest green ones and I advise chopping them so that the toughness of the skin does not create an unpleasant chewing experience.

The fruits can also be steamed or boiled in soups and even fermented. The red-ripe sweet ones are eaten as is or candied. There are two varieties of the plant that can be either sweet or bitter with no other difference than that. The fruits are packed with cucumber-like seeds.

When I asked my Indian friend if I could grow some of my own vines in my garden he cut off a thick, tan woody branch with a green vine growing from it and handed it to me. It was spring, so I figured it a good time to ask. He instructed me to stick the woody end of the branch a few inches into the ground and water it twice a day, morning and evening. I did as he instructed and the new vines began sprouting up from the branch within a week.

Coccinia grandis has been introduced and spread around the tropical to sub-tropical regions of the world and is definitely a choice edible. Although probably a rare find in any Florida woods, if apocalyptic events forces the masses to immigrate away from their cities and towns a survivalist/forager with this knowledge will have a better chance than those without. Because, if ignorant and destitute refugees discover this fruiting vine they will have no idea whether any of it is safe to eat or not—being forced to pass it up on the side of caution and continue searching for some old abandoned Twinkies factory.

TURK'S CAP MALLOW, *Malvaviscus species*

Turk's cap, *Malvaviscus arboreus* or *penduliflorus*, a.k.a. wax mallow and turk's cap mallow. This bushy shrub has been a UFO to me since my early childhood . . . an Unidentified Flowering Object.

I don't remember much from my earliest childhood—being well over a half-century now—but the sweet flavor of nectar coming straight from the back of a flower created a unique and unusual sensation of a visual-memory and taste-memory combination. When two or more of your five senses combine together in some unique way it imprints the experience into your mind more-so than other occurrences, making it easier to remember. Both of my surviving siblings remembers it as well.

The flower is unique in that it never opens its overlapping petals and when you pull off the flower from the shrub, then pull off the green calyx/sepals, the end of it now resembles a tube that you can put up to your mouth and suck in a burst of sweet nectar when there is still nectar in it. In dry conditions and as the flowers get old sometimes the nectar content will be mostly gone.

I only recently noticed the plant again after many years of forgetting about it while walking down highway 301 in Zephyrhills and recognized it. I performed the old ritual from my childhood and it was *déjà vu!*

Then, the very next day, I was given a book by my oldest friend Ray called *The National Audubon Society Field Guide to Florida* and found a photo in it of the very same plant—revealing to me at long last what it actually was. I don't remember who showed me how to get nectar from the flower; that memory did not endure time. I then asked and received confirmation on my identification of the plant from the edibles expert Green Deane along with a bonus of finding out that the red parts of the flowers are edible.

I'm not surprised that the plant is a member of the mallow family, as there's edible quality in a few other mallows. The hollyhock and hibiscus are also members. My plant is closely related to hibiscus. There are health benefits for hibiscus tea. The hollyhock, *Altheae species* has leaves reported to be edible as a salad ingredient or pot herb (raw or cooked). *Altheae* is the same genus as marshmallow—which is originally how the sweet con-

Hollyhock.

fection marshmallow was made from the root and seeds of the plant *Altheae officinalis,* commonly called, marsh mallow. The hibiscus flowers, *Hibiscus species*, are used in herbal teas commercially and most hibiscus plants have edible flowers petals. The red portions of these flowers shown here are edible raw or cooked.

The most popular wild edible of the mallow family is a plant commonly called cheeseweed from the *Malva* genus (*Malva neglecta*) because of the edible, little, wheel-shaped (with its spoke-like indentations) fruits. I haven't found any cheeseweed in Florida. The book by John Kallas PhD, *Edible Wild Plants: Wild Foods from Dirt to Plate,* has a long chapter on mallow, twenty-seven pages, with recipes and including his always remarkably clear, color photos (better than mine).

Okra, *Abelmoschus esculentus,* is another member of the mallow family—being just immature seed-pods. Many members of the mallow family have medicinal quality because they are mucilaginous—plants with a clear slimy sap or juice (like okra). The aloe vera plant produces a slimy gel-like substance that can moisten burned or irritated skin better than just about anything and has been suggested to have actual healing properties. Plants with thick sap can be used medicinally for many ailments.

The biennial plant designated *Malva sylvestris* with its cluster of pink one-inch flowers have edible seed capsules and flowers that can be added fresh to salads.

There are many flowers with edible petals. The petals are usually clipped away from the center of the flower where it is often bitter tasting. Petals are always picked as fresh as possible, often being frozen for later use—to be added to a salad or plate-entree at the last minute or as a garnish, including for desserts.

When you study the edibility of plants you focus just on which exact plants are well documented as edible. After quite a while of discovering edible species, when you see a plant you can't exactly identify positively right away, the chances become more likely that the edibility of it is questionable and you must—for safety's sake—assume that it is toxic before being presented with positive proof that it isn't.

VIOLETS, *Viola species*

A report states that there are about 850 species of violets. The "sweet" are scented while the "wood" variety are less so.

The family of plants they belong to are called *Violaceae*, or the violet family. These heart-shaped leaves are probably the species *Viola affinis*. I don't know the exact species name with so many different varieties. The plant that is called, African violet is not in the *Viola* genus, nor of the violet family, and is toxic.

However, all violets in the *Viola* genus are known to have edible leaves and flowers. The dried leaves can make a prized tea and the flowers can make a jelly. The tea is a favorite of author/instructor Tom Elpel.

For the sake of survival foraging; the leaves are high in vitamins C and A but excessive amounts can be diuretic, or at least a mild laxative effect.

The leaves and flowers make a fine addition to a swamp salad, which is simply what I call a salad foraged on Florida's wild raw edibles. The leaves are a very healthy addition to a stew, soup, steamed dish, or added to boiled greens.

As you can see from the photos, the leaves are heart-shaped to almost round that gives the appearance of a cone as they unfurl. The flowers on those are white to violet colored. My camera does not bring out the violet color as well as it should. The other violet was in deep woods and has very white flowers with leaves ranging from oblong to linear and moderately toothed. Those violets are probably the ones designated as *Viola lanceolata* but I don't know. The wild violets I've seen over the years have been of the small variety, many times in deep Florida woods. If you see any violets in a planter-pot or landscaped flower garden they may have been sprayed with poisons and best left alone. That goes for all edibles that are a little less than wild. Be cautious of landscaping.

To know a violet from other flowers (because the leaf-structure can vary greatly) notice the color of the flowers can range from blue, purple, lavender, yellow, and white (variegated) depending on the species. The yellow ones tend to have more of the natural substance that can make one diuretic, maybe even nauseous. The yellow flowered violets are best left alone.

Notice from the close-up top photo that two of the petals appear slightly larger, close together, pointing upward and curved slightly back. The other three are also together but pointing downward with variegated lines, or veins, along them. The middle petal of those three of this species is the most veined and seems to be deviated from the other two—as if being squished between them. I've been eating the leaves of wild violets as a trail nibble and in stews for years now.

My first introduction to violets was by looking at photos and sketches in books for many years before finding one in the deep woods of central Florida. Wherever you might find one, you will be likely to find more nearby.

Black Walnut, *Juglans nigra*

This is such a valuable resource not only for the food harvested from nuts, but for medicine in the nut hulls, fuel and building materials from the tree itself. It grows from New England west to Minnesota south to the Gulf of Mexico and across northern Florida. It can grow to more than sixty feet and can live past one hundred years. A large tree with compound leaves, alternately arranged on the branches. Each leaf has fifteen to twenty-tree leaflets, the terminal leaf is often missing; leaf surface is dull with a slightly hairy or downy texture on the underside. Walnut and many other nut trees have a very strong and I think pleasant scent when touched that leaves a sticky residue on your hands. There are features of all plants that help with identification. Practice and experience will make things easier all the time. Rely on all your senses, sight, smell, taste (as long as you know it is safe), as well as books and guides. Come to know your body and how you respond as an individual to the world around you. Your primal being will awaken more every day in the process.

It is such a tradition in regions where this tree grows to harvest the nuts in the Fall, and either process them, or sell them in large quantities to local buyers that you will find no shortage of methods of collecting, curing, and extracting these hard to get at, but very worthwhile nuts.

Take a burlap sack, or any bag for that matter, with you most anywhere walnuts are found, and you should be able to fill it quite easily. Press the hull of the walnut with your thumb; ripe nuts will show an indentation. Get as many as you can off the tree rather than off the ground, but those on the ground can be collected too.

Removing the hulls, while not too difficult once you get the hang of it, is a very messy process, and even though you may wear gloves to keep from staining your hands, you will probably stain them dark yellow to brown anyway. This stain, while not harmful other than maybe making your hands hurt for a while doesn't wash off either by the way and can take a week or so to wear off. I never really cared about that aspect much, although it can be a little hard on the skin leaving your hands a little raw after hulling the nuts. Even with all this effort though, all the resulting goodness is worthwhile. Harvest walnuts when they fall to the ground, or off the tree if you can get at them, and before the hulls turn black and mushy. They are still probably fine after turning black, and many people will let them turn on purpose to make the hulling process easier. Native nuts come into maturity September through October. I think it best to collect nuts as soon as possible so they don't mold, and so juice from the hulls doesn't penetrate the hard shell surrounding the nut meat. I find the best way to hull walnuts is with a sharp paring knife, or other small knife, cutting all the way around the nut and peeling the two halves away. Some people will put them in their driveway and drive over them, but this method can crack the shells and you don't want to do that. There seems to be a perfect time to remove the hulls when they are soft enough to cut and remove but before they become too mushy. This is no doubt a tedious, time-consuming process, but it doesn't take much energy, and the rewards are worth it. If a hull is too hard to remove, just set it aside and try again in a few days. Walnuts are by no means an instant food, but their nutrition and medicine are worth the time and effort. By the way, if you find worms in the hulls, don't worry; they don't affect the nut meat at all.

The next step is to rinse the hard nuts in their shells as well as possible scrubbing with a brush if necessary to get the job done. Rinse them in a container of water such as a bucket or improvised container, agitating them with a stick, or shovel, anything will do. Repeat this process until the nuts are as clean as possible. Any nuts that float are usually not any good. Do check those floating walnuts for edible grubs though, then throw the rest out and keep only those that sink. The water test gets rid of most but not all of the bad nuts. This process works for acorns and other nuts too by the way. Once clean, spread nuts out still in the shell to dry in a warm dry place, on some sort of rack or screen making sure they get air circulating all around them where they can air dry and cure for at least two weeks, and up to six weeks. This process may be done near your fire or any place warm and dry as the best drying temperature is said to be around 95 degrees. This will bring out the flavor of the nut meat among other things. Put the clean hulled nuts in a cool, dry, ventilated area out of sunlight. A nut is cured when it breaks with a crisp snap. If you don't cure them the right way, they will spoil. It is best to store them at 60°F or less. Ideal humidity is 70 percent. In the case of some things, walnuts included here, keep them in a well ventilated spot out of the sun. Make sure to protect your stash from critters as they are a favorite for squirrels and other foragers, and they will go to great measures to get them. This is definitely a long term survival food, but worth it in nutrition. Two pounds of walnuts off the tree will produce about a cup of nutmeat.

If you plan to store the nuts for any length of time, leave them in the shell in an airtight container where they will keep for about a year. When you're ready to shell the walnuts, put them into hot water and soak for about a day. Next day put them in hot water again for about two hours. Then shell. When you do crack the shells, and pick out the meat, if you have access to a freezer, you can freeze them in freezer bags for up to two years. You can also salt brine them or dehydrate them, but I've never tried that, only heard it can be done. Preserved nuts can be stored at room temperature if kept sealed up for awhile. I don't know just how long, because they are such good food they don't hang around too long.

Walnuts can be difficult to crack, but with practice and the right tools can be accomplished You can just hit them with a rock or hammer which usually manages to break the shell, but smash the nut in the process A pair of vice grips works very well on walnuts, and many other types of nuts if you are lucky enough to have some.

As nutrition goes, black walnuts are about 60 percent fat, 20 percent carbs, and 25 percent protein. If all you had were walnuts to eat, it would take about three cups, or 150 nuts cracked and picked to provide enough calories for long term survival I don't recommend making a sole diet of walnuts, but the numbers are here to give you an idea of what it takes.

Eating this many walnuts, or a mono diet of any kind, is a very bad idea. In the case of walnuts, or any nut, seed, or legume, there is an issue of phytic acid. Modern evidence suggests that at least some of the phytate can be broken down by soaking and roasting. The majority of this data indicates that soaking nuts for eighteen hours, dehydrating at very low temperatures either in a food dehydrator or a low temperature oven, if you have such modern conveniences available. It's important to note that phytic acid does not leach minerals that are already stored in the body, it only inhibits the absorption of minerals from food in which phytic acid is present. Studies show that phytic acid interferes with the enzymes we need to digest our food, including pepsin, needed for the breakdown of proteins in the stomach, and amylase, which is required for the breakdown of starch. Phytic acid also inhibits the enzyme trypsin, which is needed for protein digestion in the small intestine. Diets high in phytate cause mineral deficiencies. For example, rickets and osteoporosis are common in societies where cereal grains are a staple part of the diet. In short, don't try to live on nuts and grains alone.

Phytic acid is not all bad, so don't throw out all your nuts, grains, and other foods containing it, but do take care to soak, sprout, even roast these foods to inhibit some of the negative effects. It doesn't leach nutrients from your body, but rather inhibits the body's ability to absorb them. Also, the body needs some phytic acid to function properly. This is all a very complex issue, and needs further research beyond the scope of this writing. I think as I always have that moderation and balance is key in the meantime, there are several methods that can be used to reduce the phytic acid content of foods. This includes soaking, sprouting, and fermentation. More on this elsewhere. The main thing, is to have a variety of survival foods available. Eat a moderate amount of them, and you are a giant step ahead of the game making a difference in just surviving, and actually thriving in a given situation. Foraging is hard work, but the quality of what you get to eat makes it worth the effort. There is simply no substitute for nutritious food.

Food is the primary focus here, but the medicinal properties of walnut hulls, the green outer part of the fruit is worth mentioning especially in survival scenarios. Green hulls can be dried, pulverized, and encapsulated somehow, or tinctured in alcohol. They are an excellent human anti parasitic, and anti-fungal among other things used both internally and externally. More on medicinal properties at another time walnut wood when cured is an excellent firewood, and is also very good for making bowls, spoons, furniture, and so on. We're talking long term here though.

WATER HYACINTH, *Eichhornia crassipes*

This stuff can completely cover lakes, ponds, streams, and slow-moving, freshwater rivers in no time. Plants can double in size every two weeks as if being born pregnant.

Water hyacinth was introduced to Florida and many other parts of the country about 150 years ago. It could have been used as a resource for cattle feed, mulch, dry fuel, chicken feed, fertilizer, people food, and more but it is now deemed a controlled substance—invasive and noxious—and must be eliminated from existence no matter what. Or so says the governing body of this state.

Seriously, a famine-food resource that could feed thousands with 18.7 percent protein, 17.1 percent fiber, 36.6 percent carbohydrates with vitamins A, B1, B2, and beta-carotene is an illegal substance?

Florida statute 62C-52.011 FAC states "It is illegal to collect, transport, possess or cultivate this plant." Why? They don't want it ending up in a lake, pond, stream, and so on, where it will cover the surface in no time at all. I guess it is bad for tourism if our waterways are covered with useful noxious weeds or, since it isn't cattle, coal, gas, phosphate, sugar, oranges, uranium, or fast food no one wants to use it. It isn't profitable.

In a survival/famine/doomsday scenario, that rule would no longer be in effect when the survival of tens of thousands—if not millions—of refugees have to resort to foraging for food. There is a clause somewhere in the regulations of protected plants which allows usage in an emergency. If one is lost in the deep swamp and survival depends on harvesting a protected species, there's nothing illegal about it. I'm not absolutely sure that the clause exists but I've heard that a judge will not convict someone of that kind of violation if the person(s) had no choice. The problem that they have with this plant is its ability to spread if transported away from where it already exists. Harvesting, boiling, and eating on the spot would not be illegal.

Notice, for identification, the bulbous float or round, green gourd-like stem where the leaves grow from is unique to water hyacinth. These round floats can be deep-fried. When the flowers appear, they are violet spikes with yellow spots in the middle. The flowers are edible boiled.

This plant would have advantages in a future apocalyptic world. It absorbs chemical pollutants from contaminated water—cleaning the water. Note: Harvest water hyacinth (as all edible aquatic plants) from clean water only. Do not forage downstream from any mining operation or downhill from any interstate, power plant, major highway, cattle/dairy farm, or large factory. Water hyacinth produces methane—which could be used as a renewable energy source. It is nutritious and wholesome from wholesome water—an extra incentive to protect Florida waters.

Unfortunately, as they do with Roundup's poison around here, beware of a state, county, and their locals that fill our environment with poisons in an attempt to kill noxious, unwanted weeds like the water hyacinth. It almost seems like all of the actions of the (chamber of) commerce-driven elected officials are dead-set against having clean air, soil, or water. They continue to poison everything in some vain and misguided attempt to *make it all look pretty*—in their own shallow, shortsighted way or to profit from it somehow.

The shoots, leaves, and flowers can be boiled or fried and the youngest bulbous, round parts can be deep fried. Youngest shoots are best. A report claims that this plant can make some people itch after eating. Whether cooked or raw, they are reported to cause itching all over to some people—"the itches" it's called—so it is best to try only a little at first.

It does not soften up much in boiling so I chopped it up and boiled it separately for a few minutes before adding to a stew. YES! I'm a rebel all right. I collected, transported, and consumed an illegal substance.

WAX MYRTLE, *Myrica cerfera*

This is called wax myrtle, a.k.a. bayberry, a large shrub to small tree with thick bunches of lanceolate, alternating leaves, smooth on top but hairy underneath, with a medicinal and bay-leaf kind of smell when crushed.

These tiny BB-sized berries are light-green to bluish-white in our late summer through winter. The leaves or berries may be dried, crushed, and used sparingly as a seasoning (particularly for meat). However, the berries are very waxy—hence the name—and even used to make a wax substitute. The process consists of simmering mature berries and skimming off the waxy film from the surface as it forms, then collecting it to cool and harden. The way natives made candles was to dip floating string (cordage) along the surface of the boiling berries, hang it aside to cool, then dip the string along the surface again, repeating the process until it forms a candle. The resulting candles was made by natives for unknown centuries. The trees requires male and female trees to be in the same vicinity in order to produce the waxy fruit.

While our best natural mosquito repellent comes from the leaves of beautyberry, *Calicarpa americana*, the wax myrtle leaves are also known for their use as an insect repellent but not as good. Just rub the leaves all over yourself as you would with beautyberry leaves. The natives also dried and

The BB-sized berries are light-green to bluish-white in Florida's late summer through winter.

smoked the leaves but I don't suggest smoking anything at all in any kind of post-apocalyptic world or survival/doomsday/famine scenario. The ripe berries of wax myrtle are not exactly edible but can be consumed as a seasoning on a limited basis when dried, crushed, and ground. There are many species of *Myrica* around the world with similar uses to some extent.

WHITE SNOW, *Drymaria cordata/diandra*

When the tiny, green, sticky, Velcro type seedpods grow up above the rest of the plant in colonies they retain a whitish glow from the early morning or late afternoon sun giving the visual impression of a thin light front —hence the name that I prefer to call it, white snow. Other names consist of two-word phrases ending with the name chickweed, because of some similar characteristics to the more edible and popular chickweed, *Stellaria media*.

I've seen this weedy little plant around over the years and wondered what it was. Even though this plant is fairly easy to identify, don't mistake it for its toxic cousins that grow out west. Once you know what this one looks like you shouldn't have any problems identifying it thereafter. This plant, like many, is one that you won't know until you really know it.

Found mostly in our cooler months here, the leaves are edible raw or cooked as additions to salads, stews, or greens. Their mild flavor blends well that way but shouldn't be eaten by the handfuls. This plant has medicinal properties of which I know nothing about except for the general rule in foraging that plants with medicinal herbal constituents are usually not edible, or require preparation processes to make edible, and/or are only eaten in small amounts. Like chickweed, the stems have an elastic cord through it. Unlike chickweed, the leaves on white snow have barely any stem (petiole) at all, appearing to be attached directly to the main-stem, and the flowers on this plant are tiny and white and similar to chickweed. This is an annual plant that grows most of the year, usually about a foot long with the leaf-nodes frequently sprouting roots to attach to the ground as it crawls along. This should only be eaten sparingly.

WILD BLUEBERRY, *Vaccinium species*

Note to reader: I have reason to believe that the photo I took here of this supposed blueberry may not be a true blueberry or huckleberry and I can't be sure that this berry is even edible until confirmation one way or the other. I did not taste-test this berry when I found it and have not seen any like it since. However, there are wild blueberries in Florida and the Southeast. The leaves, however, are reported to be much smaller than these. While there are commercially grown and sold blueberries with these leaves, I don't exactly know if this is a blueberry. It sure looks like it to me.

Along one of my favorite hiking trails I found this small bush. I've seen lots of berries out there that are somewhat similar but not with the five-pointed, star-shaped calyx that stays on the fruit also known as a "crown berry" type and called "star-berries" by natives.

In general, berries that are marble-round of various colors can range in edibility according to their color when ripe. This does not include drupe berries like blackberries and raspberries or strawberries. This is not a rule, just a generalization. Red round berries are seldom edible, like the holly species, with the exception of wintergreen berries and a few others. Black berries that are round are edible species about half of the time. Round berries that are blue when ripe are usually not edible, making blueberries unique. Yellow berries are hardly ever edible. White ones are almost never edible.

In New England and Pennsylvania, I picked two basic kinds of blueberries, a high-bush species and a low-bush. While there is a species of the high-bush kind in Florida, the berries are reported to be edible but not exactly palatable.

Blueberries have been a foraging favorite of both man and beast throughout history and almost everywhere around the world. The ones I've found were few and far between and are among the upland mixed forests of sandy saw palmetto prairies, pine flatwoods, and scrubs.

Blueberries are one of the best sources of antioxidants, which are extremely important in order to maintain a healthy immune system, something a survivor will need maybe more than anything else.

However, wild blueberries are seldom easy to find in Florida's suburban, rural, and wilderness areas and there are look-a-likes that can either be unpalatable or even slightly toxic. I suggest putting one like this in your mouth, taste it thoroughly, then spit it out and wait a while to see if there is any bad reaction to just tasting it. However, if it looks and tastes like an edible blueberry, it probably is.

WILD GRAPES, *Vitis rotundifolia*

America has had a grape-killing bacteria being spread by insects and called Pierce's Disease for centuries that kills all kinds of grapes other than the muscadine species. California has been able to control the disease so that a variety of grapes can be grown there but the Southeast remains relatively free of all grapes other than native muscadines, escaped and introduced muscadines, and hybrids.

To identify them, first remember that the shape of a grape seed is that of a teardrop not the shape of a crescent moon (quarter-moon). A seed shaped like a crescent moon is a moonseed, *Menispermum canadense* which is not a grape, has very different leaves, and has a poisonous seed. Some native wild grapes have a seed that could be shaped more like a half-moon than a teardrop and is edible, so it can vary.

Look for tendrils along the vines and near the tips of the vines—a forked tendril (or "split") is an escaped cultivar while a single tendril is a native—to be sure you have a grape vine. Most vines have tendrils which allow them to crawl and climb. The leaf shapes are not the best identifier either because they vary somewhat between varieties. There are fruits of grape ranging from blue to black with reds and greens and frequently get almost as large as the large cultivated, store-bought grapes. The native muscadines ripen to black and are usually among the smallest.

From Florida to Texas and northward wherever grapes grow you will find native grapes and escaped cultivars of muscadines fairly exclusively. Pierce's disease is known to kill off different species of grape and trying to grow any kind other than the many varieties of muscadines and hybrids will not work here in the Southeast US.

I've noticed over the years around here that we have tons of wild grape vines—absolutely invasive—but finding the ones producing fruit is very difficult. It is reported two specific reasons for it. About 90 percent or more of the vines of natives around here are male and the few females there are will only fruit sporadically. Only the non-native, introduced and escaped species produce almost every year.

Other notable information on grapes include drinkable sap from the woody sections of vines. If you cut through the vine and then cut halfway into the vine further up. Then step back and watch for the sap leaking off the cut to the ground and place a container underneath it. If that doesn't work, try cutting another vine off completely at the lowest point and place the container under that somehow. This and other methods can be used successfully for obtaining drinking water from other kinds of woody vines. If the sap from a vine is very bitter, it should be discarded. Use your best judgment on that one, weighing the risk versus the reward. I don't have enough information on water-vines to make absolute statements on them. In general, there are vines in the Southeast here and around the world that produce drinkable water.

Even though the seeds are not the kind that contain cyanide I don't suggest swallowing them. The seeds can, however, be pressed for their oil. Even though the young leaves of the more delicate hybrids are edible boiled I won't suggest it for two reasons: One, they all generally look too fibrous, and two, there will usually be better wild greens around you if you know what to look for. The photos above show our main species, one of which is also called Southern fox grape and what appears to be another species. Be aware that the fruit of the very toxic vine called Virginia creeper, a.k.a. woodbine, looks similar to native grapes but the leaves are very different and are deeply lobed and erratically toothed.

WILD MUSTARDS, *Brassica species* & *Raphanus species*

The photos show the *Brassica* mustard or wild mustard. The mustards include well known members of the Brassicaceae family called, crucifers (for the shape of the four petaled, yellow flower which resembles a crucifix) and include broccoli, cabbage, cauliflower, kale, and bok choy. They are as nutritious and important in our diet as any vegetation could be. The wild mustard of the genus *Brassica* looks very similar to the wild edible plant of the genus *Raphanus* called wild radish. We get both species here at the same time.

It appears the two species might be interbreeding around here. The differences between *Brassica* and *Raphanus* are:

Raphanus—low growing, sprawling.
Brassica—four to six feet high, upward growth.
Raphanus—individual flower stems for single flower buds.
Brassica—bunches of flowers along stems.
Raphanus—flower petals with veins.
Brassica—flower petals without veins.
Raphanus—leaves are thick and dark green.
Brassica—leaves are thin and light green.

Most of my thick *Raphanus* mustards clled wild radish have fuzzy leaves that hold shape well—too well—when boiled or fried. The thick fuzzy texture is a little off-putting—like eating *fillet-of-sponge*. Many guides report that mustards gets bitter with age. The fuzzy texture of the wild radish leaves prevents me from even considering putting it in my salads. This wild mustard above has delicate leaves that works better. The green immature seedpods of both species that point up as they grow are good chopped and added to my salads, soups and stews. If the greens turn out too bitter, they can be boiled twice (changing water) to calm the bitterness. Certain parts, like the seedpods, have a mild peppery flavor.

The whole plant (while still in the ground) can be blanched by covering it with newspaper or cardboard for a few days to also calm the bitter flavor. The same procedure can be done with dandelions. For a mustard spread, mix flour and ground-up, mature (they will be black) seeds with half and half water and apple cider vinegar. Pepper and salt can also be added to taste along with other spices. There are aging processes for preparing the seeds for making the mustard condiment. Some guidebooks with recipes include that info. I just want to know what I can eat in a survival situation. Recipes don't concern me that much.

Like many boiled greens, there is a cleansing of the liver and digestive system when eating mustard greens. Medical research suggests that all members of the formerly known as Cruciferae family are natural cancer fighters and preventives. Mustards are high in important minerals like calcium and potassium and full of vitamin C. There is also a report concerning species of the *Brassica genus* (kale, collards, broccoli, and cabbage included) that components in the greens can suppress thyroid function and possibly lead to fatigue and weight gain. Oil that is pressed from mustard seeds can produce a powerful antiseptic—used in ancient Greece to fight fungal infections. Strong bitter mustards can even expel intestinal parasites. The roots of the *Raphanus* mustard (wild radish) can be peeled, boiled, and added to stews. This *Brassica* mustard above has a root that can be baked or slow-roasted as-is and ground into a substitute horseradish.

There's protein, fat, carbohydrates, iron, calcium, potassium, vitamin A, ascorbic acid (vitamin C), with riboflavin, niacin, and thiamine in wild mustard.

My central Florida wild mustard and wild radish around here comes up in the fall and continues until our early spring (a snowbird edible). It needs disturbed, rich, sunny, well-drained soil—frequently along roadsides and fields. I'm attempting to plant the seeds of this plant in other locations to find out where or if I can produce them where they might be needed someday.

WILD ONION, *Allium canadense*

In central Florida, I have a particular variety of wild onions that only Euell Gibbons seems to properly describe in his landmark book, *Stalking the Wild Asparagus* (1962).

The *Allium* genus contain many species and varieties of wild onions that is sometimes called a garlic even though it has the telltale onion-like bulb, taste, and odor. When my local wild onions pop up in our fall season they appear as single blades of firm standing flat grass that smells and tastes exactly like green onions. You can't necessarily smell the onion odor until you crumble-up or break off pieces of a blade. When very young they look like grass, or young small scallions, a.k.a. green onions, just not round and hollow. They call this species a wild garlic or field garlic even though it is clearly an onion.

The general rule I've been taught and have surmined is. If it looks and smells like an onion, it is an onion. (I would add taste to that equation/rule, just to be sure). The risk of getting this plant mistaken with that equation/rule is nearly impossible. I say, nearly, because the subject of edible wild plants is still very much an undiscovered science that relies on multiple sources of information and a certain amount of risk. What is safe to eat and what is not when it comes to wild plants are fraught with hazards and uncertainties.

The bulb grows from the size of a pea to a dime, then to a nickel and then to a quarter. They can get larger if you dig around enough and look. The bulbs are very hard to eat raw without chopping them up or boiling excessively. As its growth progresses, the single blades give way to a solid, round, solid stem slightly larger than the original lone grass-blades, which produces these clus-

The bulb grows from the size of a pea to a dime, then to a nickel and then to a quarter. They are very hard to eat raw without chopping them up or boiling excessively.

The flower is pinkish white with four to six smallish petals. The bulblets without flowers looks like they have tails coming out of the seeds.

ters of bulblets/seeds/cloves at the top of the stem which has little rootlets growing out of each one, sometimes with a flower on the end. The flower is pinkish white with four to six smallish petals. The bulblets without flowers looks like they have tails coming out of the seeds. Again, the bulb is hard to eat raw without chopping it into pieces first, or you can boil them for a half-hour and then use the broth for onion soup—adding whatever ingredients you may desire. The seeds/bulblets on the top of the plant can be pickled or placed into a chopper or cooked until soft enough to eat (it varies).

WILD PLUM, *Prunus species*

This is a cherry-size plum that turns from green, to yellow and finally, ripens to this unique shade of red.

At the beginning of the previous century there were already some three hundred species of plums cultivated from native plums.

My first impression of this tree was of the chickasaw plum, *Prunus angustifolia* but on closer inspection it didn't have the thorns associated with the chickasaw or the red or yellow tips on the ends of the teeth of the leaves. This could easily be a cultivar of the American plum, *Prunus americana* sometimes known as the hog plum, not to be confused with the hog plum of the flatwoods plum, *Prunus umbellata* which is sometimes referred to as hog plum because the ripe fruit of that species is reportedly too hard and bitter to eat raw but works well in jellies and pig-feed with its black and yellow ripening fruit.

This species in the photo of the yellow fruit on the tree was very tart even when turning from this yellow to pink and then to shades of red before falling to the ground. The ones I picked off of the ground were reddish, tart and sweet while any fruit still on the tree was just too tart no matter what color.

The seed is a small plum-pit, making it easy to see that it is in the prune family and of the *Prunus* genus but the taste reminds me of a tart peach—also in the prune family. As I just stated, the ones on the tree are very tart but the ones on the ground were sweet and much less tart. Just fight the ants for them, never mind a little split in the skin and discoloration but maybe discard what appears to be tiny chunks eaten off by whatever. If appearing satisfactory, just blow any dirt off or rinse it off or even collect them to take home and wash before using. Save the pits, dry them on a reasonably dry day in the sun for planting in your backyards, food-forests, or bug-out sites.

The chickasaw plum (so named by the native First-Peoples tribe) and American plum can hybridize. While the chickasaw produces fruit in our spring here this American plum (or hybrid of) is ripening now in early August and looks to continue for a while. You probably will not find these species fruiting south of central Florida but the range extends north to about Pennsylvania, west to probably the Rocky Mountain states and down to Oklahoma and Texas (possibly in California as well).

I would imagine this fruit makes a very good jelly, jam, preserve, pie, sauce, wine and other related recipes. This is definitely a choice edible to look out for when the art and science of foraging for food becomes a necessity for survival.

WILD RADISH, *Raphanus species*

A cousin to our *Brassica* wild mustard, this plant is of the *Raphanus* genus and commonly called wild radish. It produces a very edible root—peeled of its outer shell and thoroughly cooked—as well as edible greens that are best when young. However, the members of the mustard family contain sulfur glycosides which ingested in small amounts is just bitter and stimulating to the digestive tract (as all fibrous foods normally do) but in larger amounts (sulfur glycosides) is reported to be too acrid and irritating. This acrid quality can be used in medicinal herbal remedies to stimulate healing.

The cultivated vegetables; cabbage, Brussel sprouts, broccoli, cauliflower, kohlrabi, and kale were all bred from the same family of the wild mustard. *Brassica* and *Raphanus* are beneficial in small to moderate amounts for their ability to help prevent cancer, just as all of those common produce vegetables listed above. The greens of the *Brassica* wild mustard have a much more palatable texture than this *Raphanus* plant. When I eat small portions of the young leaves I get the impression that I'm eating *filet of sponge*. The seedpods look similar for both and can be eaten raw or cooked as is while still green.

Consuming large amounts of these plants can cause harm- -if not just heartburn. However, the sulfur in them can help metabolize and excrete the active ingredient in Tylenol (Acetaminophen) and thereby prevent toxic levels of it from building up inside our livers. In small to moderate amounts, these mustards also help prevent the ailment known as goiter, an enlargement of the thyroid gland - but excessive amounts may actually cause it. There is also a report concerning species of the *Brassica genus* (kale, collards, broccoli, and cabbage included) that components in the greens can suppress thyroid function and possibly lead to fatigue and weight gain

Why call it wild radish? Many parts smell like a radish. Pull up the tap-root, clean it off, peel off the outer layer or just break the whole thing in two. The smell from it reminds one of radishes. Peel off the outer layer of the roots (discard the outer layer) and chop into small pieces and boil for at least thirty minutes to soften them up. You might learn tricks to soften up the hard, edible roots, like adding something to the water while boiling (maybe baking soda) that might help soften up the root quicker. The peeled root can also be wrapped in foil and placed into the hot-ashes of a campfire to bake overnight. They can then be added to stews for a pleasant boiled vegetable flavor or eaten as is. They can otherwise be hard to soften up if not chopped and boiled extensively.

There are plenty of health reasons to get a little bit of greens into your diet every day. Fortunately for the future survivors of human folly, there will be ample amounts of wild greens of various kinds growing wild—if they know which ones are edible.

WINGED SUMAC, *Rhus copallina*

If a person has an allergy to mangos they might be allergic to sumac. Our local species is called winged sumac. Another species you might find in the South is called smooth sumac, *Rhus glabra*. The berries of all edible sumac species grow on the ends of the stalks in

what is called terminal clusters and are always dark red. They are always found in dry soil like our sandy palmetto prairies and pine flatwoods. The northeastern US has a taller and somewhat different species called sumac, *Rhus typhina/hirta*. The berries from those are less effective at making the beverage Sumacade because they will be less acidic and therefore less tart.

Staghorn Sumac.

The leaves turn red in the fall before falling off for the winter and the berries dry up and shrivel to a hard and crusty unusable mass which sometimes hangs on to the tree until the following spring produces new berries. The berries are not edible raw because of its tiny hairs. Do not mistake sumac for Brazilian pepper.

To make sumac-ade (the taste when sweetened a little resembles lemonade), cut off a few full spikes of dry, dark red, ripe berries (best to wait for a long dry spell or at least a week of no rain) and drop them into a bowl or pot of warm (not hot) water to soak for an hour or two while stirring and lightly mashing periodically. Then strain the liquid through cloth, preferably cheese-cloth at least once and then again through a coffee filter.

Staghorn Sumac in winter.

When it rains, it washes off the flavorful malic acid, a shiny look to the berries, so waiting for a dry spell is the best bet for harvesting. In my survival gear I keep coffee filters for filtering groundwater before purifying. You will want to make sure that you have removed all of the fibrous, tiny hairs out of the liquid. Using coffee filters to strain out any remaining hairs or fibers will insure a clean final-product. That resulting liquid can be used as a tart beverage (sweeten to taste if you want) or with pectin and sugar to make a jelly. You can also mix other fruit juices with it to make a multi-fruit/berry jelly, like elderberry. Around here you can probably find lots of beautyberries to simmer, strain, and then mix into it for jelly. The sumac-ade will usually have a pinkish hue to it but not always. It is reportedly suggested that one can hang some cut stalks of berries into a dry place for storage for over a month until needed. Do not mistake Brazilian pepper, *Schinus terebinthifolium* for sumac. The local Brazilian pepper is toxic and has been mistaken for a pink peppercorn which comes from a different species from Madagascar, very different from our Brazilian pepper species here. No matter what any local-yokel tells you, the Brazilian pepper plant that invades Florida's landscapes are toxic and unusable in any way. Once you know what edible sumacs looks like you shouldn't mistake it for something else.

The seeds of sumac can be ground up to make a bitter, tannin-filled tea or used as a lemony spice if ground thoroughly. The leaves and stems were used to make a tannin solution particularly good at tanning animal hides.

There is also a plant called poison sumac which is so toxic that the sap can burn or irritate skin worse than its cousin poison ivy but it only grows in wet places (the edible sumac likes it dry), the poisonous berries of poison sumac grow along the leaf axils (nodes) rather than the terminal clusters at the tips of our edible sumac branches, and the berries of the poison sumac are white, poison sumac is somewhat rare in these parts. The winged sumac is widespread and found deep into Florida woods. The differences between the two is such that mistaking them would be somewhat stupid and the consequences of such a debacle might just thin the herd a bit as natural selection is apt to do.

WINGED YAM, *Dioscoria alata*

The vine in the top photos above is *Dioscoria alata*, the winged yam, that will be prime pickin' year-round, but particularly when the vines die off for the winter as the starch collects in the roots. While the roots are edible boiled at any time of the year, most roots contain more of the carbohydrate-rich starch when the aboveground parts die off for the season. The vines grow in colonies near other similar vines, but only this one has edible potential.

Note the long, arrowhead shaped leaves.

It is a prime foraging food that will provide a fairly large group of people with much needed starchy carbohydrates. It tastes so much like potatoes I mash it with a little milk, butter, and salt. These twin, opposite, arrowhead-shaped leaves grow in pairs (after the sprouts get longer) along a square vine with purple tinge along the edges of the vine. Always look for that identifier for positive ID. The leaves are predominantly in pairs on the very square vine that has purple coloring on its edges and purple shading where the vine meets the root. The hanging, misshapen, brown bulbil is not edible but can be planted to produce a new yam. The following photos are of the toxic, and very invasive cousin that you'll see in many a wooded lot around here. . .

Note the square stem with purple tint.

Don't mistake the edible yam for the deceptive, *heart-shaped leaves* of the toxic species, *Diocoria bulbifera,* also called air potato, the poisonous cousin with single, alternate leaves (one leaf at a time along the stem) along a *round stem completely green*. If you made a mistake and boiled the wrong root it would taste bitter. The edible *D. alata* will not be at all bitter. It tastes like potato.

Always remember that the edible *D. alata* has the arrowhead-shaped leaves in pairs along the square vine with a purple tinge on its edges. The root is the only edible part, boiled, and can become very large. Some roots are reportedly over fifty pounds. The roots often come in two sections attached on one end. The usually larger older section is spongy—best for using to make flour. The usually smaller, firm section is the prime part— chopped, sliced, and boiled after peeling. The spongy section from the yam in the photo was very thin and long which I removed before taking the photo.

Note the heart shaped leaves of the air potato. HIGHLY TOXIC!!!

Bumpy, round bulbils of toxic air potato. DO NOT EAT!!!

The natives long ago tried to use the root of the toxic cousin, *D. bulblifera*, during lean times, by boiling in multiple changes of water until all bitterness was leached out. Even then, it was just used for extreme famine and was still dangerously acidic. One writer describes the resulting yam to be barely fit to feed to the dogs.

The round, beige/tan, bulbils of the toxic species was rarely used if at all. You should consider all parts of the invasive, toxic air potato, *D. bulblifera*, as too toxic/acidic to be of any use to us. If you cut a potato-like, round, beige, hanging-bulbill that we call an air potato and look at the insides you'll notice that it becomes discolored within seconds with a bright tint. This acidic reaction varies depending on how acidic it is. Just touching this substance to your tongue can cause a burning sensation that can last for a week or more. It is one of the most acidic substances in Florida's natural environment.

Winged Yam tuber, eight to ten pounds.

The very edible yam, *D. alata,* was cultivated and then escaped, but not nearly as invasively as its toxic cousin. Yet, the bugs around here eat the leaves in the fall of the toxic *bulbifera* but not the edible *alata*. I also noticed that with the fall season, the toxic *bulbifera* vines die off well before the edible *alata* vines. In one wooded area, it was very hard to find the edible vines among the very invasive toxic ones. However, as the bugs ate away at the leaves of the toxic vines and death occurred to them well before the leaves of the winged yam, all I could see remaining in the late fall was the edible-plant vines of the winged yam. Point out the locations of the winged yam vines to remember for the future and use the misshapen, dark-brown bulbils to plant new yams with. I was able to plant some of the edible yam species around my trailer by picking their dark-brown, oblong-shaped and misshapen hanging bulbils, which are like hanging seeds along the vine. These bulbils are misshapen and dark brown while the bulbils of the toxic air potato, *D. bulbifera,* are round and light brown or beige.

To the best of my knowledge, the hanging bulbils of both species are not edible. There may be some vague reports of some of them being edible after precise and extensive boiling procedures but I wouldn't bother with that. If you take a bite of the boiled yam and it tastes even a little bit bitter, spit it out. It could be a hybrid between the two or the toxic one and absolutely not edible. The edible ones are never bitter. Again, don't eat any of it at all if it is at all

Inedible hanging bulbil of Winged Yam.

bitter. Some of the edible yams will have purple flaking in the flesh of the yam while others will be as white as a potato. A species of imported yam from China is deep purple inside.

It has come to my attention that some people in Florida are mistaking the edible yam for a native wild yam of Central America which may have the effect of causing sterility in both men and women. There is even a species of *Dioscoria* that is used medicinally for women's health issues. Our winged yam, *Dioscoria alata,* is a foreign invader from overseas, not native to the Americas. Over the thousands of years or so that people around the world have been eating our edible wild (introduced and escaped) yam there has never been any problems. Our edible wild yam is the most cultivated yam in history worldwide. Some people actually believe that the native yam of Central America is responsible for the Mayan extinction. You can be assured that ours here is not the native species of Central America. Ours is a species that was introduced around the world and perfectly edible. Once boiled, it can be prepared as you would any potato dish. To fry it or bake it, boil thoroughly first (just to be safe. I don't know of specific info that states boiling as an absolute requirement but most info seems to suggest that it might be necessary).

WOOD SORREL, *Oxalis species*

There are around five hundred species of oxalis (or oxalises) around the world. Getting the exact botanical names of these plants here has been somewhat of a challenge for me.

Oxalis violecea, or *O. dibilis, O. stricta, O. acetosella, O. Dillenii;* just to name a few of the species found in America. On the west coast of the US are a couple of oxalis (which is also one of its common names) such as *O. oregano* and *O. corniculata.* There are too many and too many versions of names within the assorted guidebooks that I possess.

There are a few specific species in this area, some are introduced species with pinkish-violet flower blossoms and the native species with yellow flowers called *Oxalis stricta* All species have edible leaves and leaf-stems that taste like mild rhubarb. Some species might have an edible, fleshy, icicle-like, water-storage root/tuber.

The leaves are used in salads in many parts of the world. Most, if not all, guidebooks state a warning about something called oxalic acid, the same as the high concentrations of it called calcium oxalate crystals that are found in plants like skunk cabbage (both eastern and western versions), Jack in the pulpit (*Arisaema triphyllum*), and dumb cane (*Dieffenbachia seguine*). Those plants present somewhat of a challenge to make edible, but most plants with concentrations of oxalic acids and crystals can be rendered almost completely harmless through boiling or drying procedures (depending on the plant).

There are many edible plants with oxalates that are perfectly safe *in moderation and accompanying any normal and diverse diet, and with varying degrees of oxalates.* sheep sorrel, purslane, lamb's-quarters, (*chenopodium album*), docks (*Rumex*), Japanese knotweed, just to name a few wild species, as well as common foods like spinach, rhubarb, Swiss chard, beet leaves, cocoa and others.

The misconceptions about oxalic acid goes back a long way and continues in several ways to this day. Your best bet is to eat as many different kinds of healthy food in your diet as you can. Any normal human being with a normally diverse and healthy diet can consume these foods on a regular basis with no ill effects. And, most modern foragers will only consume a very moderate to small amount of it at any one time anyway. Too much sorrel at once might cause a queasy stomach and those who are prone to kidney stones, gall stones, and gout should limit their intake of these foods to small amounts on rare occasions. This means also that when faced with famine and survival, eating large amounts of these foods and little else would be harmful to some degree to anyone. These plants are perfectly fine to consume (prepared properly where necessary) in moderation and especially within the parameters of a normal diet.

The leaves and stems of wood sorrel can be juiced for washing external skin problems. The plants are also fermented and placed on skin tumors in the form of a salve being held in place to actually burn off the tumor—painfully, I might add.

As a trail nibble, there is hardly anything better. The tart flavor of the leaves and stems have the same basic flavor as sheep sorrel leaves (for the same reason) and resemble a tiny mild rhubarb. One recipe includes making an ice tea from the plant. The astringent nature makes this plant a washing agent or used as a soak for getting tarnish off silver.

The edible parts include the leaves, flowers, and seedpods by most accounts, so I was thrilled to see that it might include an edible root.

While sorrels resemble some clovers, the most obvious difference is the tartness of the sorrel. Clovers are bland, edible with some cautions, and better for making a tea from the flowers or left to the cows. However, I've tasted the nutty flavor of the northern red (looks more purple) clover's (*Trifolium pratense*) flower petals. They are edible and nutty flavored.

YAUPON HOLLY, "*Ilex vomitoria*"—The Caffeine Fix

If you are anything like me, you like—practically require—a cup of coffee in the morning. If not coffee, any caffeine product will do. In some future Great Depression, post-apocalyptic America, imports of coffee will be disrupted indefinitely and any that does get through to here will be very expensive. Coffee is grown in equatorial regions of mountainous South American landscapes with deep, rich, fertile soil; not the Florida shell and lime-rock of near sea-level elevations. With a little luck, you might be able to successfully grow coffee in South Florida but you'll have to work at it. So, we must ask ourselves: Are there natural sources of caffeine in Florida's environment?

The Florida survivalist can forage on a native plant used in landscaping in the holly family, a small tree known as yaupon holly or the shrub, dwarf yaupon holly. They are popular now in landscaping and can be found wild as native species as well as introduced and escaped species. Scientifically called, *Ilex vomitoria*, only the leaves are used. Air-dried sufficiently and brewed or steeped for a caffeinated tea almost the same, if not exactly the same, as the South American drink called yerba mate. The accompanying photos show a *Ilex vomitoria var.* (cultivar) *pendula*. This plant and its variations have more caffeine than any other plant in North America and is loaded also with healthful antioxidants.

The berries are toxic and cannot be used, only the leaves. Thoroughly dried and crushed leaves can be placed in a cup and steeped in hot water for ten to fifteen minutes or simmered or brewed for five minutes. The more nitrogen in the soil where the plant grows the stronger the caffeine will be. It is also high in antioxidants, which is needed to maintain good health in stressful times.

I would strongly suggest to doomsday preppers to order one of the many variations of the species called *Ilex vomitoria* for their properties—if they want a tree with leaves that make a caffeinated drink.

The *vomitoria* part was named after a ceremony by Seminole Indians (First Peoples/First Nations). The warriors and high-ranking tribesmen fasted while drinking large amounts of very, very strongly brewed tea until vomiting it up. The vomit symbolized purifying the body and the one that held out the longest—vomiting the most fluid—was deemed the purest. As long as the leaves are thoroughly dried and not too strongly brewed (a few dried and crushed leaves should do) you should be okay.

The leaves of *vomitoria* are the best identifier. The plant can be a shrub used as a well-man-Icured hedge (*Ilex vomitoria* var. *nana*, or dwarf yaupon holly) or a small tree sometimes manicured/trimmed in the shape of an upside down bowl (weeping holly, *Ilex vomitoria* var. *pendula*), heavily branched small trees with branches pointing down, almost like a weeping willow.

The leaves (both photos) have gently toothed margins around simple, slightly oblong, alternate, slightly leathery leaves. It will grow fast and healthy throughout the Southeast and beyond. They might even be drought and salt tolerant. Someday the old expression a cup of Joe might be changed to, a cup of Holly.

YUCCA, *Yucca filamentosa*

I know that it looks like one of the yucca and agave plants that you might see in the desert southwest but it isn't, it's closely related though. Most foraging books report the uses of it, particularly the uses by Native Americans, describing the variable prepara-tion techniques of the yucca plants of the Southwest, which may or may not be compatible with our local species that does not grow in the Southwest.

This is *Yucca filamentosa*, a.k.a. Adam's needle, which ranges in the US from Florida north to about Michigan or southern Canada and west to the conti-nental divide of the Rocky Mountains and down to Texas. While I have identified them along the con-tinental divide (the east side of the Rocky Mountain range in Montana, Wyoming, Colorado, and New Mexico). That's as far west as they go—unlike the *Yucca baccata,* the Spanish bayonet of the Sonoran Desert. Another yucca species, *Y. glauca,* a.k.a. soapweed, can also be found along the continental divide in the high prairie and plains states, but not east of the Mississippi River. At least one guidebook on edible plants states that all yucca species are edible with the stipulation that flower and bud uses work best to the dry-fruited species and the edibility of the fruits work best in the fleshy-fruited species. I don't have experience with the fruits of these species, so that's up to you to look into.

Of the opportunities I've had to inspect and forage off of these species it has always been when they were in flower, not yet fruiting, and I have eaten the young, green, tender stalks after boiling.

The relative agave (not native to Florida) also has edible uses. A good source on our yucca reports that the very young flower stalks are boiled twice to be edible. Another source reported that the core of an almost mature stalk is edible as well—but my sources don't mention that for our local yucca. I can only state at this point that I have eaten the flower petals raw and cooked and the young stalks boiled which are edible on all yucca species as far as I know. However, some people might experience mild nausea from eating the flowers and a second boil to the tender, young stalks might be necessary if they taste rank.

I've eaten the dull-white flower petals from the *Y. filamentosa* species and the *Y. glauca* species. I pulled them off and ate them raw or mixed them in with a salad or omelet. The *glauca* species tasted soapy, which is part of the reason it is called, soapweed. That soapy flavor is attributed to a chemical in yucca species called saponin, which in higher concentrations (like the roots) is toxic but can be used with water to create suds for washing everything from yourselves, your utensils, dishware and pots, and your clothes. The roots were crushed by natives and pioneers and mixed with water, fat, or oil for a natural soap, even to end up being included in some of today's all natural shampoos.

As you can see, the leaves of the basal rosette are long, sharp on the ends, and so fibrous that cordage can be made by stripping or cutting the leaves and weaving or braiding it into cordage. The seeds of some species might have a laxative effect, but our species is reportedly edible when boiling the whole seedpods enough to remove the seeds, shell the seeds, and then boil them until soft to mix in with stews or eat as a side dish.

However, the reports on the seeds is not completely clear. They may require roasting before boiling. Either way, roasting, shelling, and grinding can make flour from them. Be sure of the method of preparation for boiling the seeds into a cooked vegetable and try to get at least two sources of information that agree on their edibility and method of preparation. Consider it your homework.

The old, dead, woody stalks are used for making hand-drill sets for fire-starting. However, the high humidity of our Florida climate most of the year makes all primitive fire-starting methods much more difficult than in drier climates. I keep several butane-lighters, flint & steel implements, and plenty of matches in Ziploc bags in my survival supplies. All Floridians of sound minds and bodies should have the same modern fire-starting methods stashed away for emergencies. The dead dry stalks of this yucca can make good tinder and kindling because the temperature needed to ignite it is not nearly as high as most other natural material here. Of the flower petals (any green parts should be removed), they probably should be boiled for a dozen minutes or so, and then added to soups, omelets, and stews in small amounts.

Getting comprehensive information on our yucca species was not easy when most foraging books focus specifically on the other species of the southwestern desert. Keep in mind that a recipe for a southwestern yucca may or may not work so well on our eastern species here.

12
Poisonous Plants

Poison ivy.

Extremely toxic castor bean.

Wild foraging for food is determined by a plant's edibility and availability. Wild mushrooms have the same determinations, but there is a much higher chance of poisonous, toxic, mildly toxic, or just unpalatable mushrooms than there is for wild plants. For edible wild plants, it is usually easier to distinguish particular species from others compared to wild mushrooms. However, there are extremely poisonous and toxic plants out there, usually adorned with colorful foliage or blooms, that any student of foraging should learn about. These are just a few examples of dangerous plants.

The poke is only edible when

Mature poke.   Rattlebox.

under seven inches high and boiled at least twice. In this fruiting stage of several feet high (I've seen them get up to twelve feet high) the whole plant is very poisonous.

The showy crotolaria, a.k.a. rattlebox, *Crotalaria species* is toxic throughout its life cycles for every part of it. The name comes from the rattling of the seedpods when shaken while mature.

The tropical plant, coontie, *Zamia pumila*, has reports of being used as a root-starch by natives around tropical and sub-tropical areas after an elaborate and extensive washing process which was refined by these people over hundreds of years. The waste-water that resulted from the processing of this plant poisoned some of their cattle as well as wild animals. For modern survivors/refugees to

Coontie.

167

attempt to make this and other toxic plants useful is very dangerous even under expert supervision. Besides, the only real experts on how to make coontie edible are all pretty much gone and didn't write any guidebooks.

Water lettuce.

This aquatic plant (photo above), water lettuce, *Pistia stratiotes*, might look like a garden lettuce floating on freshwater lakes and ponds in warm climates but it is far from edible raw and even then, used only as a famine food after cooking (I don't know the specifics) in India, China, and Africa. Any bite of a piece of this lettuce will bite back harshly unless cooked by expert, experienced people. If eaten raw or under-cooked, expect to experience intense irritation in the mouth, throat, and upper digestive tract, also described as a burning. There are other plants with the same problem. Our local taro root and elephant ear has the same problems. I advise staying away from them unless supervised by only the most knowledgeable of experts.

When a potential food source is referred to as famine food, it usually means that its palatability is in question and should only be attempted in an emergency. However, one may not want to risk getting sick at a time of deprivation and hunger. Knowing exactly what one can eat is imperative. There really are many tasty plants that are edible out there if one knows what they are and how to use them. If you know of a wide variety of good ones to choose from, you might not have to resort to drastic measures and eat the famine food kind.

Here is a list of subtropical and tropical plants that are definitely, absolutely poisonous, not at all edible!

- AMERICAN MISTLETOE, *Phoradendron serotinum* (fatally toxic).
- ANGEL'S TRUMPET, *Datura candida*.
- BUTTERWEED, *Sencio glabellus* (Can cause fatally toxic liver damage). This plant, Butterweed (photo in LESSON B) is similar in appearance as the wild Mustards (*Brassica species* mostly).
- CASTOR BEAN, *Ricinus communis* (bottom photo above) Swallowing even one seed can be fatal, many people have died from this plant. Its presence can even cause allergenic problems and induce asthma attacks. Just because you make an oil from the seeds for lubricating things doesn't mean it can be safely consumed internally.
- CHALICE VINE, *Solandra maxima*.
- CHINABERRY, *Melia azedarach*.
- CORAL PLANT, *Jatropha multifida* (eating one seed may cause seven to eight hours of violent vomiting and purging).
- GLORY LILY, *Gloriosa rothschildiana*.
- JERUSALEM CHERRY, *Solanum pseudocapsicum*. To be safe, never assume that a red round berry is edible particularly in tropical and subtropical climates. They usually aren't edible.
- OLEANDER, *Nerium oleander*, (even the smoke from burning it is highly toxic).
- RATTLEBOX, *Sesbania punicea* (not the same rattlebox as the next one).

- SHOWY CROTALARIA, *Crotalaria spectabilis* (also called rattlebox).
- RED SPURGE, here in Florida. According to Dr. Julia Morton, "Shrub or small tree. Plant and sap irritate skin. Sap a serious hazard to the eyes; it was introduced into the nursery trade of South Florida in 1959 because of its usually colorful foliage" (even though it sheds all of its leaves during the coldest part of our dry season) "and is sold to the unsuspecting public with complete disregard for its harmful potential." (From the book, *Plants Poisonous to People in Florida* by Julia F. Morton).
- ROSARY PEA, *Abrus precatorius* (even one seed can be fatal).
- WATER HEMLOCK, *Cicuta mexicana* (very deadly).

There are many other plants with harmful potential, but the fact is that many of them are harmful in many ways and yet, because of the colorful or otherwise aesthetic appearance of many of them, they are sold and marketed as landscape plants without any regard for the potential harm from them.

At the same time, for some stupid reason (to me), people purposely poison, contaminate, and kill the most useful plants around them because of a foolish conception of surrounding oneself with a distorted aesthetic appearance in order to heighten one's self image within a culture obsessed with wealth, social status, and appearances. Social circles, especially of middle and upper-class people, put irresponsible value in preferences of beauty at the cost of safety and security—like the safety in not exposing very young children to poisonous plants and the security of knowing that you have wild potherbs and other useful plants scattered around your neighborhood, half-acre lot, five-acre property, or multiple acreage.

The fact is, most plants that society considers "weeds" have edible and/or medicinal uses. Unsightly they may be to some, they are your emergency food supply if you just let them grow and know them. To me they have a similar appearance of usefulness to a vegetable garden. DON'T BE POISONOUS—BE RESPONSIBLE!

As an emergency food-source, I would feel somewhat safe consuming edible plant parts that grow a certain distance from a road (depending on how close, what elevation to the road, and how heavily traveled the road is). As for how close to someone's flower garden I would forage, I would be more hesitant because of people spraying herbicides and pesticides that are extremely carcinogenic.

What most people don't know is the benefits of partaking in wild food. Rather than the grocery store and restaurant, wild food provides an abundance and variety of nutrients fresh from the soil for free. It also provides one with a unique sense of self-reliance. That was the main reason for my interest when adulthood forced me to realize my dependence on low-paying employment—leaving me vulnerable to homelessness and deprivation.

There is no better reason than knowing you can always find food to eat in almost any situation. To me, anyways. It just makes a lot of sense. Here are a few very toxic plants that could be mistaken for edible ones.

BLADDERPOD, *Glottidium vesicarium* (or maybe) *Sesbania vesicaria*

The name bladderpod is used for other wild plants with no relation to this one. The little yellowish-red flowers on multiple branching stalks with hanging seedpods that resemble snap-peas is not just poisonous to us but has killed hundreds of cattle within a single herd when

little else was available for them to eat. Members of
the bean or pea family in the wild are often poisonous regardless of how edible the seeds or beans may
appear to the untrained eye. In some cases, the seeds
or beans of the pea family are edible; it's about half
and half. That's not good odds to risk your life with.
The Mesquite of the Southwestern deserts and Texas
areas has edible beanpods while the beanpods and
seeds of the coral bean are deadly poisonous.

There is another plant with the same common
name, bladderpod, which is very different and grows
out west. It ranges from eastern Texas, southeast
Oklahoma, and across to parts of North Carolina,
south to Florida.

To humans, even one bowl's worth of cooked
or uncooked portions consumed has and will cause

Bladderpod.

death or make one violently ill. The scientific name was/is once *Sesbania vesicaria* at some
point before the printing of one guide-book and is different in other guide-books. It does
seem as if changes in scientific names sometimes affect the name of the genus instead of the
particular species and/or variety. In many cases, the genera's name is completely changed
while the species' name is not changed. It involves the words in the dead language of Latin
(which all life is scientifically named with) and usually to describe particular characteristics of
the plant. Another reference book has bladderpod listed as *Sesbania vesicaria* even though it is
a later publication from the other book. From the way some guidebooks on flowers and plants
present their information, it appears that the scientific name of this plant has been switched
from one to another and back, or it just depends on where a particular author gets his/her
info. According to one book, chickens, hogs, and sheep, as well as cattle have been poisoned
from this plant, particularly by eating the green or mature seeds.

This plant comes up in the hot Florida summer in low clearings of roadsides, fields, and
vacant lots. The seedpods form around late August to mid-September and after the plants die
off in the fall the seedpods can lie around intact for quite some time. This plant appears to
be invasive in the places where they get a foot-hold and serves no purpose for us that I know
of other than being an example of not letting a poisonous plant that looks like it might be
edible fool us.

Local relatives of this, the bequilla, *Sesbania herbacea* and the purple sesbania, *S. punicea*
have flowers ranging from yellowish-red to reddish-purple, all having similar "legumes"—the
seedpods—and with similar size and structure to the overall plant.

As tempting as this plant may look to the average Joe American, to pick, boil, and consume the seedpods or to shell and soak those seeds for cooking would be a huge mistake.
Unfortunately, many Americans (and humans in general) are prone to making huge mistakes
and probably will continue to do so because of a combination of hubris, ignorance and delusions. This plant is an example of how important it is to know your wild edibles and how
devastating it will be for many people when their money becomes useless, their banks close
down, and their grocery stores are empty. Desperate people commit desperate acts, like sam-
pling an unknown seedpod for consumption when they have no idea if it is edible and they
are not prepared at all for the calamities of their self-inflicted anarchy.

COFFEE SENNA, *Cassia species*

The *Cassia species* are members of the bean family or pea family and usually have thin seedpods with common names like sicklepod, coffee senna, coffee weed, partridge pea, and wild senna. I have learned over the years not to completely trust guide-books that report a plant as having a coffee substitute potential. Most (if not all) of the first-hand accounts that I've read or heard about with these coffee substitutes are that they do not really taste like coffee and none of them have caffeine. What is coffee without caffeine other than hot, colored and flavored water?

As modern Americans, most of us need a caffeine fix in the morning or sometime during the day or the caffeine withdrawal symptoms of headache and irritability will soon inflict us. The fact is, none of the so-called coffee substitutes (that I know of) contain caffeine except for a tea made from some of the hollies in the *Ilex* genus like the yaupon holly—which would not make it a coffee substitute but rather a natural caffeine source that one could forage on by making a caffeinated tea. Growing the actual coffee plant in the States might be possible in southern-most Florida but doubtful in other parts of the country because of the tropical nature of the plant. Plus, the coffee plant requires the kind of rich tropical soil that is not naturally found in southern Florida.

In the case of this coffee senna and the *Cassia species* you might assume it to be safe to roast and grind the mature beans into a non-caffeinated coffee substitute, right? Guidebooks even report it to be a coffee substitute. However, these plants might contain alkaloids that are proven toxins in large amounts and can cause liver damage. Some people may have tried eating the prepared beans, as they are reported to be toxic when eaten in considerable amounts by one report. Bottom line for these plants is to just stay away from them. If there are useful purposes out there for these plants, as well as the bladderpod also mentioned, I will need more than one reliable source to convince me.

If one has entered a serious famine/doomsday/survival scenario, that individual should never compromise their health by taking chances consuming wild plants that might be even just a little toxic. In the case of some seeds in the bean/pea family, some are so toxic that a few seeds ground up or chewed, swallowed, and ingested can kill. The rosary pea is a good example of that.

CHINABERRY, *Melia azedarach*

All parts of this tree are very toxic. This colorful tree in the fall shows shades of green, yellow and pink. The brightly-colored warning of foraging applies. The fruit, bark, leaves, flowers and roots contain very high concentrations of *saponin*, the toxic substance that can be used to make suds for cleaning clothing. It also contains at least one other deadly alkaloid that attacks the central nervous system and causes severe gastroenteritis. In this case, I would refrain from using it to wash yourself unless you guarantee that you don't consume any at all in any way. The large, green to yellow berries stay on the tree even after the leaves fall off and are a well-known pig-killer, including cattle, sheep, goats, and poultry as well as people. Incidents of poisonings of human beings are rare because of the very repulsive and bitter taste. The leaves and the fruits have been used as insect repellent in drying and storing fruits and other produce. The fruits have been used to make a flea-powder insecticide. Overripe fermented fruits intoxicate birds and have rendered them unconscious for hours.

A New Deadly Algae

A new toxic algae called *Aetokthonos hydrillicola* has just recently been discovered growing on an invasive, fresh-water, aquatic plant called hydrilla. Hydrilla is native to Africa and Southeast Asia and was introduced to Florida canals in the 1950s. The plant itself has spread since then to throughout the Southeastern US and grows as much as an inch per day. I have no previous knowledge of this aquat-

ic-plant nor have I been able to obtain a photo of it. As far as I presently know, it is not one of the many aquatic-plants that has edible and/or medicinal uses to humans. However, I am fairly certain that this plant has no edible or medicinal uses.

The algae being discovered growing on this particular plant is not the same as the blue-green algae being reported on lately in Florida's southern region. That's a different story that is probably not related to this *Aetokthonos hydrillicola* bloom.

Aquatic birds, waterfowl, that feed off the hydrilla and the birds of prey that feed off them are being killed fairly quickly by this toxic algae. This particular algae growing on the Hydrilla affects the brains of entire flocks that feed on the aquatic plants, causing a complete neurological breakdown within 24 hours of symptoms. The birds begin to show signs of madness by flopping around and acting erratically. Predator birds that usually eat fish are finding sick birds easy prey, causing the predators themselves to get sick and die.

The Florida apple snail, *Pomacea paludosa*, lives in and around lakes and ponds as far south as the Everglades and is being exposed to the toxic algae, putting the Limpkin, *Aramus guarauna* and the snail kite, a.k.a. Everglades kite, *Rostrhamus sociabilis*—birds who feed off of the snails—at risk. This will also put all those who might forage on these snails at risk as well.

To this point we know that eagles are dying from feeding off sick waterfowl but in order to know which animals and how many are being killed by it we must be able to examine the brains of the victims within 24 hours of death and freezing them doesn't work. This makes it difficult to track the effects of the toxic algae.

The Everglades are the most at risk of this toxic algae for now, affecting both the wild-life that feeds on the hydrilla and the wildlife that feeds off of the wildlife that feeds off the hydrilla. So far, that list includes eagles, mallard and ringneck ducks, horned owls, coots (a waterfowl), and kites. However, we are only now discovering this toxic algae and it could easily spread to other wildlife on the food-chain. Even the manatees are at risk, as they also eat the hydrilla as well.

Other fresh-water snails as well as slugs and mollusk species may also be at risk of being infected, making it risky to harvest these wild edibles anywhere that hydrilla grows. According to a recent University of Florida study, the State of Florida spent $66 million over seven years, on mitigation efforts. Researchers do not know where the algae came from or how to get rid of it. They can only suggest at this time that we get rid of the hydrilla, which is easier said than done.

To find this toxic algae on a hydrilla plant you'll need to shine an ultra-violet light on the bottoms of the leaves. If the *Aetokthonos* algae is there it will be lit up bright red.

Even though the plants themselves are spread out around the southeastern US this toxic algae is limited (thus far) to the Everglades and could be caused by the same problems that has caused the blue-green algae bloom in south Florida where over-development and the sugar and phosphate industries have been polluting with impunity.

It is very unlikely that Florida's Anti-environment/Pro-pollution-for-profit political leaders are going to do anything about the problem anytime soon. It could create a health hazard for hunters and foragers in the near and distant future.

We don't know if the algae will affect us if we eat something infected, for now. For something new to be killing birds and possibly other wildlife this way thus far it is likely that it will eventually affect people.

Consuming rats or snails in parts of Florida is already risky with a possible subtropical parasitic nematode called "rat lungworm" that can cause eosinophilic meningitis, possibly causing severe infections in the brain leading to coma or even death.

13
Medicinal Plants

Reading anything comprehensive about medicinal, herbal medicine gives me a headache. If there are wild plants around that can help relieve a headache, there probably is something to it but I don't know what it is.

Broken down into basics that we dummies can learn to use in survival/famine/doomsday scenarios, there are characteristics in plants to look for in herbal field medicine. If the need to treat a burn from fire-making, tending, or cooking, or getting stung by an insect, you want at least one specific kind of plant. That would be a plant that has something that would both cool, moisten, and protect the skin. This is where the aloe vera plant is a good example. It has a thick, heavy sap or, mucilage that will moisten burned or stung skin. Aloe has been established to strengthen the body's healing function, making it an excellent skin lotion for cuts, scrapes, burns, and even insect bites.

The aforementioned plant spiderwort, *Tradescantia* species has a thick mucilaginous sap also used to treat insect bites as well as other skin problems. A tea or poultice made with the leaves of this plant and others like it, including its cousin dayflower, *Commelina* species, can be used for a number of problems that include both internal and external needs. The sap can be made into a tea used for sore throats. The leaves of the plant called plantain, *Plantago* species has been used in folk medicine for generations as a poultice to cover the skin for burns, cuts, and stings or taken as a tea (with ripe seeds) for constipation. The seeds from plantain are used commercially for laxatives. The thick sap of these and other mucilaginous plants is just one of the basic applications used in medicinal remedies and is the most common needs in outdoor survival.

The willow tree provides the substance that is the precursor for aspirin. Cut a twig off of a willow bush and gently crush it to release the bark from the wood. Now chew the bark. That very bitter aspirin flavor will rush to your senses and relax your aches and pains at the same time. Just don't overdo it.

A practitioner of herbal medicine is called a CAM, "Complementary and Alternative Medicine." In Canada, the federal government regulates botanical medicine in how they label the products sold, which isn't much for regulating an industry as large and complex as alternative medicine but more regulation than in America. The Canadians have a government agency called the Office of Natural Health Products (ONHP). They regulate specific requirements on labeling and packaging with some attention directed at manufacturing and distribution. These recently enacted regulations are specifically about labeling a wide range of information about each product sold in Canada for brand names, designated licensing numbers, dosage, amount of weight, measurements or number of doses recommended, storage requirements, conditions, and even other ingredients—all the key data on a product and displayed in both French and English.

The United States is much less regulated. Herbal products of any kind are lumped together with dietary supplements ranging from nutritional vitamin and/or mineral supplements to botanical medicines, yet very limited on what kinds of information must be printed on a product's label or package. Enacted in 1994 by the Dietary Supplement Health and Education Act (DSHEA) and yet they are not required to seek pre-approval for products by the Food and Drug Administration (FDA).

As a disclaimer from the consequences of these faulty, inadequate regulatory requirements (practically non-existence; commerce is king in America) you'll see this statement on the products sold commercially, "This statement has not been evaluated by the Food and Drug Administration. This product is not intended to diagnose, treat, cure, or prevent any disease." That leaves the market wide open to fraudulent or deceptive practices. The lack of regulations over any industry that affects the public health is only beneficial to the industry's bottom line, to make profit at the cost of public safety and fairness.

Medicinal Applications: herbal teas, liquid dosage forms of tinctures and fluid extracts, and solid dosage forms.

Herbal teas include both decoctions and infusions. An infusion is your typical tea made with the more delicate parts of a plant, such as flowers and leaves (usually dried)—by steeping in hot as well as cold water depending on the constituent/s (the natural substance in the plant being extracted into the water for medicinal use) that are being extracted from the plant. A decoction is used for the more fibrous plant material (roots, bark, etc.) and involves boiling down the material to a specific volume—a concentrated amount.

If that wasn't tricky enough to measure and administer, liquid dosage forms called "tincture" and "fluid extracts" can get even more tricky and even dangerous when using plants that require exact measurements of the constituent being extracted because of toxicity. Many plants that are used medicinally are often toxic—not edible—and require carefully measured amounts and potency of dosage to be safe. If you purchase one of these forms you must depend on the manufacturer or herbalist that the preparation you're about to ingest was prepared properly and accurately—not just to avoid harmful side-effects caused by improper preparations but in terms of whether the extract will even be potent enough to be useful, provided your metabolism and body chemistry is compatible with the constituents and its potency.

When something is referred to as an art and a science—such as herbal medicine—it is usually because the science on it is not well established enough to be a cut-and-dry process and requires a degree of skill that is learned, honed, and perfected as much as one can under the limitations involved. The main limitation being that we don't know enough about the science and there is no governing body overseeing the industry within a free (to be greedy) market economy.

It comes down to the other form of dosage . . . taking a pill, the solid dosage form. We would like to think that it is the most reliable and trustworthy form, but we would probably be wrong. Again, because there is no viable governing body or well-established science involving the standards and practices of this industry in America. The pill-form includes capsules, tablets, freeze-dried products, and lozenges also dependent upon the manufacturer or herbalist to be wholeheartedly concerned with the accurate production of their product. The biggest concern by the consumer being whether the product actually has enough of the actual herb in it—given the fact that the industry is not regulated in this pro-commerce-capitalist America and barely regulated in Canada.

This is why you should look for the phrase "standardized extract" to have at least some level of confidence in a commercial product. It's a product in which a specific concentration of a particular constituent or group of constituents are supposedly guaranteed. However, while some preparations may be standardized to a marker component guaranteeing that the correct plant was harvested and used, this marker agent need not necessarily be the active constituent. As long as they use the right plant, the product doesn't have to guarantee that it is the right part of the plant or even include the particular medicinal substance of the plant.

Also, unfortunately, the standardized practice is not well established because of the lack of—once again—the science behind it. Specific dose regimens of herbs range from different traditions—Chinese, European, natives local to numerous climates and environments, and the questionable claims of clinical and pharmacological evaluations.

These safety issues involve non-existent uniformity over the practice of herbal medicine. There is no viable regulatory governing agency in either the US or Canada that oversees the industry. Allergic reactions, mis-identifications of the herbs being used, adulterations of the products with heavy metals and even pharmaceuticals, and unintended interactions with conventional medicines are all problems that can make the practice of herbal medicine a risky business—but so can conventional medical practices and pharmaceuticals as well. The pharmaceutical industry has the same issues when they are being regulated by agencies being run by opportunistic for-profit entities. To de-regulate an industry you just put people in charge of it who benefit directly or indirectly from the profits of that particular industry. Or you can just cut the regulations themselves in order to increase profits to the industry and then get a job with that industry when you leave the agency. It's common practice in America to put people with past or future employment in an industry to regulate that industry for the supposed purpose of public safety.

A particular therapy in either conventional or alternative medicine can also aggravate the condition being treated. The bottom line is to be very cautious about the use of medicinal herbs. Study it thoroughly if you intend to use it in some future apocalyptic world where there is no choice but to trust someone other than an established health-care system, even one like America's that operates on a pay-to-play, survival of the richest, for-profit-only objective.

In herbal remedies, the practice of field medicine is profitable to use in the absence of, or in addition to, doctors and hospitals with conventional, chemically derived medicines as long as the practitioner is well learned, honed, and perfected in the *art and science* of herbal medicine. Otherwise, there are a few plants around that can help with some of what ails you for some things, but not much.

The bitterness in some raw greens is helpful for digestion but too much can have a laxative affect, stomach cramps, and/or vomiting.

Poke roots, while extremely poisonous internally, can be used as a topical antibiotic for fighting infection. The decoction made by boiling the roots extensively can either be used by dipping a cloth bandage into the boiled liquid (after cooling) and placing on the infection as a poultice (held on the spot by wrapping strips of cloth around it) or soaking the infection right into the decoction.

Sheep Sorrel tea might help reduce high blood pressure. Violet leaf tea might help with pain. A liver cleansing tonic can be made with the dried leafy material from violets, gota kola, Caesarweed, chickweed, and plantain.

Dandelion parts have many medicinal advantages, probably the healthiest weed of all. The "bitters" of the bitter greens help the digestion of food while other constituents can clean toxins out of the glandular system. Dandelion's proteins and iron provides help to blood circulation and flows of the kidneys and pancreas.

Stinging nettles can help to increase circulation and stimulate the efficiency of both liver and kidney function. This plant is well known among herbalists for its many medicinal uses.

An alterative is a substance or constituent used as an internal cleansing of the liver, digestive tract, urinary tract, and other systems.

Curly dock is another with a wide range of medicinal uses. As an alternative, it can cleanse the liver, bowels, lungs, and purify blood with a simple tea made with one teaspoon of soft material.

14
The Nibbles

There are a large number of plants that may not sustain you in quantity, but when approached as trail nibble, and eaten in small quantities, or used to spice up your main fare, make up in quality what you may not have in quantity. As with everything we consume, always test for your own personal edibility no matter how commonly edible it may be with the Universal Edibility Test. With that said, here we go on our list of what you might call supplementals or we like to call trail treats.

CLOVER

White clover (*Trifolium repens*) and red clover (*Trifolium pretense)* are two common edible varieties of clover that seem to grow wherever people are throughout the world. This is great, because they grow in abundance in yards public parks, open fields, roadsides, open meadows, and other similar spaces. I have rarely seen clover in any wild spaces or wooded areas. The closest to wild places are farm fields. The bad side to this, is because they grow where people are, they are far more likely to be contaminated by herbicides and other chemical, and even biological contaminants as in animal excrement, runoff from storm sewers, and agricultural runoff in rural areas. Clover is a common, easy to identify edible that is high in nutrition. Both the red and white varieties are edible, but not yellow clover.

A white clover.

The leaves, flowers, seeds, and roots of clovers are all edible. The young leaves, taken before the plant flowers, can be eaten raw. As the plant matures, cooking the leaves is recommended. You might call it a survival food, and perhaps rightly so for only the blossoms taste good. The leaves are an acquired or tolerated taste In reference to the blossoms, don't select brown ones. You only want young and fresh whether white or red, though red clover tastes best. The leaves are another matter. Young ones are fine raw in small amounts, less than half a cup. Older leaves should be cooked as should the roots.

Red and white clover can be eaten either raw, fried, boiled, cooked in with other edibles, or thoroughly dried, ground into a flour, or used as a tea. I have fried white clover in butter and sugar to make a delicious dessert not unlike caramel corn. Raw clover flowers, either red or

A red clover.

white are slightly sweet. Brew fresh flower petals into a mildly sweet tea, or add fresh ones to a salad. You can also use the flowers thoroughly dried either in the sun, or an oven if you have access to one. Enclosed in a hot car is a good way spread out on some sort of improvised cookie sheet. You can then either grind them into a flour, or make a tea. You can dry the leaves to use also. Slow drying them separated out like the flowers and the leaves removed from the stems. They should crumble easily when ready. Dried clover leaves make a very good tea.

What clover leaves don't have in taste, they make up for in nutrition. They are high in protein, beta carotene, vitamin C, most of the B vitamins, biotin, choline, inositol, and bio-flavonoids. Clover does come with three words of warning, however: One is that quite a few people are allergic to it and don't know it, so go easy at first until you know one way or the other. Make sure your clover either completely fresh or completely dried, never in between. Never, and I mean NEVER ferment clover. It can be very dangerous to eat any part of this plant if it is suspected of being fermented in any way, or has any mold growing on it causing you to run the chance of sweet clover disease, which reduces your blood's clotting ability. I personally would steer away from sprouting too as that could cross over into fermentation. If you eat it raw, make sure you have a source of fresh clean water to wash the plant before consuming as you would any raw plant. Cooking is best if you are in doubt. In addition, clover in warm climates can produce small amounts of cyanide, although would have to eat a lot of it to feel any toxic effects. Like any food, moderation is the key. Eating more than a half a cup, and you will likely throw up. Try to mix up your diet including numerous different food, and remember to use the Universal Edibility Test on every part of every plant you are going to use. Follow this practice, and keep accurate notes including how you feel, time of year, location, everything you can think of. This way when the going gets tough, you will have an arsenal of food and medicine to get you through. Think about it, you wouldn't wait to learn how to drive a car until you absolutely had to would you? The same applies to survival skills. Although clover is a very easy plant to identify, go through the process of identifying every part of the plant, and follow its life cycle. This applies to all plants in general.

Also, avoid using any seeds that contain a purplish, pink, or black discoloration or spur. This is particularly so if the discoloration appears in the form of a spur on a grass or herb seed when observed closely with a magnifying glass. It may turn out to be a very dangerous fungal infection called ergot. All seeds of grassy plants are susceptible to fungal growths that must be diligently scoured and purged from the potential grain that most of the grassy plants provide. Yellow sweetclover, *Melilotus officinalis* and white sweetclover, *M. alba* may not be edible in any way because it is reportedly very susceptible to Ergot.

Recapping, while clover is easy to identify, and it is clear that you only want it fresh, or dried, and then in small quantities. There are possible poisonous look-alikes. My advice is to stick with what you know. Perform the Universal Edibility Test. Remember moderation is key.

SPICEBUSH, *Lindera benzoin*

This is an aromatic shrub and puts me in the mind of sassafras, rightfully so as it is related. It grows in wooded areas in eastern North America, north from New York, west to central US and south into Florida. It seems to like the cool, damp bottoms of wooded areas near creeks and ravines. It is a bush that grows to about twice the height of an average man, and about the same in diameter, and has multiple narrow trunks. I see it growing among the hickories and

Poplars often in the same area as mayapple, sweet cicely, wild hoary mountain mint, trilliums, and other plants that love this moist bottomland.

It's aromatic, oval, leaves have a spicy, citrus scent, growing alternately from a thin branch. Small oblong green berries emerge in the spring, and turn red toward fall. The spicy, somewhat pulpy berries have one seed. They are a favorite of birds, and other critters, so harvest what you need early on, and leave some for the competition. I like them as a trail nibble and I pick them and have them in my pocket, having one every now and then to stave off hunger a little.

You can collect leaves, twigs, and bark all year, although they are best when in flower, and can make a nice tea by steeping in hot water The berries can be nibbled as is, or ground, seeds and all to make a nice seasoning. There are no poisonous look a-likes and Spicebush is easily identified by its wonderful citrus, woods scent.

Here is an interesting quote from *Grit* magazine that speaks of spicebush. "During the Civil War, spicebush tea often substituted for coffee when rations ran short. Dried leaves were often used for this purpose, but young branches were also steeped to make a tonic. This spicy beverage had medicinal qualities as well. It was used to reduce fever, to relieve colds and dysentery, and to destroy intestinal parasites. *Lindera benzoin* is considered a warming herb that improves circulation and increases perspiration rate."

PARTRIDGEBERRY, *Mitchella repens*

This a low-lying plant with red berries when ripe, and is unique because one berry comes from two flowers. It has up to eight seeds and is easily identified.

The vine itself grows low to the ground, and doesn't climb, but rather hides out under the cover of leaves, has pairs of opposite leaves with a yellow vein running down the middle, growing along the vine on short leaf stems close to quarter-inch long. All partridge berries have two dimples because each berry grows from two hairy flowers. The plant flowers mid to late spring and sometimes again in the fall. The small, unique bright red berries with their distinctive two dimples ripen from mid-summer to mid-fall often through winter, making them a nice little find in bleak winter months, if other critters don't get to them first. They grow in damp woods among mostly deciduous trees, likely in mountain areas.

Partridge berries are a favorite food of grouse, hence their name, at least that is what they say. It is an uncommon find, but makes a good trail nibble, and the leaves and berries can be used in salads, pies, or ash cakes, and teas. Although nutritious, partridgeberries are somewhat bland, their reward is the role they play in our health as a cancer preventative, vitamin C, antioxidants, and tannins. They are found in the Appalachian mountains, and other areas in the eastern US.

The partridgeberry has no toxic look-alikes, and although it won't provide a lot of sustenance, it might keep you going long enough to get through, and provide a little comfort.

TEABERRY, *Gaultheria procumbens*

This goes by many names: checkerberry, johnny jump ups, or wintergreen. I know it as teaberry. It is an evergreen perennial that spreads by a stem just under the surface of the ground. Each stem will produce three to ten leaves and possibly a few red berries. It has small sort of bell shaped flowers that hang from short stems starting in mid-summer, send the red mild wintergreen flavored berries ripen in late summer and will overwinter if they don't get eaten by something first. The ripe berry has a star-shaped depression on the bottom A network of woody stems attached to each other allow teaberry to grow in what look like large patches through a network possibly all from a single root.

Teaberry is often found in poor, acidic sandy soil in the eastern US, sometimes under white pines or in moss, and in mixed forests. It ranges from Newfoundland through New England, across the Great Lakes and down to Alabama.

I have seen several sources that tell how to make teaberry tea the traditional way which allows the teaberry to release its active ingredients better than just steeping in hot water. You can pick leaves anytime of the year, fill a jar or sealable container with them, then cover with pure water for a few days until you notice them bubbling from the fermentation process. You can then drain the leaves, and use six or seven of them wet, or dry them for later use, to make a tea that not only tastes good, but works as a pain killer as it contains methyl salicylate, the active ingredient in aspirin. You don't want to drink too much of it for this reason, because of its possible blood thinning properties, but it is good when you need it. I use the small shiny, leathery oval leaves and red berries as a trail nibble, chewing them for their wintergreen flavor. I don't know if they still make teaberry gum, but the flavor is very similar. I realized after first chewing the leaves, that that was likely where teaberry chewing gum got its name.

Because of its characteristic wintergreen scent, that could be a good distinguishing feature for a positive ID. Wintergreen oil is a very powerful substance, and can be toxic if used in quantity extracted from the plant, so this plant, while making a great nibble in small quantities isn't good to make a meal out of.

MAYAPPLE, *Podophyllum peltatum*

This has a very short window of opportunity as food, and the edible portion is surrounded by so many poisonous elements, that I was reluctant to include it in this list. I decided to include it though with the statement to USE EXTREME CAUTION WHEN CONSUMING THE FRUIT OF THE MAYAPPLE. ALL PARTS OF THIS PLANT ARE POISONOUS EXCEPT THE VERY RIPE FRUIT, INCLUDING THE SKIN, AND SEEDS.

That being said, it is definitely no more than a trail nibble. ONLY THE PEELED SOFT FULLY

A large mayapple patch.

RIPE FRUIT WITH SEEDS AND SKIN REMOVED IS EDIBLE. Only eat this fruit in small quantities as too much as too many can have a mild laxative effect. At this point, you may ask, what's the use then? Well, this delicate fruit when fully ripe is well worth the effort, and wait. It has been used traditionally to make jellies, jams, and pies, but is good on its own. If you do find mayapple, the fruit fully yellow and soft, and the leaf starting to wilt is just right. It is quite easy to eat raw or cooked when done properly. Remember to remove the skin and seeds before cooking. There is a lot of competition for mayapple fruit, as a lot of critters like it as well. If you do happen on one of these, wash it, peel it, remove the seeds, and enjoy its refreshing goodness. As with everything, make sure to take it through the Universal Edibility Test If you are very careful, the fruit of the mayapple, can be a wonderful, unique foraging experience, and a great addition to your trail nibble list during its brief window of edibility. Oh yeah, as a final note, don't eat this fruit if you are pregnant.

Toxic unripe mayapple fruit.

Mayapple is one of the first plants to appear in spring. The fruit usually ripens in late summer, early fall, depending on climate. It is found throughout eastern and much of central US. It usually grows in colonies in shady damp deciduous woods. Mayapple grows one- to one-and-a-half-feet tall, some with a single leaf on a long stalk, others produce two leaves. Stalks are light green, round, and hairless. Leaves, umbrella like, to one foot long and across; palmately lobed, five to nine lobes per leaf, deeply divided, and hairless. Each plant has a single waxy, creme-colored flower with six to nine petals, under the leaf. The mayapple fruit itself is egg-shaped, green when unripe, turning yellow when ripe.

Mayapple may sound dangerous, and if not treated properly, it is, but when eaten at just the right time, following the rules of consumption, it is a true gift from nature's bounty.

WILD MINT, "*Pycnanthemum incanum*"

Wild mint or hoary mountain mint in this case is a plant I have used to add flavor to other foods, as well as using it as a tea. It is only one of many mints that can be found growing wild that are edible and medicinal. I mix a little in with stinging nettle to add flavor to it either as a tea, or wild green. I also will sometimes mix in a little dried mullein leaf as well if making a tea. I am always able to find nettles and wild mint fairly close to each other as both like rich wooded damp areas near stream beds, and ravines in the eastern woodlands of the US. It is found north into New England, south into parts of Florida, and west at least to the Mississippi.

Hoary mountain mint is easy to spot, partly because of its distinctive mint smell, square stems covered in fine white hairs, opposite toothed leaves with short leaf stems, clusters of small pinkish white flowers, and in this case, leaves that seem to be dusted in a fine white powder. This plant is about knee high, and stands out among others in its natural area It is often seen in the same areas as mayapple, sweet cicely, stinging nettle, and spicebush to name a few.

This mint has a number of uses. It is excellent as a flavoring for other foods such as meat, other wild greens, and as a refreshing, and healthy tea. Along with its edible uses, the strongly aromatic quality of mint works as a good insect repellant when used by itself, or in conjunction with other plants such as lemon balm lavender, and other strong smelling plants. I rub it on my clothes, put it in my pockets, in my hat, etc. to keep the bugs at bay.

Although you can't live on mint alone, it will add flavor to your food, and can help sustain you along with other plants in small quantities.

Sweet Cicely.

INDIAN STRAWBERRY, *Potentilla indica*

This was one of those plants I was told was poisonous, and when I finally learned it wasn't toxic, I was told by an authority that it was essentially useless with no value whatsoever. Turns out both of those assessments were wrong. Neither poisonous nor useless. Tasteless for the most part, but not without value and therefore useful as a food, at least as a nibble. The fruit is 3.4 percent sugar, 1.5 percent protein and 1.6 percent ash. It has 6.3 mg of vitamin C per 3.5 ounces of juice. Granted that isn't that impressive, but it is something, and in a dire situation could prove valuable not just sustenance wise, but psychologically as well.

Probably the best way to describe this plant would be to say round tasteless strawberry, which is pretty

Lemon balm.

much true. The round red strawberry like berries look slightly different, and the seeds on them protrude rather than laying flat as they do on strawberries. They can provide a little relief from thirst, and can be added in with other edible berries or juice for those hot summer days. And the leaves can be used as a potherb, eaten raw, or dried and used to make a nice tea.

It is found throughout the US, and other places I'm sure. It is most commonly found in yards, and more manicured areas it seems, but I have seen it in wooded areas too. It has a low, trailing vine with a single yellow flower with five petals. Long stemmed leaves have three toothed leaflets. A strawberry like fruit emerges after the flower that ripens in late summer with seeds on the outside. The berries are eaten raw, leaves raw in salads, leaves cooked as a green, and leaves dried for tea.

Take care when consuming this plant to be mindful of agricultural chemicals, herbicides, pesticides, and the like, also for animal contaminants, and other pollutants, as this plant is found often in urban areas. Indian strawberry, as unassuming as it is, just might help you get through a tough situation.

HACKBERRY, *Celtis laevigata*

Hackberry is often thought of as a weed tree. The wood is stringy, not considered practical for lumber, and is an inferior firewood. The tree is abundant, and grows most anywhere. It is easy to identify because of it very rough light gray deeply furrowed irregular bark. The leaves also have a rough sandpapery quality often with warts, or galls on them. The part we are after are the small berries, about the size of chokecherries, that are varying hues of dark red, with a somewhat dry texture that consist mostly of a large hard seed surrounded by a sweet pulp, and thin skin. Their sweetness gives them one of their common names, sugarberry.

The berries make an excellent, but somewhat meager snack even though they were a main source of nutrition for thousands of years. They are somewhat hard to collect in quantity, so I classify them as a trail nibble. They will provide a few easy calories and protein. The whole berry is high in calcium, up to 20 percent protein, and has a high amount of fat, fiber, and other nutrients. They can be eaten raw, or dried, seed and all, if you grind them first. They are found most everywhere on the planet where people live, and the berries are the oldest known foraged food, and main nutrition source until modern times where it is considered an invasive weed tree.

Don't confuse the hackberry with prickly ash, known also as a toothache tree because chewing their leaves numbs the mouth and gums providing relief from a toothache. Prickly Ash has medicine smelling leaves, which hackberry does not. Hackberry grows along edges of fields, parks, waste areas, and yards, both urban and rural areas. In other words, it can be found most anywhere.

Berries ripen in the fall, and although hard to reach sometimes, will remain over winter, making them an excellent winter food.

KOUSA DOGWOOD, *Cornus kousa*

This bears one of the strangest looking fruits I have encountered outside the tropic regions. A little research, and finally the Universal Edibility Test, and it turns out it is edible, at least for me. Turns out, some people report adverse reactions from eating this strange fruit. A testament to the UET, also universally important. The fruit of the kousa dogwood is sold commercially in some parts of the world, and there are recipes to be found as well. To include it in a book of wild edibles may be a bit of a stretch, but the only way to find it here at least, is to forage it. I guess that would be considered cultivated foraging. Anyway, if you are caught in an urban area when the excrement contacts the turbine, then you may just encounter this tree.

Like most dogwoods, the kousa dogwood is an ornamental tree, small as trees go, usually not over twenty feet in height, with a thin, flaky bark and long lasting flowers. The fruit is a strange red, round fruit, slightly smaller than a golf ball, and in a way similar, but opposite in texture, that is to say, where a golf ball has indentations on it, the kousa fruit has bumps all over it. The skin is somewhat leathery/gritty, with an orange pulp and seeds. I squeeze out the pulp, eat it raw, and spit out the seeds. I don't think either are toxic, but am not sure about the seeds, and the skin just isn't fit for good eating.

I first encountered the kousa in a cemetery, and was hesitant to do much more than try it due to the likelihood of the area being treated with some sort of agricultural chemical. I did try a couple of them though once I knew i didn't react adversely to it, after the UET.

I finally decided it deserved mention at least as a trail nibble, and if I found one of these escaped into the wild, I would not hesitate to incorporate it as a full side dish. The fruit while a little weird, is available when ripe, and the leaves are edible at least when young, as a cooked potherb. Incidentally, many varieties of dogwood are edible, however, many aren't, so do your homework, and testing in advance so you will know which is okay for consumption. As this is an urban cultivar for the most part, exercise common sense, and caution by not collecting near the road, due to toxins from car exhaust, and whatever else may end up running off the road. Also avoid where the presence of agricultural chemicals or other pollutants may be found.

That said, happy foraging. That pretty well sums it up for me as another valuable contribution to wild edible in the journey through life in the natural world of America.

Acknowledgments

My participation in this work is dedicated to my bro, sis, and grandpa—Rene Boudreau (Bro), Nancy Fike (Sis), and Leslie D. Carr (Grampa).

Special thanks to John Nason, for his technical assistance and inspiration; to Ray Canales, for some photos and for being an old friend who continues to be; and to Green Deane of Eat The Weeds for being one of my heroes.

Thanks also to Skyhorse Publishing: Jay Cassell, Lindsey Breuer-Barnes, and Helena Nadazdin.

Also Prepper Dan, Marcy Dunnigan, John Rose, Paul Roy, Debbie Cagle Albertson, Vicky Lin (Living Food Bakery), Carole (Herbal Kitchen), Dr. Wang, Janice Taylor, Cissa Monteiro and Steven DeFalco, Tom Elpel, Stephanie Bratter, Gudrun Malers-Scheider, Franz Scheider, Katarina Lauver (Indie FM), Mike M. Gibson, Christopher Nyerges, the band called "The War On Drugs" and, of course, Mykel Hawke and family.

—Doug Boudreau

I would like to thank my family from childhood, as they did their best, and as a result of our hardships, I became a Green Beret and survival expert.

I'd like to thank the US Army Special Forces (a.k.a., Green Berets) for all the great men who taught me, the amazing men with whom I had the honor to serve and learn from, and for all the training and experience they gave me, which did not make me, but it did make me better.

A very special thanks to the US Army Survival, Escape, Resistance & Evasion (S.E.R.E.) School, for all it did to encourage me to learn more and to share knowledge with civilians.

This one is from way back, but I'd like to thank the tribal elders from varied American tribes, where my father brought us to play and learn as kids. Special thanks to Chief Custalow and his wife, Mini-haha of the Mattaponi tribe.

It would be unfair of me to not give thanks to the great many indigenous leaders and elders from various tribes and people around the world, who shared with me in my travels, some of their old ways, often no longer practiced by their own youth. We humbly try to honor their memory.

My most special thanks goes to my Kentucky brother, John Rose. Not only did he serve in the military, but he endured a childhood that made my harsh upbringing look like an easy ride. John shares my love for music and makes some of the best my ears have ever heard. But most important, many of the plants I cover in this book with Doug, come from what John shared with me. When it comes to foraging for wild vittles, John is a supreme master. And above all else, he is one of the kindest souls I've ever been blessed to get to know and such, I count him as a spiritual brother. My family is so grateful to him and his lovely lady, Julie.

A unique thanks to my Special Forces Brother, Sam Coffman. Not only does he share my keen enthusiasm for survival but he took the study of survival medicine to a whole new level. Learning from him has been a great challenge and joy.

My deepest love to my blood brother, Jon Loneman, former 101st in Serbia, French Legionnaire in the Pyrenees, contractor with me in Haiti and Sierra Leone. and contractor in

Iraq, seven rotations, thrice blown up, twice with fatalities, and now residing in Texas with his wife, Pam. Jon was the one who truly took to learning the ways of the medicine man and tried to teach this bonehead some of the powerful medicine he had learned while on the reservation that I shunned back then.

And a most special thanks to Doug Boudreau for partnering with me on this book.

And last but not least, I am thankful for my family, both my grown sons who put up with a tough dad and my wife, Ruth, and son, Gabe, who put up with and share in all my survival shenanigans.

—Mykel Hawke

Bibliography

98.6 Degrees: The Art of Keeping Your Ass Alive by Cody Lundin.

Botany in a Day, by Tom Elpel.

The Complete Medicinal Herbal by Penelope Ody.

The Complete Wilderness Training Book by Hugh McManners.

The Dictionary of Useful Plants: An Organic Farming and Gardening Book by Nelson Coon.

Eating On the Run by Fred Demara.

Edible Insects by Fred Demara.

Edible Plants of North America by Francois Couplan.

Edible Wild Plants: A Falcon Field Guide by Todd Telander.

Edible Wild Plants: A North American Field Guide by Thomas S. Elias & Peter A. Dykeman.

Edible Wild Plants: Eastern/Central North America by Lee Allen Peterson (1977).

Edible Wild Plants by Oliver Perry Medsger.

Edible Wild Plants: Wild Food from Dirt to Plate (2010 Gibbs Smith) by John Kallas, PHD.

Field Guide to Edible Wild Plants by Bradford Angier.

A Field Guide to Edible Wild Plants of Eastern and Central North America by Lee Allen Peterson (aka the Peterson Guide).

Florida Wildflowers and Roadside Plants by Richie Bell and Brian J. Taylor.

Florida Wildflowers: In Their Natural Communities by Walter Kingsley Taylor.

Florida's Edible Wild Plants: A Guide to Collecting and Cooking by Peggy Sias Lantz.

Foraging Flavor: Finding Fabulous Ingredients In Your Backyard or Farmer's Market by Tama Matsuoka Wong & Eddy Leroux.

Handbook of Edible Weeds by Dr. James Duke.

Hawke's Green Beret Survival Manual by Mykel Hawke.

Hawke's Special Forces Survival Handbook by Mykel Hawke.

The Herbal Drugstore by Linda B. White MD, Steven Foster and the staff of *Herbs for Health*.

National Audubon Society Field Guide to Florida.

A Naturalist's Guide to Cooking with wild Plants, by Connie and Arnold Krochmal.

The Neighborhood Forager by Robert K. Henderson.

Outdoor Emergency Survival Guide by Byron Dalrymple.

Outdoorman's Handbook by Clyde Ormand.

Outdoor Survival Guide by Randy Gerke.

Plants Poisonous to People in Florida by Julia F. Morton.

Practical Outdoor Survival by Len McDougall.

The Search by Tom Brown.

The Self-Reliance Manifesto: How to Survive Anything Anywhere by Len McDougall.

Southern Wildflowers by Laura C. Martin.

Stalking the Wild Asparagus by Euell Gibbons.

Taylor's Pocket Guide to: Herbs and Edible Flowers by Ann Reilly.

The Tracker by Tom Brown.

Tom Brown's Field Guide to Wilderness Survival by Tom Brown.

Trees (Taylor Guides) by Susan A. Roth.

The Ultimate Survival Guide by John (Lofty) Wiseman.
The US Armed Forces Survival Guide by John Boswell.
The US Armed Forces Survival Handbook by Sergeant First Class Matt Larsen.
The US Army Survival Manual, Department of the Armed Services.
When All Hell Breaks Loose: Stuff You Need to Survive When Disaster Strikes by Cody Lundin.
Wild Edibles: Identification for Living Off the Land by Mariam Van Atta.
Wildflowers in Color by Arthur Stupka.
Wildflowers of the Southern United States by Wilbur H. Duncan & Leonard E. Foote.
Wild Foods by Lawrence Pringle.
Wild Harvest by Alyson Hart Knap.
Wild Plants for Survival in South Florida by Julia F. Morton.

Index

190